Humanism and its aftermath

Humanism and its aftermath

The shared fate of deconstruction and politics

Bill Martin

HUMANITIES PRESS
NEW JERSEY

First published 1995 by Humanities Press International, Inc.,
165 First Avenue, Atlantic Highlands, New Jersey 07716

Library of Congress Cataloging-in-Publication Data
Martin, Bill, 1956-
    Humanism and its aftermath : the shared fate of deconstruction and
politics / Bill Martin.
        p.   cm.
    Includes bibliographical references and index.
    ISBN 0-391-03893-1.—ISBN 0-391-03894-X (pbk.)
    1. Derrida, Jacques. 2. Deconstruction. 3. Political science-
-Philosophy. 4. Social sciences—Philosophy. I. Title.
B2430.D484M368   1995
194—dc20   94-39400
                                                        CIP

A catalog record for this book is available from the British Library

Printed in the United States of America

For Bascenji

Contents

Contents

Nothing can save us that is possible.

—W. H. Auden

Preface

I said a moment ago: it only appears that deconstruction, in its manifestations most recognized as such, hasn't "addressed," as one says in English, the problem of justice. It only appears that way, but one must account for appearances, "keep up appearances" as Aristotle said, and that is how I'd like to employ myself here: to show why and how what is now called Deconstruction, while seeming not to "address" the problem of justice, has done nothing but address it, if only obliquely, unable to do so directly. Obliquely, as at this very moment, in which I'm preparing to demonstrate that one cannot speak *directly* about justice, thematize of objectivize justice, say "this is just" and even less "I am just," without immediately betraying justice, if not law [droit]. . . .

It is this deconstructable structure of law [droit], or, if you prefer to justice, as *droit*, that also insures the possibility of deconstruction. Justice in itself, if such a thing exists, outside or beyond law, is not deconstructable. No more than deconstruction itself, if such a thing exists. Deconstruction is justice. . . .

I think that there is no justice without this experience, however impossible it may be, of aporia. Justice is an experience of the impossible. A will, a desire, a demand for justice whose structure wouldn't be an experience of aporia would have no chance to be what it is, namely, a call for justice. Every time that something comes to pass or turns out well, every time that we placidly apply a good rule to a particular case, to a correctly subsumed example, according to a determinant judgment, we can be sure that law [droit] may find itself accounted for, but certainly not justice. Law [droit] is not justice. Law is the element of calculation, and it is just that there be law, but justice is incalculable, it requires us to calculate the incalculable, it requires us to calculate with the incalculable; and aporetic experiences are the experiences, as improbable as they are necessary, of justice, that is to say of moments in which the decision between just and unjust is never insured by a rule.

—Jacques Derrida, "Force of Law"

What if deconstruction is simply this, the *possibility* of justice? The whole aim of the following text is to explore this "What if" in terms of systematic social theory. To simply formulate a conception of justice is difficult, perhaps impossible. This is Plato's problem, especially in *Republic*. Indeed, Socrates develops an entire plan for a utopian social order predicated on the possibility of justice, even as he must admit in *Republic* and elsewhere that he has not succeeded in grounding this possibility. Already in Plato there is an aporia and a dynamic interaction, a relational ontology, of justice and its possibility. Knowing justice, having it, defining it, implementing it, all this is problematized by Plato, who all the same goes on to ask, "What if . . . ?"

Either this possibility or nothing: this is the whole force of Socrates' discourse in *Republic*. The dialogue is essentially an all-out attempt to answer Thrasymachus' definition: "Justice is the interest of the stronger." Socrates cannot help but admit that his attempt fails in practice and quite possibly in theory as well; and yet, either this or nothing, either there is an answer to Thrasymachus or there is no point to being human. For, after all, Thrasymachus' conception of justice applies equally well to animals and possibly to plants and inanimate objects as well. This universality of the struggle to survive and (therefore?) dominate has been touted as the virtue of political philosophies from Thrasymachus to Hobbes to contemporary Hobbesians, who have systematized this "ethic of calculation" (as Derrida puts it) by means of game and decision theory, modeling all social interactions on the two-person prisoner's dilemma. Finding myself—for it must be my *self*, in this dilemma, no wonder that I might say "Hell is other people." One can only hope that this is the final assault of positivism on political thinking.

Please pardon the thumbnail sketch of Plato, which merely repeats what every student of philosophy and western intellectual culture already knows.

In asking whether deconstruction might be the possibility of justice, Derrida is asking whether there might be another conception of politics, another thinking of the polis. This book aims to sharpen the sense of the alternative conception, theoretically and practically, and to show why it is necessary to political thinking and praxis. In pursuing this aim I connect especially with central themes in the Marxist tradition (or traditions). However, I am greatly concerned here with the fate of deconstruction. I worry that it may not be able to do all of the work that it could do, because of its tendency—the tendency, at any rate, of "what is now called deconstruction, in its manifestations most recognized as such"—to get bogged down in etymological play. This tendency gives way, with some proponents of deconstruction, and sometimes with Derrida's work as well, to a kind of silliness lacking any political edge whatsoever. This silliness seems to me a preoccupation that a tired and even cynical Eurocentrism might indulge in. There are better possibilities in deconstruction, especially when Marxist and Kantian themes are engaged. In some respects this text is a workbook for such an engagement.

Much of my thinking in this text grew out of two opportunities which arose in fall 1991 and spring 1992 at my home institution, DePaul University of Chicago. First, my colleague Michael Naas asked me to collaborate on an introduction to the translation of Derrida's *L'autre cap* that he prepared with Pascale-Anne Brault. Michael and I think somewhat differently, in form and content, and the collaboration, at least in the practical form we sought, ultimately did not work out. This happened for the further reason that I produced a fifty-page contribution rather than the fifteen-page piece requested. In any case, my mind was set to thinking about Derrida and the inseparable questions of humanism and the trajectory of Europe (the translation of *L'autre cap* bears the subtitle, *Reflections on Today's Europe*). I want to thank Michael for many wrangling conversations concerning these questions. The discussions have now become Part 3 of the present text, "From Other Shores: Derrida and the Idea of Europe, apropos of *L'autre cap*." Second, Michael and I jointly led a graduate seminar on Derrida and social theory (spring 1992). I see the impact of the seminar on every aspect of this book. I wish to thank the seminar participants for their provocative contributions.

This is my second book on the subject of deconstruction and social theory (the first was *Matrix and line: Derrida and the possibilities of postmodern social theory*). Roger Gottlieb has played a major role in both projects. I thank him now and I will thank him for many years to come. Although I argue in this book to some of the same points I attempted to establish in the earlier book, I have made every effort to avoid covering the same ground. Where I do discuss the earlier book directly I aim to highlight points where more work is needed and where my views have changed.

For a little while it appeared that the Derrida fad had faded and that it would be possible to simply get down to work on the texts of an important thinker. This was before the controversy over Political Correctness and multiculturalism was initiated by neo-conservative ideologues and institutions, a controversy in which Professor Derrida is often portrayed as the arch-nemesis of western civilization. Although the present text shows that Derrida is no such animal, its aim is not to demonstrate this to neo-conservatives, who do not value careful reading or thinking in any case. (Paul Bove's recent critique of Allan Bloom's

The Closing of the American Mind as "unreadable" is to the point; see pp. 67–79. Michael Berube's excellent article on the anti-PC phenomenon, in the *Village Voice*, also makes the important point that if the likes of Dinesh D'Souza are the caretakers of western civilization, then we're in a lot of trouble.) Still, the atmosphere in which the question of Derrida and politics must be discussed is again in a state near Brownian motion. This has had the effect, ironically, of politicizing a question that was supposedly already politicized, and that is all to the good ("To be attacked by the enemy is a good thing," Mao once said), even if most of what must be dealt with in a controversy stirred up by neo-conservatives has little to do with what Derrida has actually written. (I use the term neo-conservatives as Habermas does, to draw a contrast with traditional conservatives, i.e., conservatives who, for all that they may be wrong, still care about values and may generate useful and accurate critiques of modernism and consumer capitalism. Alisdair McIntyre is a good example of the latter.) The problem is to ride this wave of politicization in a way that extends the possibilities for deconstructive political thinking both practically and theoretically. It has been difficult to find the space for something like thoughtful reflection. In this search I have had a number of companions, to whom I am very grateful. The good people at Humanities Press have been very helpful: Keith and Beatriz Ashfield, Cindy Nixon, and Stacey Anolick. William Zeisel, who did the copy editing, which can be a thankless task, performed a major service in sorting out my often tangled sentence structures and frequent parenthetical digressions. This book was originally proposed in a quite different form and for quite different purposes, by Professor Roger Gottlieb, whom I (and many other social theorists) regard and revere as a patron saint of radical philosophers. My gratitude toward him, on so many levels, is ongoing. I would especially like to thank some of my contemporaries, friends who are also pursuing "marginal" social theory: Alison Brown, Andrew Cutrofello, Craig Hanks, Patricia Huntington, Tamsin Lorraine, Martin Matustik, Dianne Rothleder, Chelsea Snelgrove, George Trey and Cynthia Willett. I remain, as always, most grateful to my companion in life and thought, Kathleen League (also numbered among this group of marginal social theorists), who grappled with the arguments of this book every step of the way, providing crucial input on all of the most important questions. This book is dedicated to her.

The seminar on Derrida and social theory mentioned earlier was often a contentious scene. Indeed, the final session was the most intense and disquieting class I have experienced as student or instructor. Remembering that session, which took place on June 2, 1992, I would like to mark the date of this text. Derrida marks the time of his public presentation of "The Ends of Man" as that of the assassination of Martin Luther King, Jr., the U.S. war in Vietnam, and the "Events of May" 1968. He marks the time of *L'autre cap* as that of the Gulf War and the declaration, by President George Bush, of the New World Order. The date of this text, the time of its composition but much more than that, is that of the Gulf War and the uprisings in Los Angeles and the attendant shockwaves felt nationally and internationally in the wake of the Rodney King verdict; the time of this text is the declaration, through the murder of thousands of Iraqis, of the New World Order, and the declaration of war against that order initiated in the streets of Los Angeles.

This book is in three parts (followed by a brief afterword). Most of the first part is taken up with clearing the ground, so to speak, for the articulation of deconstructive social theory. The first six sections interrogate the institutional and social bases of deconstruction, especially as it has been practiced by literary theorists and philosophers in the United States. One of the chief aspects of this interrogation is to raise questions of class that have been ruled mostly out of bounds in a good deal of recent discussion of marginal subjects. Although I work hard to avoid a reductivist sense of class and especially of the proletariat, I also try to show that these notions are absolutely necessary for capturing the reality of marginalization in the world today. Part of the effort here is to show how much of what is called deconstruction is politically crippled by its avoidance of class. Another aim of Part 1 is to set up the encounter with Marxism that is present at almost every point in the book. In particular, I try to show the sorts of questions that Marxism, as a radical social theory tied to radical social movements and revolutionary uprisings, has historically encountered. I argue that if deconstruction has a contribution to make to radical social theory and practice, it must also encounter these same historically generated questions. In the seventh (final) section of Part 1, I push this Marxism-deconstruction encounter to at least one kind of limit, what I call "the ethical moment in politics." In this encounter both Marxism and deconstruction are transformed, the former toward a greater sense of alterity, the latter toward a greater sense of historical concreteness. I hope that in this encounter neither Marxism nor deconstruction are dirempted of their respective essential strengths. On this point, however, the reader must judge.

Part 2 enters more directly into the question of humanism, its past, present, and future. The circuits of thought and practice encountered

in this part run from Descartes to Richard Rorty's postmodern liberalism, with discussions of Kant, Nietzsche, and Habermas in between. I
discuss the meanings and languages of humanism available to humanity.
In the final section, I take on some of the mean-spirited attacks directed at Jacques Derrida and his work in recent years. It is worth
considering that if Derrida has inspired this motley crew of neo-conservatives to line up against him, he must be doing something right.

In Part 3, I take up Derrida's arguments concerning the language of
humanism, focusing especially on a recent text that bears directly on
this issue, *The Other Heading*. Again, I encounter Marx and Habermas,
as well as Hegel.

Much in this text is personal—not simply "about me," personally,
though I think it appropriate that there is an inescapable element of
autobiography, especially given that I have tried, in the past ten years,
to take deconstruction personally. This is to say that I have tried to
engage with deconstruction and to practice an engaged deconstruction.
Deconstruction happens, as Derrida has remarked many times. This
text, in some sense an open letter, attempts pointedly to raise the question,
"Deconstruction happens: Now, what are *we* going to *do* about this?"

Part 1

Amicus brief: De-sedimenting deconstruction, its possibilities for social theory

A world that is objectively set for totality will not release the human consciousness, will ceaselessly flatten it to points it wants to get away from; but a thinking that blithely begins afresh, heedless of the historic form of its problems, will so much more be their prey.

—Theodor Adorno, *Negative Dialectics*

That a "case" has to be made . . . .

What is deconstruction? We who have been using the term in recent years have often been asked this question, often with the added request, "in twenty-five words or less." Not exactly the sign of real intellectual quest, and most in academia who ask the question in this form know better. Here is a non-answer that uses far fewer words than twenty-five: this text uses "deconstruction" primarily as a name for the philosophy of Jacques Derrida. His work must be read in its own right (I strongly suggest starting with either *Speech and Phenomena* or *of Grammatology*, not *Glas* or *The Post Card*); no brief formulation will do justice to this or any other interesting and sophisticated work.

However, having issued this warning to narrow-minded professors and neo-conservative journalists who don't have to read Derrida to know he's no good (paraphrasing Dale Spender's pithy book title), I should immediately say that of course I intend to discuss various aspects of Derrida's work in detail, and especially to articulate those aspects in connection with the "What if?" that opens the Preface and that motivates this text.

1

In this book I offer many arguments and readings that I would characterize as deconstructive. I aim to open a space for reading the writerly dimensions of western political modernity and some of its canonical texts, as well as to open a common space for diverse voices that have recently begun to make themselves heard. The aim, indeed, is to open the "archive" of difference as found in both the canon of western modernity—even if in the form of a repression of the other that must be read in the margins—and in the experience of the masses. Even in the western and especially U.S. atmosphere of historical amnesia, nothing is truly or fully forgotten. There is an archive of difference and the strivings of people toward justice that may not be in books (or the books may not always be in the hands of the people), that may not be in people's minds (or in their conscious thoughts), but that exists in their hearts, their lives, their forms of life, and the social institutions that they inhabit and have marked with their lives. This characterization of the archive and the need to open it, and to let it open itself, is deconstructive in both the letter and the spirit of Derrida's work.

My entire text must be the argument for this last claim, and I hope that the reader will be convinced. The problem is truly that of showing the coterminousness and compearance (co-appearance) of deconstruction and justice.

However, the case presented here cannot simply be a matter of hanging the argument on the hooks of quotations from Derrida. Even the most expert testimony cannot be the full basis for judgment; there are two further questions. To keep with the legalistic terminology, these are the questions of circumstances and motives. There are other possible contextualizations of Derrida's work and the work of deconstruction more generally than what I offer here. These contextualizations are rarely offered as such, relying instead on the weight of the contemplative tradition in philosophy. This is quite an irony in the case of Derrida's philosophy, when Derrida is well known (perhaps best known) for arguing that there is nothing outside of context. (Of course, what he is best known for is a willfully ignorant caricature of this argument.) This being the case, however, it must be admitted in the court of theoretical opinion that the evidence of the circumstances of Derrida's work offered here is itself circumstantial.

Arguments for these circumstances, that is, the particular contextualization offered here, will be presented. But there is also the question of motive. Discussion and theorizing of the marginal is nothing if not practical. This theme will be presented from various angles in the remainder of Part 1. The general outline of the theme is captured well in Lawrence Grossberg's *We gotta get out of this place*; knowing the reference of this title might be significant for understanding the present text as well:

> In the last instance, theory can only be judged by what it enables, by what is opens up and closes off (and any theory always does both) in the contemporary context. Theory is of little use if it does not help us imagine and then realize better futures for ourselves and future generations. (p. 13)

A little further on, Grossberg comments on the need for analysis that is "speculative . . . because it does not have the comfort and security of a completion." In my view, there is much writing on Derrida and deconstruction that, despite a certain rhetorical adventurousness, seems finally to seek this comfort and security. This sort of writing is too "Heideggerian," especially in its tone of religiosity, its jargon of authencity—even if this formulation is itself too comfortable and secure, answering none of the relevant and important questions. (Discussion of "comfortable deconstruction" appears below.) The aim of this book is to travel light years away from comfort and security.

To delimit deconstruction to the work of Jacques Derrida and to work that bases itself in his philosophy has its strengths and weaknesses. I will focus, for the moment, on the latter. Derrida was long reluctant to call what he does deconstruction. He still often refers to "something called deconstruction," in part out of recognition that he does not own the term (nor does anyone else), nor can he legislate its use. (Derrida does recognize, all the same, that he is in some sense responsible for all of the uses of the term.) As Derrida has remarked, deconstruction is a North American phenomenon. In North America, and first of all through university literature departments, deconstruction has been "invented" as an approach, and then primarily as an approach to reading "literary" texts.

Derrida argues that deconstruction is not a "method" or a "concept." "Approach" is a word that is also problematic, but it has the virtue of capturing the sense that deconstruction is the activity of letting something happen. "Deconstruction happens," Derrida says, apart from whether he or anyone else gives that name to what appears in the space of deconstruction.

How could such an approach, which I still have to describe in detail, function as a key concept in critical social theory?

Interestingly enough, the term critical theory has come to serve as another name for literary theory, at least in academic circles, and not just the name of a school in social theory initiated by Max Horkheimer and Theodor Adorno. Deconstruction is undoubtedly a key concept in

literary critical theory. Perhaps there is still an argument needed concerning why deconstruction should be a key concept in literary studies, but there is no doubting that the practice of literary deconstruction
is now an established part of literary studies. The question might be,
then, the relation between the two types of critical theory. How is it
that a term might move from one type to the other? Surely a theory of
literature cannot do without a theory of society, because the former
theory concerns the production of meaning. Only a purely formal theory
of literary meaning could avoid the social dimension. Such a formalism would have to be a Platonism beyond anything that Plato himself
conceived. Not only literary deconstruction but all of the critical methods
in literature that have emerged and developed over the past several
decades—structuralism, semiotics, psychoanalysis, and of course feminism and Marxism—are, in the first place, a refutation of the asocial,
pristine formalism of the New Criticism. This is not to say that there
is nothing good in the New Criticism, which promoted a rigor in thinking
about literature that had not existed, although it also set literary studies on the road of professionalization. The attempt to isolate the "ver-
bal icon," its "meaning," from the social network that generates meaning
is, however, itself a product of the social network. All of the critical schools
in recent literary studies recognize this, deconstruction among them.

There is, then, at least a bit of social theory in literary deconstruction.
But this does not explain why social theory proper would benefit by
importing a term that has developed, for the most part, in the context
of academic literary studies.

Would we consider, for example (and to take as an example a term
that has a much longer history in literary studies), "irony" as a candi-
date for the status of key concept in critical social theory? Could we
think of irony as having the same importance as, say, democracy or
autonomy? On the face of it, this seems unlikely—but perhaps that is
the problem.

New Criticism, among other things, manifested in literary studies
the same positivism that seemed to grip all of the disciplines ("hard
sciences," "social sciences"—the very terms are manifestations of positivism, the humanities) for much of this century. If anything, in the
New World Order this positivism is even more pervasive. Derrida, in
his concern with the question of literature (and with this "question"
before "literature itself") the question of how "literary meaning" is
different from meaning in philosophy, or in the sciences, has been
preoccupied with the critique of positivism since his first publications.
Literary meaning, on Derrida's view, even if different from meaning
in philosophy or the sciences, cannot be separated from meaning "out-

side" of literature. If Derrida is right, we have good reason to think that what might be called a literary theory of society would be a good thing to develop. At the very least, we might think that a term, deconstruction, that has been articulated for the most part in literary circles might be very useful in thinking about politics.

In due course I will specify what is involved in "thinking about politics." An important argument of this text will be that the critique of positivism must be accompanied by, indeed, accomplished through, the development of a different thinking and a different politics. Positivism, I will argue, is not simply an intellectual or academic trend, it is a culture and a form of life, and must be addressed as such.

In asking of what use deconstruction might be to social theory are we not already on the terrain of asking that deconstruction become a methodology? Are we not asking after the pragmatics of deconstruction? This text attempts to develop a social theoretical deconstruction that is not a pragmatics, not simply a proceduralism for the adjudication of political questions. And yet, when the parameters of this task are actually set out, I find this an almost impossible task. On the one hand, it is the entire point of deconstruction to ask after the possibility of justice without closing off the possibility of the unprecedented. On the other hand, it seems not only impossible but wrong and unjust to conceive of a politics that is unable to make judgments, to make distinctions between justice and injustice. Impossibility is not the problem here; after all, in Kant's view, ethics sets an infinite task. This is also to encounter a certain impossibility. For Derrida, it is this impossibility that draws us out toward responsibility. But this drawing out, contrary to what some purely academic deconstructionists might think, cannot be a mere intellectual exercise, even if certain forms of intellectual work are necessitated by our impossible responsibility.

How might deconstruction work with both hands? The activity of social theory, at least in a sense that is not purely academic and which I would still call engaged, demands that this question be answered. Derrida does sometimes use "strategy" in place of "methodology" (e.g., in *Positions*, where he discusses "a general strategy of deconstruction"). If there is a strategy, how does it work? Are there "strategists"—does deconstruction require a kind of agency? Then what is the meaning of "deconstruction happens"?

Even accepting that deconstruction cannot be made into a methodology, or that to try to do this is to foreshorten the possibility of deconstruction and its strategies, and even accepting that deconstruction might have some other way of talking about and acting on the possibility of justice, wouldn't deconstruction have some dues to pay in order to prove itself in the arena of political theory? What's more to the point, how might deconstruction present itself to politics? Is this not the real test, the test of reality, of presence, of any concept in social theory? Here, if nowhere else, a theory of irony would serve us well.

The class for deconstruction: The emergence of deconstruction in North American literary studies

Although recent literary theory has evidenced a better, more developed sense of politics and political responsibility, this has come about, as with most everything good that has come out of the academy since 1970, because women, people of color, and others from marginalized groups have entered the fray. The first years of deconstruction's emergence in North America were marked by the somewhat puerile aestheticism of the Yale School, well documented in Frank Lentricchia's appropriately titled *After the New Criticism*. Although this "school," consisting in Paul de Man, Hillis Miller, Geoffrey Hartman, and Harold Bloom (and purportedly Jacques Derrida, who held an appointment at Yale in the seventies), was never really as coherent a camp as most onlookers initially thought, the theoretical efforts of de Man and the advertizing efforts of Miller convinced the academic world at large (and *Newsweek*, the *New York Times*, etc.) that Yale was deconstruction and deconstruction was Yale.

Harold Bloom, a formidable critic, was least identified with the philosophy of Derrida, though there are interesting comparisons to be made. Bloom and Derrida both have had longstanding engagements with Jewish themes; the sources of these engagements, however, are quite different and Bloom already had his own well-developed system and terminology when Derrida came on the Yale scene (see de Bolla). Paul de Man, also a major thinker in his own right, was by far the closest to Derrida in his approach to texts. Indeed, taking deconstruction in a narrower sense, in which it is simply one aspect of Derrida's practice rather than the name for the whole of that practice, de Man is arguably more the deconstructionist than Derrida.

Paul de Man, who died in 1983, was certainly one of the most influential literary critics of recent decades. His many students exercise a considerable influence in academic literary studies, and some of them have developed the political possibilities of deconstruction. These possibilities are fully present in de Man's work, if rarely thematized, and I hope that they will be developed further. For instance, there are whole political manifestoes to be derived from key essays such as "The Rhetoric of Temporality," "Autobiography as De-Facement," and "The Resistance to Theory" (not to mention all that de Man wrote on Rousseau). I will not develop this deconstructive social theory here, but not, however, for the reason that the reader might assume.

The question of Paul de Man's wartime collaborationism has been adequately discussed. (See, e.g., Norris, *Paul de Man*, pp. 177–98; Lindsay Waters', "Introduction"; the many articles collected in Hamacher et al.; and my "Blindness and Hindsight".) Neo-conservatives, such as David Lehman, as part of a general attack on feminism, Marxism, deconstruction, Black studies, and 'PC' and multiculturalism (referred to in the Preface), have convincingly revealed that de Man was at the very least an opportunist and scoundrel as a young man, and most likely a dissimulator in later life concerning his activities in the early forties.[1] Not only de Man's wartime collaborationist journalism but also the abandonment of his first wife (whom he never officially divorced) and family are condemnable acts, and his relations with colleagues and students at Bard College do not bear much scrutiny either.

And yet, even though the question of collaboration and complicity is very important, no one who is really concerned about fascism and the Holocaust would restrict discussion or inquiry to the question of Paul de Man. Nor would this inquiry be restricted to the even more difficult case of Martin Heidegger, which is not to deny that the question of the intellectuals and fascism is very important. Surely one has to suspect this sort of restriction of the discussion, particularly at a time when fascist winds are blowing again. Clearly, coming to grips with fascism and how to fight it is not the aim of the neo-conservatives, who have their own fascist and fascistic associations to worry about or hide: I'm thinking of such entities as the Nationalities Council of the Republican Party, which has many members who were former members and even leaders of central and eastern European fascist organizations. Enough said on this time-consuming topic. (A principal part of neo-conservative strategy is to formulate texts in which, to paraphrase Lillian Helman, even the punctuation marks are false, so that refuting such texts is a very tiring and unrewarding task.)

My reason for not taking up the social theoretical aspects of de Man's work is quite different and has little or nothing to do with his activities as a young man or his dissimulations in later life. Frankly, my own estimation of de Man's main body of work, in *Blindness and Insight*, *Allegories of Reading*, *The Rhetoric of Romanticism* and *The Resistance to Theory*, has not decreased by one iota as a result of the "revelations." The *line* (I use this term with all of the overtones it must necessarily have after Lenin) I take here is that something called social and political theory must have a fundamental orientation toward practice. Although there is certainly a politics of de Man's practice of deconstruction, and although that politics should be pursued, there seems little orientation toward practice evident in de Man's work. Terry Eagleton once quipped, in an article that was not especially hard on de Man ("The Critic as Clown," in *Against the Grain*), that de Man was another of those intellectuals who had a reputation as a man of the left without ever having done anything to earn that reputation. (Few of the major Marxist literary critics, Eagleton, Fredric Jameson, and others, made a big commotion over the de Man affair. They have a fundamentally different sense of what the stakes of this question are than the neo-conservatives, who do not evidence any real concern about fascism.) What is more important, once one has studied in detail de Man's many essays (something David Lehman claims to have done, although he doesn't demonstrate it), one finds that the brilliance of the work, much of which consists in readings in English and German Romantic poetry, is not matched with any apparent political project.

Subtlety and nuance are themselves important, to be sure; and, as Theodor Adorno points out, especially in *Aesthetic Theory*, stylistic innovation can be more politically efficacious than explicit political statement. Indeed, on Adorno's view, artworks that depend on the latter often undermine themselves through reinscribing an authoritarian gesture that it is the whole purpose of autonomous art to challenge. De Man, too, seems to possess a negative impulse in common with Adorno, an impulse that seems not much present in Derrida's work. (I will discuss the question of negativity and affirmation, vis-à-vis Adorno and Derrida, in Part 3.) Still, despite all of this, one looks in vain to find what de Man was finally after, what his "project" was, other than to create ingenious readings that discover the fundamental aporia in diverse texts. This judgment may be harsh, and I am impressed by the way that Christopher Norris (in *Paul de Man* and elsewhere), especially, weaves various threads from de Man's *oeuvre* into a coherent "critique of aesthetic ideology." Derrida's sense of his own work, which aims "to let the other speak" and "to clear a space for the other," comes through, one is tempted to say "shines forth," even if that is a funny expression to use in connection with Derrida and his critique of the language of presence, in any careful reading of most of his works. (Derrida does get bogged down in wordplay from time to time, just as analytic philosophers sometimes get so caught up in microscopic technical details that it is hard to see the point.) De Man always seems to rest with finding the aporia in the text. Although there is an important sense in which the other (or the specific other, if not alterity as such, which by definition does not "come into" the world) comes to the world through various aporias, the political dimensions of alterity are not developed as such by de Man.

One point of this discussion has been to show that, although there are important connections there is also a world of difference between "deconstruction is Yale" (or Yale deconstruction) and "deconstruction as the possibility of justice." It is the second deconstruction, largely undeveloped—to some extent Yale deconstruction has stood in the way of this development—that my text attempts to unfold.

A debt of gratitude is owed to the Yale School. It was the pathway through which Jacques Derrida's work came to be disseminated in North America. I do not wish to engage in crude or reductive analysis. However, launched as it was as a North American movement, deconstruction bears the marks of its elite class origins. There is the need, then, to extend deconstruction beyond the halls of the Ivy League academies and far beyond the academy in general. There is a further need for a kind of "recovery" (another word that seems funny in this context) of deconstruction, a return to Derrida's texts and to their position in relation to the canons of western philosophy and literature. I need not ignore or disparage the work of the Yale critics in order to move this agenda. Finally, there is the need to deepen the project of deconstruction, which again means taking deconstruction beyond the academy, particularly beyond the academy's superficiality with regard to the most significant questions facing humanity. Here the class character of much deconstruction as practiced in the academy, and the class character of the academy, as stamped upon much of the practice of deconstruction, stands as a major obstacle in the way of a deconstruction that really works, on every level, to let the other speak.

Theory and practice: The challenge of Marxism

I have gone a short distance in setting the terms of the case that must be made if deconstruction is to be useful to social theory. Before approaching what might be called the question of a deconstructive "theory of justice," let me explain the methodology of the present text.

"Making the case" is legalistic language. Anyone who remains fundamentally indebted to Marxism believes of course, that the "case" for any sort of social theory must finally be forged in the crucible of social practice. Below I will turn to the obvious and justified question, "If Marxism is so helpful, why fool around with deconstruction?" We who work at the intersection of Marxism and deconstruction have been asked this question repeatedly, in one form or another, for the past ten years or more. For the moment, however, I will stay with the model provided by Marxism, in order to raise some important questions about the tasks of social theory.

Marx saw his own theoretical work as a necessary intervention into an unfolding process of class struggle. Marx did not invent the contradictions of capitalism, or the labor theory of value, or the idea of a social class consisting in propertyless wage-workers. His modifications to all of these categories, and his theoretical matrix for understanding the intermotivations of them, were all proposed within a basic orientation to practice. That is, the point of Marx's work was to further the development of the revolutionary practice of the proletariat. One central question for my study is: Can the deconstructive project of letting the other speak be put on the same footing? In other words, can I develop this project in terms of an understanding of the social system (or systems) at work in silencing the voice of the other (or making us deaf to this voice), the agents and forms of agency involved, the practice necessary for straining toward alterity and thereby changing society, and changing society and thereby straining toward alterity? Can deconstruction provide more than an ethical norm, however admirable that norm may be? These questions, which occur naturally to anyone thinking in a Marxist mode, are absolutely crucial, regardless of how one judges Marx's work in dealing with similar questions concerning the proletariat.

If "proletariat" annoys some readers, fine. Part of my task is to show that the proletariat has been excluded from more fashionable conceptions of the other. This exclusion again reveals the class character of much that calls itself deconstruction; it also reveals the academy's overwhelmingly middle-class character, which permeates it not only in what is taught, who is taught, and who is teaching, but in many other ways that add up to an integrated form of life. It is difficult to get outside of a form of life, to see, for instance, the proletariat and other others, even though these others may be cleaning the restrooms and offices of the university and mowing the lawns. The point is that deconstruction has to be deepened, made more powerful, by criticizing everything in it that can render deconstruction merely academic.

Although it would not hurt for deconstructionists to engage in some "practice" in the flatfooted sense (of course, it is not a matter of just any practice, but the point here is that there are many people writing in deconstructive politics in recent years who have never been active in politics per se), the point is not that deconstructive practice cannot get off the ground until more practice is generated. Yes, there is a need for engagement, a term not very much in favor with the, shall we say, post-Sartre generation. (I will soon turn to the question of the supposed impossibility of praxis in light of Heidegger and Derrida.) But the prior, more significant question is: What sorts of practice of the invisible, marginalized other have already brought forth deconstruction?

"Deconstruction happens." It is not a matter of Derrida or anyone else calling forth deconstruction. In Marx's view, the proletariat must liberate itself and all humankind. This the proletariat does by pursuing its basic interest in resolving the contradiction between socialized production and individual accumulation. This contradiction, in Marx's view, must be understood, confronted, and resolved on diverse levels: economic, political, military, cultural, theoretical, institutional. The proletariat, in its practical existence and struggle, finds the theoretical and organizational forms necessary for the replacement of capitalism by socialism and, eventually, communism. Marx does not first of all attribute a moral character to the emancipatory struggle of the proletariat. Any "ethic" that the revolutionary proletariat has it picks up along the way, so to speak. Furthermore, the role that the proletariat plays in emancipating all exploited and oppressed people is, similarly, not in the first instance taken up for ethical reasons or impulses.

Here two problems emerge, from a deconstructive standpoint. First, there is seemingly no space in Marxism for the ethical as such. ("The ethical" and "ethics" are not necessarily the same thing in this formulation.) Second, there has been a pronounced tendency in Marxism to reduce the particularity of different oppressed peoples or groups (e.g., women, dominated nationalities and ethnic groups) and the particularity of different forms of oppression (e.g., male or masculinist domination) to a single class logic. Even if the way to end all forms of oppression is the working out of the logic of the proletariat through the class struggle—itself a point of contention, but it is not an argument that should simply be ignored, as it often is in much deconstructive political writing—this does not mean that the form of that working out, the sense of what constitutes different forms of oppression, or even what is meant by the proletariat should be dealt with in monological terms.

These questions will undoubtedly be familiar to anyone who has thought about the subject. I will return to them in a moment and will deal with various forms of them repeatedly in this study. My point now is something different, namely, that a major strength of Marxism is that it has encountered these and other major problems, and not just in theory.

Some readers, if they really think about what is implied by this last comment, may be taken aback. For the implication is that the practical manifestations of reductivism, the best examples of which are the determinism of the Second International and the catechismic dogmatism of Stalin, actually exemplify a strength of Marxism. This is a large debate that cannot be engaged with at length here. I draw a distinction between the former example, which to me represents an abandonment of the revolutionary spirit of Marxism in the name of a reformist reading of its letter, and the latter; I agree with Sartre and Mao that Stalin represents a deviation *within* Marxism. Even so, why say that this deviation represents a strength? My answer is that the Stalin period and experience shows what can happen to living (even if becoming ossified) Marxism in the crucible of practice. Only in that same crucible can the revolutionarily transformative aspects of Marxism be restored, and it is in that crucible that the revolutionary possibilities of Marxism can and must be developed. These possibilities are being and will be developed, regardless of how much triumphalist rhetoric is broadcast by capitalist ideologues and regardless of how much defeatist rhetoric is heard in the moanings of moping liberals, because the contradictions of capitalism are certainly still with us. None of this is to say that there are no problems with Marxism or that there are not forms of capitalist contradictions (and other social contradictions) that Marx never dreamed of in his worst nightmares. (It is weird, however, that some people raise this latter point as though it is somehow an indictment, rather than a vindication, of Marx.) The point is not even that Marxism necessarily has all the theoretical resources for dealing with these shortcomings. The point, rather, is that any social theory should look forward to the same sorts of tests, and any social theory that avoids all these problems in order to remain pure is not really a theory of society or a theory about how to create a better society.

Living Marxism, as revolutionary critical theory, will not only encounter many problems—failures, defeats (it is important to not confuse the latter with the former, even as the two are closely, dialectically related)—in the struggle to overcome capitalism and all forms of oppression, it will also, of necessity, learn how to think, think about, and deal with these problems. In the best sense, that is what Marxist theory is, a set of "notes" on struggles that have been and are being waged in all of the spheres where capitalism dominates. Numerous revolutionary intellectuals and intellectual revolutionaries (Lenin's distinction), not all of them Marxists (strictly speaking), have contributed to this effort.

I have thematized, in a shorthand form, certain aspects of the model offered by Marxism because it is necessary to raise the question, Would deconstructive social theory, if such a thing is possible, be able to encounter problems similar to those encountered by Marxism? Should it? This is one way of posing the question of a fundamental orientation toward practice.

Here, I think, a dividing line can be usefully drawn. Those who think that deconstruction either cannot or should not encounter problems of the sort outlined also tend to believe that deconstructive social theory is neither possible nor desirable. Actually, the claim is broader; on this view, politics as project, program, praxis, or line is also impossible and undesirable. Ultimately, in this view, there is no such thing as social theory; there is no sense in trying, to quote Marx, to "grasp the inner connections," so that "theory becomes a material force."

Urgency

Here is another way of posing what has just been claimed as a strength of Marxism as a test for any possible deconstructive social theory or, for that matter, any social theory—and quite possibly any philosophy— at all. Marx was both more and less than a philosopher. There is a certain urgency about Marxism that often seems lacking in other philosophies. Certainly, critical thinking should not always nor often be thought in a hothouse environment. Real critical reflection requires a certain distance and calm. (I will say more on this question in Part 3, when I consider the meaning of tempo and speed for philosophy and for the polis.) I would still draw a distinction between a *certain* distance and a *certain* calm, on the one hand, and what might be called, on the other hand, a fundamentally contemplative, quietistic attitude. But I am actually driving toward something else. People who are Marxists in all but the most academic of senses confront the following question: Knowing what I know about the world, thinking what I think about the world, how should I live my life? Yes, this question should exist for any serious, developed philosophy, and I believe that it is raised by the philosophy of Jacques Derrida. But it is no secret that, if one compares the "Derrideans" with Marxists, the question certainly can be seen to exist with much more urgency for the latter. There is much writing by vaguely political Derrideans that seems to promise to make something out of the call to responsibility and the call to, as Derrida puts it in *The Other Heading*, "responsibility to responsibility," but, after twenty years of preliminaries, things seem to be at a bit of an impasse. Of course, things in general are at an impasse, a condition that Derrida speaks to very well in *The Other Heading*. In *Matrix and line* I discuss this impasse as fundamentally characteristic of postmodernity and what I call "postmodern capitalism"; see especially Chap. 2. Furthermore, it is true that we, who believe that only fundamental change will address the major questions that humanity now faces, must try to work toward, in Gayatri Spivak's words, "revolutions that as yet have no model." Or, to give a little more credit to the experience of revolution from the Paris Commune to the Cultural Revolution in China, even where we have models and experiences that should be built on, even when, as with many aspects of the Stalin period, we are learning through negative example, we must still attempt to clear a space for the unprecedented.

This is the meaning of the idea of "Marx after Derrida."

A Marxism that is closed to the unprecedented has simply capitulated to the impasse. A dialectic in which everything is fully determined, in which nothing new can appear—this could serve very well as a definition of the impasse.

By the same token, a deconstructive politics that simply casts aside, does not even begin to dig into and investigate, the historical experience of revolution, even where that experience has gone seriously wrong, cannot possibly clear a space for the unprecedented. Where is this space to be cleared, if not in history?

Quite a few people who call themselves Derrideans or at least invoke Derrida and speak of deconstructive politics get stuck on the mere phraseology of "responsibility to responsibility," as though it were a hamster's treadmill. They often express a belief that fundamental change is necessary, only to add that it is also impossible—and they often take Derrida's use of "impossible" as authorizing this belief. They, along with a significant segment of the middle classes of western countries, have found their way toward a fairly standard conservative position, albeit paralleled by a certain amount of philosophical sophistication and deconstructive terminology. The corollary is that this "sophisticated" conservatism does not and cannot believe in the possibilities of the masses, in their ability to make history. Why is this cynicism any different from that which generally pervades in the present impasse? It is certainly no better for the fact that it may be more sophisticated.[2]

My question is: Does this conservatism really encompass all that is possible in and with Derrida's philosophy? Am I simply being old-fashioned in wanting philosophy to "mean something," and not in a merely contemplative sense?

This has gotten quite personal, I realize. I warned you in the Preface! Although many parts of this study will be impersonal, retreating into a coldly analytical mode, I still would like to see this study as constituting a kind of open letter, to the following audiences.

To those who believe in the possibility of deconstructive social theory but are frustrated, as I am, by the failure to get beyond preliminary gestures. Michel Foucault once called his own work a "tool-kit for revolutionaries." I do not want to frame the possibilities of Derrida's philosophy in quite those terms, but I do not want to provide some building blocks that radicals could creatively take up. We who believe in the idea of a deconstructive politics need to get our act together. I attempted to make one kind of contribution to this project with *Matrix and line*; this text is an attempt to make another kind of contribution.

To those who are skeptical of this project, including those who are skeptical because it is a "project." This category divides into two parts. To the deconstructive conservatives, whom I sometimes also call aesthetes, I address some thoughts about Derrida's work that will make it difficult to rest with conservatism. To the Marxists, I show that there are not only some other answers that have not hitherto been considered in Marxism, but also some other questions.

To those who have been so flummoxed by the posturing of some deconstructionists that they have given up on the idea of Derrida's work mattering very much, I want to show why it does matter very much, despite the way that some people have fooled with it. (Some people have done crummy or trivial things with Marx also.)

I don't want to name the aforementioned "some people" or castigate them personally. Who am I to do this? No one. Nor do I subscribe to Habermas's claim that Derrida is a "young conservative," although some of the Derrideans fit that description. (It is interesting that Habermas's claims about Derrida, put forward mainly in *The Philosophical Discourse of Modernity*, are not based on textual analysis of Derrida's works.)

Materialism, the spiritual poverty of secular society, and alterity

I agree with Habermas about a few things, two of which are important here. Habermas has more than once remarked upon "the non-existent Marxist theory of politics." Habermas may be more right about that than even he is aware. Habermas believes that a political theory worthy of the name must address the condition(s) of political modernity. In this respect it is important to consider Marx and Marxism's fundamentally ambiguous relationship to modernity. By now most Marxists are willing to part ways with economism for long enough to

consider the spiritual poverty of contemporary life. But there is little
in Marxism, either of the classical type, western Marxism, or the traditions of Lenin and Mao, that provides for a systematic critique of
this poverty. This aporia of Marxism, argues Habermas and numerous other theorists gathered under the banner of "radical democracy"
(e.g., Laclau and Mouffe), has opened the way to the emergence of
the "new social movements." There are also problems with some of
these movements, especially in the fact that they tend to be based in
the middle classes and to reflect that basis.

An example, a very important one in the present historical juncture
that people in United States find themselves itself in, might be the
overwhelmingly "pro-choice" rhetoric of the mostly liberal abortion
rights movement. This rhetoric simply mirrors that of consumer capitalism, thereby contributing to the further spiritual impoverishment of
life under advanced capitalism. Such forces have to be united with—
but also struggled with—in the general struggle for women's autonomy,
in which abortion rights play a key role at this point. But this should
blind no one to the fact that "choice" is not at all the same thing as
autonomy and is not the basis for human community; quite the opposite. Interestingly, the other side of this coin is that the question of
community—and, indeed, questions of values more generally—is then
ceded to the anti-abortion rights movement, which also has no interest in women's emancipation or autonomy. (Some work that goes beyond this narrow horizon is found in the ongoing debate on abortion
in *Tikkun* magazine, as well as in Marlene Gerber Fried, ed., *From Abortion
to Reproductive Freedom: Transforming a Movement*.)

The fact remains, however, that these movements have thematized
dimensions of human life as social concerns in ways that quite possibly would never have arisen from Marxist theories or strategies in
themselves.

Secularism is an overarching historical development that does not
only have to do with the rejection of religious authority. Secularism,
furthermore, maintains that there are no fundamental mysteries about
the world, nothing that in principle cannot be known. In this sense,
Marxism is fully and proudly secular. It is common in Marxist circles
to denounce any challenge of this principle as either fideism or agnosticism. (An especially concentrated example of the use of this rhetoric
is Lenin's *Materialism*.) Furthermore, Marxism, like other secularisms,
takes knowledge (or "science") to be the highest principle) which can
only be claimed on the basis of a Hegelian move that reconciles knowledge and freedom). The problem is that there is a difference between
agnosticism and the rush to know too soon, the rush to claim too soon

that the dialectic is going to work out one way or another. The latter seems to be a kind of reduction of the dialectic to mechanical materialism, the very sort of thing that Marx wanted to avoid. How can the dialectic open a space for difference, for the unprecedented? This is a crucial question in general and a crucial question for Derrida in particular.

Pursuing historical and dialectical materialism, people may indeed be able, in principle, to know everything about the world, even if that knowledge does not necessarily issue in a fully predictive science. There really may be no fundamental mysteries in that sense. But I wonder. For example, if all of the physical, and even chemical determinants of a loving relationship could be specified, and if such a relationship could be fully contextualized in terms of economic, political, and other material factors, would we have really described even one instance of love? Derrida seems to raise this question by setting Hegel and Genet side by side in *Glas*.

Wittgenstein once said that it is not *how* the world is that is a mystery, but *that* it is. I've often asked my Marxist friends, in particular my activist friends, what a Marxist answer to the "question of being" would be. That is the question, Why is there something rather than nothing? Besides being told to go find something better to do, it seems the Marxist answer is the same as the logical positivist answer: that the question does not make sense, "something" (i.e., everything) cannot be quantified, and therefore the question of being is not a question at all.[3] That Marxism and positivism converge on this question does not necessarily mean that the former is simply a species of the latter, but it does reveal something about the tendency of Marxism toward an artificial closure and totalism. And it certainly tells us that there is a strong tendency toward positivism in Marxism, a tendency that is strong in all forms of materialism.

Marxists, in avoiding the question of being or, in actuality, suppressing it, have sought to suppress religious influences on Marxism. There have been exceptions, such as Ernst Bloch and Walter Benjamin, but they are, to say the least, very unorthodox Marxists. Ironically, the result has been just the opposite: the extreme case, the Stalin period, had the outcome of making Marxism into an unquestionable religious dogma.

The liberation theologians of Latin America have done the most to foreground the question of being within a Marxist economic and political framework. (I would be willing to say quasi-Marxist, for the purists, but I prefer a Marxism that is open to certain contaminations.) These theologians are primarily activists and not ontologists or metaphysicians. Their example shows that the confrontation with or, better, appreciation of the question of being by Marxism is not the road to quiescence that Marxists often tell us it is.

Of course, their example, and the example of Marxism in a headlong rush toward closure, should also demonstrate that it is not religious mysticism in itself but rather engagement with the world, more specifically with the oppressed, that makes the question of being an empowering question. In other words, Heidegger and Wittgenstein, for all that they say that is provocative and useful on this point, were still light years away from the liberation theologians.

A somewhat reductive sketch of what Derrida is up to in his work might help to draw together the diverse strands of this discussion. Derrida, it might be said, is concerned with two main types of questions and their interrelation. On the one hand (it is important not to prioritize these types by saying "first" and "second"), Derrida examines in great detail the material operations and effects of sign-systems. Like Roland Barthes in *S/Z*, Derrida looks for different codes at work in texts. In some ways, Derrida's work is not so different from structural linguistics, semiotics, hermeneutics, and other disciplines that attempt to discover how the movement of signs can give rise to meaning. (I will turn to an important difference shortly.) On the other hand, Derrida is interested in the question of "is," the function of "is" in "What is?" It is not hard to see that this is thinking in the vein of the question of being. Heidegger had already argued at length that this question, which seems to have no answer, underlies every other question and indeed every other statement. Every other statement takes this "is" for granted and, indeed, generally suppresses the "is." Derrida's seminal (another funny word) work on this question is found in three essays in his *Margins of Philosophy*: "Ousia and Gramme: Note on a Note from *Being and Time*," "The Supplement of Copula: Philosophy Before Linguistics," and "White Mythology: Metaphor in the Text of Philosophy." Most of the other essays bear on these questions, but these are the key texts.

Now, what could be the relationship between these two fields of inquiry? What makes Derrida's work not simply a form of semiotics or hermeneutics is that Derrida pursues sign-systems to their limit. The popular caricature is that Derrida seeks this limit in order to destroy meaning. The truth is that Derrida finds at this limit the place, or non-place, where meaning finds both its possibility and its impossibility. The question of being, on the other hand, is the limit question of questions; it is the question that must be suppressed so that other questions may be asked in a univocal, seemingly fully present voice. Derrida's project may be described as taking off from the place of convergence of these semiotic and ontological limits. As he puts it in "The Voice That Keeps Silence" (from *Speech and Phenomena*),

> The sense of the verb "to be" ... sustains an entirely singular connection with the *word*, that is, with the unity of the *phone* and sense. Evidently it is not a "mere word," since it can be translated into different languages. Moreover, it is not a conceptual generality. But since its sense designates nothing, no thing, no state or ontic determination, since it is encountered nowhere outside the word, its irreducibility is that of the *verbum* or *legein*, the unity of thought and voice in logos. The prerogative of being cannot withstand the deconstruction of the word. *To be* is the first or the last word to withstand the deconstruction of a language of words. But why does using words get mixed up with the determination of being in general as presence? And why is there a privilege attached to the present indicative? Why is the epoch of the *phone* also the epoch of being in the form of presence, that is, of ideality? (p. 74)

But there is more to this convergence than simply a new kind of metaphysics. My own belief, as one Derridean among others, is that Derrida has an emancipatory sense of clearing a space for the other, that he does see this as a politics and not simply as an opening to endless wordplay. But the politics has to be worked out, it has to be concretized, even if then it also has to be unsettled anew, again and again, in a continuing revolution. That many intellectuals, while noisily proclaiming their radicality, seem to strenuously resist this concretization, seems to indicate that they have become new theologians, without the liberation.

If I thought that the only possibility for Marxism was a repeat of the Stalin experience, I would not be a Marxist. If a thought that the only possibility for deconstruction was to create ingenious psychoanalytic-etymological analyses of canonical texts or movies such as "Who Framed Roger Rabbit," I would not be a deconstructionist. But I see possibilities that go far beyond this.

The reader may have surmised from this first part that I intend to create a synthesis or interaction of Marxism and deconstruction. This will indeed be a possibility opened by this text, an important one I think, but not the only possibility. Sartre, in *Critique of Dialectical Reason* and *Search for a Method*, attempted a synthesis of existentialism (à la Sartre, of course) and Marxism, even going so far as to say, in the latter text, that existentialism must become simply parasitic on Marxism. This brings to mind Derrida's notion of the "dangerous supplement" (set out in *of Grammatology*). Deconstruction is always parasitic; Derrida's dangerous supplement to Marxism, however, if fully ramified, would bring about a transformation of Marxism. My sense, though, of what it means to fully ramify any idea or theory or way of thinking through Marxism is that this ramification must encounter practice and issue in praxis. This is why I have discussed Marxism at such length here. My larger aim is to see what the dangerous supplement of Derrida's work will do to the larger tradition of western humanism, of which Marxism is a part.

Critique of "project" in Bataille, Blanchot, and Nancy

Let me now confront this question of a political "project."

For the generation who came of age in the 1960s, this idea is associated most of all with Jean-Paul Sartre. His voice was dominant on the French philosophical-political scene from 1945 to the late sixties. Perhaps it is a peculiarity of some intellectuals of my sub-generation, people who either caught the tail-end of the sixties or just missed it, but the year 1968, not only in France and the United States but from Prague to Shanghai, has remained significant for me, both politically and philosophically. I read books such as Mark Poster's *Existential Marxism in Postwar France* and Arthur Hirsh's *The French New Left* with great enthusiasm, feeling inspired by the idea of "philosopher-activists." If some of this activity was seriously overrated at the time, it is seriously underrated now, and works such as Luc Ferry and Alain Renaut's *French Philosophy of the Sixties* have appeared as neo-conservative attempts to cancel everything that was great and liberating about "68 Thought."

Today, many of the important voices in philosophy and intellectual life more generally, the senior figures, are still from the Generation of 68. Although some of these voices have mellowed, few have capitulated. (The ultra-left, quasi-anarchist "Maoists" who became the self-styled "New Philosophers" were never philosophically significant. The identification of Maoism with this group by many in North America who remain fixated on Europe is simply a form of intellectual and political laziness.) When Derrida speaks of "the impossible," I cannot help but hear a resonance with a popular slogan of the Events of May, "Be reasonable, demand the impossible!" Perhaps that's just romanticism, but we could use a little romanticism.

The underestimation of Sartre today, the avoidance of him, has been accompanied by a concomitant promotion of the liberal figures of the French sixties, especially the later Merleau-Ponty and Raymond Aron. The former, however, was to some extent pushed into a corner by Sartre and his often hyperbolic rhetoric. Still ignored, except by the very specialized and politically isolated, somewhat self-isolated researchers of contemporary continental philosophy, are Sartre's earlier critics on what might be called the other existential left, the Nietzschean left, namely, Georges Bataille and Maurice Blanchot. Jacques Derrida, as he has repeatedly acknowledged, owes a considerable intellectual debt to this pair. In Bataille we find the critique of "project," its reductivism. Speaking a language that positivists cannot hear as discursive (in other words, as anything other than "poetry," perhaps good, perhaps bad—recall that Carnap praised Nietzsche as a poet but referred to Heidegger's writing as "bad poetry"), Bataille asks, "What could be more ridiculous than reducing what is—the universe, if you like—to analogies with useful objects!" (*Guilty*, p. 16).

Derrida, in his essay on Bataille's reading of Hegel, "From Restricted to General Economy," discussed the idea of a "perfect" economy, in which every coin is accounted for. This economy is, of course, Hegel's system, which, while supposedly accounting for everything, exercises a radical reduction on "what is" (a theme well-developed by Kierkegaard, Nietzsche, and other nineteenth-century existentialist thinkers). But what is the "outside" of this economy, and what is its relation to the "inside"? Given that Hegel's economy is diachronic, the succession of historical stages from a well-defined origin to a well-defined end, the "remainders" of this economy must necessarily be outside of the structure of history and historical time.

This interpretation of the remainder as "momentary" seems to be supported by Blanchot, in *The Unavowable Community*, and Jean-Luc Nancy, in *The Inoperative Community*. The first half of Blanchot's text is a post-Bataille, post-Derrida analysis of the Events of May 1968. Blanchot takes it as a virtue of the young militants that they were not "going anywhere," that they put forward no positive programs or projects. It seems that, for Blanchot, May 1968 was the big "love-in" that fits in well with the present wave of apolitical sixties nostalgia.[4] Thus,

> it was not even a question of overthrowing an old world; what mattered was to let a possibility manifest itself, the possibility—beyond any utilitarian gain—of a *being-together* that gave back to all the right to equality in fraternity through a freedom of speech that elated everyone. Everybody had something to say, and, at times, to write (on the walls); what exactly, mattered little. (p. 30)

Actually, in the context of the times, this attitude was refreshing, especially as compared with the actions and pronouncements of the French Communist Party, who declared that the rebellious youths of Paris were making a big mess of things and were an element "alien" to the working class. (Behind the scenes, the PCF was acting in a far more sinister way.) But within the present context, and in light of the anti-project framework, this characterization of the events almost necessarily reads as hippie nostalgia.

Consider, too, the notion of an event, contrasted to the notion of unfolding process. The problem with Hegelianism is that an event has no real existence (remember the exclusion of sense-certainty from the system); indeed, it simply drops out. I will return to this point, to look at the flip-side of that coin, in a moment.[5]

Nancy, whose *Inoperative Community* was the immediate inspiration for Blanchot's text, focuses especially on the notions of "being toward death," which he takes from Heidegger, and "singularity." Where Heidegger, however, describes death as "that possibility which is one's ownmost" (*Being and Time*, section 50), Nancy is concerned with the death that summons one's finitude toward community. As Patrick Hayden puts it, characterizing Nancy's position,

> The finitude of community, the finitude of beings summoning community, is also the very absencing of community through this finitude. That which calls oneself into question most radically is the death of an other; not one's *own* death, which cannot be experienced as such, but an other's death that concerns one, that one *shares*. The sharing of the other's death brings out most forcefully the differences of beings-in-common. Someone else's death removes me from myself, and their absence, impossibly, is the very openness of community, its very possibility. Without death (which is the absolutely other, the most irreducible alterity), community would not be possible. (p. 21)

Who is this "one" who is concerned with the death of the other? In Nancy's view, this one is not the atomistic individual of liberalism but rather the "singularity." Nancy's remarks on the "absolutely detached for-itself" seem aimed not only at liberalism but also at Sartre's radical individualism. In the place of the traditional, self-conscious subject of Descartes, the "being without relation" (p. 4), Nancy proposes the singular being, whose "consciousness of self turns out to be outside the self of consciousness" (p. 19). Kathy Dow refers to this reconfigured subjectivity as "intrinsically extrinsic." (In *Matrix and line* I use "positionality" and "externalism" to name this social ontology.) Furthermore, Nancy declares that "whereas two subjects merely confront each other as objects in opposition, singular beings encounter each other through the mode of "compearance" ("co-appearance") or mutual exchange" (ibid).

It is unclear to me, however, that these formulations, coupled as they are with Nancy's rewriting of "being toward death," really go so far beyond Sartre's existentialism. They remind me of the earlier existentialism, devoid of the later political understanding. This is the result, I think, of Nancy's and Blanchot's efforts toward avoiding any sense of personal transcendence; it seems they think transcendence is an opening to Stalinism. (A more direct exposition of this issue by Nancy is found in "The Compearance: From the Existence of 'Communism' to the Community of 'Existence'." The major source on this question is Vol. 3 of Bataille's *The Accursed Share*, "Sovereignty.") They are right, it does open that possibility. What, however, is the cost of foreclosing the possibility? To my mind it is a notion of "mutual exchange" in a community that does not have to be created because it is "always already" here, that simply reminds one of liberalism.

Nancy's "compearance" is not a "union," for the latter would assume "already given subjects (objects)." Rather, compearance "consists in the appearance of the *between* as such" (pp. 28–29). Nancy would have done well to have left the words "as such" out of this formulation, as they undermine the idea of "the between," or what more properly should have been called "between-ness." (Martin Buber's term *das Zwischenmenschliche*, the "interhuman," and the analysis that it is embedded in is helpful here; see Paul Mendes-Flohr, *From Mysticism to Dialogue*, esp. pp. 31–47.) One assumes that the notion of solidarity, especially in tension with autonomy, would have problems similar to those ascribed to union. And yet, I find nothing in the terms that accompany Nancy's "between" that really serves as a replacement for dialectically related notions of solidarity and autonomy, especially if this dialectic is structured, as it is in Sartre's *Critique*, as a totalizing process without a totalizer, without a transcendent spirit that provides the final meaning of history. The same goes for Blanchot, especially when he speaks of a "mutual contestation" that "deepens [the aware-ness of being isolated] in a solitude lived in common" (*Unavowable Community*, p. 21). If the only thing that makes this kind of talk not simply a form of gloomy existentialism is the lack of a "project," then perhaps we should say, "Long live the project!"

This kind of talk *is* gloomy existentialism, nihilism, *because* of its lack of a project.

Perhaps it is easiest to see Sartre's more Cartesian side in the "dialectics of boxing" example from the unfinished second volume of the *Critique of Dialectical Reason*. But this side is only predominant if one focuses on each boxer individually. An existential individualism is also readily apparent if one focuses on Sartre's choice of "sport." All the same, a sense of between-ness here structures the event as it develops in time. (For perceptive analyses of Sartre's dialectics of boxing, see McBride, pp. 163–68, and Aronson, pp. 51–75). There might be better analogies to use than boxing. I like to think about a group of children on the playground, who not only have to divide into teams but have to make up the game itself. Some people may find this example problematic, but I also find the dialectics of American-style football more reflective of the overall social dialectic, especially when one takes into account the role of the spectators and the larger socioeconomic conditions of the contest. Sartre, of course, was seeking the simplest example of a contest, but his example seems to leave him with two separate, opposing subjectivities. Is "mutual contestation" any better, however? Furthermore, where Blanchot and Nancy focus so much on the momentary, "always already" structure of these contestations and exchanges, which collapses in their work into its own kind of Cartesianism, Sartre is concerned in his latter work to absorb the moment in a network of social processes.

In favor of Sartre, too, I would say that while there remains a Cartesian kernel to even his later work, his social theory must be applied to a culture that is itself thoroughly Cartesian. The "always already" community of Nancy and Blanchot ignores this. Their always already might be a powerful way of overcoming the Cartesianism of western liberal societies if it were integrated into a project. I have admittedly overstated my case against Nancy and Blanchot, whose conceptions of community are an inspiration in some respects. Some readers will say that the problem with my critique of these conceptions is that I want to use them. That's right! But even beyond the question of integrating Nancy and Blanchot (and the general project of rethinking community in the way that they do) into the project of reconfiguring the polis, or bringing the polis into being, I find three basic problems in their approach. First, their work exhibits the typical insularity of much philosophy from France. Nancy and Blanchot (and Bataille's conception of "literary communism," which Nancy takes up in the final part of The Inoperative Community) have to be understood in the context of the response to Sartre. Apart from this context, and even somewhat within it, their work seems to generate a momentary excitement that has no orientation toward practice and a longer-term contribution to what might be called the project of quietism. Second, apart from the example of the Events of May in Blanchot's work, there is an overarching rationalism here. There is no empirical consideration of traditional communities or so-called elective communities. There is little sense that liberalism is more than merely a conception to be philosophically dissected, that atomism is a culture and a form of life and must be addressed as such. A little attention to the notion of ideology, especially in Althusser's sense, wouldn't hurt either.

Third, Nancy and Blanchot seem to get a positively existential high from considering the pathos of isolation and death. There is, certainly, a very important point to emphasizing the meaning of isolation and solitude, as Sophocles does at the conclusion of *Antigone*. Creon, having lost all respect from his subjects because of his hubris and his self-involved emptiness, says, "Take me away, quickly, out of sight. I don't even exist—I'm no one. Nothing." But it seems a kind of morbid sensibility, typical of Blanchot (and one thinks especially of the "Acephale" group, which contemplated a random murder as a way of forging their "community"; see Allan Stoekl's "Introduction" to Bataille, *Visions of Excess*), to focus exclusively on the death of the other as the other side of an isolated individualism that never gives rise to "singular being." One gets little sense from Nancy, especially, that "life is with people" (as Jews of the eastern European shtetls used to put it). In "Problems of Deconstructive Communitarianism," Kathleen League makes the point forcefully:

> In speaking of and for community, many deconstructionists are one-sidedly promoting, emphasizing, and affirming the concepts of lack, absense, death, loss of the subject, nothingness, and unworking. They are doing this to the near total exclusion of, reference to, evocation of, and concern with life and its affirmation and nurturance.
> Perhaps the selective emphasis on death is merely strategic—perhaps it does not connote a dark fascination with death, but is merely used against the counterproductive or facile tendency toward mere emphasis on life. I am not convinced that this is the case, however. [This selective emphasis] on death and absence not only reinforces the binary oppositions that deconstruction is supposed to challenge, . . . it also is no more healthy or helpful than a selective emphasis on life, . . . it probably also does bespeak nihilist tendencies and fascinations. (p. 2)

The Bataille-inspired fascination with death often seems the flip-side of a sanguine affirmation ("The future's so bright I gotta wear shades"). There are useful, sometimes profound images here, but where is the negativity in this nihilism, where is the critique?

There is some force to the critique of project, and the question still remains: Can there be a political project that does not close the way to the advent of the other, of the impossible? The question remains, for me at any rate; for Nancy the question does not seem to arise.

Is Nancy's inoperative community the only political possibility of deconstruction? It is the possibility that one encounters in making a deconstructive end-run around Marx and Sartre, among others.[6]

The project of deconstructive social theory must be developed in terms of formal characteristics quite different from the work of Nancy, Blanchot, and others working in the same vein. This is not to say that no one should do that sort of work; there are many genres of philosophy, many of which can be pursued fruitfully. For that matter, one might learn some things about community from, say, Ursula LeGuin's *The Dispossessed* or Marge Piercy's *Woman on the Edge of Time* that could never be gleaned from "theory." To my mind, in order to construct a social theory, one must deal with five basic categories: 1) social ontology and ontology more generally; 2) descriptive analysis of the *Zeitgeist* (to put it provocatively), that is, of the character of our time; 3) the question of mediations (which may also mean the question of why "mediation" is an inadequate category); 4) the question of agency and subjectivity (again, this may mean showing the inadequacy of the categories); and 5) a vision of a just or substantially more just social formation. Admittedly, the first, third, and fourth categories are closely related; the third and fourth categories come under the general provenance of social ontology. The point is to emphasize certain specific features of each category: the relation of social ontology and ontology (a classic example would be the relation of historical materialism to dialectical materialism), the specific character of mediations, the specific characteristics of agency—if such a thing is possible.

The fifth category is not found in all social theories, and here no simple distinction can be made between social theories that are "descriptive" and those that call themselves "critical." Positivist social theory, such as Chicago School sociology, prides itself on being coldly descriptive. Adorno, who is worlds away from positivism, argues that the proper place for the presentation of utopia is the work of art, not philosophy or social theory.

Deconstructive social theory cannot afford the "luxury" of doing without a vision of a more just society (I am not sure that any social theory can afford this anymore). If deconstruction already had a well-developed history of social theorizing and engagement, perhaps it too could operate through the first four categories. But, in the spirit of speaking to those who are frustrated with a promised deconstructive social theory that never gets beyond the preliminaries, I would argue that deconstruction must not only show where the aporias are, and clear a space for alterity in the spaces of these fissures, but must pose concrete alternatives.

Styles of theory

The open letter aspect of this text, discussed earlier, will come to the surface frequently. Amid these personal interventions, however, I do some analytic readings, sticking to "straightforward" descriptions of the texts of others and "straightforward" arguments of my own. There is such a thing as healthy, deconstructive suspicion of the supposed straightforwardness of arguments and descriptions, that no voice can truly be univocal, and that supposed univocity or the attempt to impose it is a dangerous and bad thing. The deconstructive argument concerning univocity is a cornerstone of the analysis in this text. If, however, there has been at times a terrorizing, reductive, positivistic fetish with a supposedly univocal logic of argument in some quarters of philosophy and social theory, there has arisen in certain other quarters of post-Hegelian, and especially post-Heideggerian philosophy a fetish that is the reverse image of this reductivism: an expansionism so great, and a concern with "marvelous images" so "playful," that the result is the, however exalted, mere aestheticization of values, life, the universe, everything. In the hands of the "masters" (in some cases, the mandarins), in particular Nietzsche and Heidegger, this aestheticization maintains a critical edge that should be harnessed by social theory. Reductive analytic philosophy, turned on its head, often results in texts that read like a very long song from the sixties psychedelic opportunist Donovan. "First there is a mountain then there is no mountain then there is" is fine for a two-and-a-half-minute pop song; in its extended version playfulness often becomes dull and wearying and has no edge.

Some texts of deconstruction are both playful and very serious. In *Glas* Derrida is as much a master of the art of writing as Cecil Taylor is the unsurpassed master of the piano. What may appear as nearly chaotic is, upon closer inspection by the careful, caring listener evidence of a wide-ranging intelligence, a text in pursuit of its connections.

Paul Bove, in his *In the Wake of Theory*, discusses three kinds of critics. His tripartite scheme, "of differing relations of . . . practice and ideology to the active forces of anomie and repression in our civilization," is insightful. Although Bove is specifically concerned with academic literary criticism, his characterizations are useful with regard to philosophy and social theory as well.

> In the first of these crude categories we find those who know not what they do when they ignore the anomalies of their professional and social situation and train their students——or hope to—in the no longer marketable skills of their own specialized paradigm. Such educators are functionaries of an ideology they do not perceive as

such: they take their position to be natural and unquestionable, although mysteriously and sadly under attack. They grow depressed.

The second group is allied to the first: they are the priests of the dominant ideology engaged in defining its power and expanding its influence. They study the "crisis" of our culture and profession but do so only to reform the "flaws" and "misdirections" that have, as they see it, led to the loss of stability, order, values, and "common sense." They frequently mistake elements of the third group—if I may be allowed a prolepsis—for the *cause* of the crisis they perceive. They cannot seriously think through the idea that the questioning existence of those they call "radicals" or simply "barbarians" indicates the real illegitimacy of the social organization and cultural values they defend or, in their fantasies, hope to "return to." (pp. 30–31)

Bove describes the second group as a "priestly class" that has as two of their functions "to simplify and to lie." These descriptions fit well both the unconscious and the conscious champions of reductivism. I should add that I do not believe that micrological reductivism is any more a professional danger for analytic philosophers per se than macrological flabbiness is a danger for continental philosophers. (Actually, these dangers seem to be mirror images of one another.) Both categories in philosophy, in any case, have largely outlived their usefulness and are themselves reductive toward the many areas of philosophy that do not fit into the categories. From the canonical analytic philosophers, from Frege to Quine and Davidson, we should take the concern for argument and for employing the fallibilistic model of the natural sciences. From the canonical continental figures, from Kant and Hegel to Derrida, we should take the concern for history, historicization, and temporality, the concern for embodiment, and the concern for truths that are not captured in the model of the natural sciences, and conceptions of the good and the beautiful that were set apart from philosophy by the Vienna positivists. Both "kinds" of philosophy can be done rigorously. Although I disagree with Habermas on many points in his massive synthesis, he has shown that it is possible to combine the virtues of the two canons.

Given the fact, however, that the subject matter of this book fits more into "continental" philosophy, I will turn to Bove's third category.

Of the third group—which is multifaceted—many descriptions might be offered. I am most interested in one feature that easily distinguishes this third group from the other two: its members often critically study the history and structure of intellectual language and practice to draw attention to its effects and to the traditional intellectuals' interest in playing certain roles. At times they go beyond even such critical history and suggest different kinds of language and work more likely to be of use, especially to others, in their struggles against power and domination.

Such critics try to invent new tactics to reduce the ease with which intellectuals can be taken back up into the hegemonic institutions that, in large part, have formed them. Because of this need to resist the acceptable forms of language and practice, critics of the third group often produce work others call "alienating," "elitist," "threatening," or simply "absurd." (p. 31)

Bove well describes a risk that needs to be taken, the risk of creating new genres of theory that resist the homogenizing logic of the Same that is the law for the first two groups he describes. But, in the sentence that immediately follows, he perhaps unintentionally describes a fourth group: "Of course much 'theoretical' work in criticism and composition is simply narcissistic, obscure, or pretentious and prissy." Where does one draw the line? There can be no hard-and-fast rule, nor should there be, but we might still look for the following characteristics: critical negativity, an orientation toward practice (what used to be called engagement), attention, respect, and a certain humility toward the other, an avoidance of mere wordplay, an avoidance of obscurantism; in short, the qualities that would make theoretical work useful to oppressed and marginalized people "in their struggles against power and domination."

Again, without making any final pronouncements on what styles and genres of theorizing might be most useful in these struggles, my intention is to provide analytical tools contextualized within the historical trajectory of humanism. My one concession to a more imagistic writing is Part 3, "From Other Shores," where I mentally rove the globe in trains, planes, automobiles, and fiber optics.

Justice, prudential Marxism, and deconstruction

Deconstruction can be understood, I believe, as a form of historical materialism, an argument I make in *Matrix and line*, Chap. 1. The distance between deconstruction's intertextual materialism and Marxist historical materialism, however, can be gauged by considering the question of justice. The final discussion of this first part is organized around the question of justice because here lies the intersection of ethics and politics or the ethical and the political. That is, while there are differences between ethics and politics, and their domains, the meaning of justice is the same for each. That, at least, is the view of Plato. Other views were dominant in Plato's day and are dominant in our own. While some modern political thinkers have attempted to create a separation between ethics and politics such that justice is the key term in ethics while power is the key term in politics, this separation cannot stand. To admit that the polis should be structured by a conception of justice in which might makes right is to accept that ethics is no more than the window-dressing of seemingly polite societies.

And yet, neither ethics nor politics can do without a theory and understanding of power. Marx emphasized this dimension one-sidedly. Analytical Marxism brings out this side by simply ramifying Hobbesian social contractarianism through the class struggle. I take much analytical Marxism to be a good teacher by negative example, showing one possibility for Marxism that has to be replaced by another possibility, more difficult to grasp. The dilemma for Marxism is to maintain the struggle for justice, on the one hand, while understanding, on the other hand, that "without power we are nothing." Perceptively, Sartre once remarked, somewhere, that with Stalin we see what Marxism is as a theory of power. One might say, "as a pure theory of power," or "merely as a theory of power." I do not wish to contribute to the conveniently reductive view of the Stalin period that is frequently peddled by liberals, opportunists, and others who are trying to do everything but understand, but there is certainly something to Sartre's claim. It would seem that Stalin thought that, if the proletariat conquered power, justice would take care of itself. To the contrary, I wonder if, without attention to justice and without attention to the ethical moment in politics, the oppressed are condemned to be conquered by power. Stalin also serves here as a teacher by negative example, in that his *histomat* and *diamat* did reveal a side of Marxism that is undeniably there. For, how is Marx to speak of justice? How is Marx to speak of the ethical moment in politics?

To shift gears: Kant, the astronomer, was one of the first philosophers to speak of the possibility of conscious life on other planets, in other solar systems. In *Groundwork for the Metaphysics of Morals*, Kant argues that the universal moral law, the categorical imperative, applies to all conscious rational beings, whether they be on earth or on the Dog Star. No leap of faith is required to assert that the universal moral law also applies to relations between beings from earth and the Dog Star (or what-have-you).

In her novel *The Word for World is Forest*, Ursula LeGuin describes the colonization of a planet that the colonizers call New Tahiti. The colonial-military expedition aims to exploit the natural resources of the planet, primarily trees, which have been entirely used up on Earth.

There is a glitch in the colonization plans, of course: the planet is already inhabited, by beings the colonists call creechies, "a meter tall and covered with green fur." The natives call themselves Athsheans. The novel is structured around a conflict between two of the colonists, Captain Davidson, a self-styled Conquistador, and Raj Lyubov, the colony's chaplain who also takes an anthropologist's interest in the Athsheans. Davidson uses the Athsheans as slave labor. Here is his characterization of the creechies, spoken to one of the logging foremen (named Ok) in charge of working them:

> "They're little, all right, but don't let 'em fool you, Ok. They're tough; they've got terrific endurance; and they don't feel pain like humans. That's the part you forget, Ok. You think hitting one is like hitting a kid, sort of. Believe me, it's more like hitting a robot for all they feel it. Look, you've laid some of the females, you know how they don't seem to feel anything, no pleasure, no pain, they just lay there like mattresses no matter what you do. They're all like that. Probably they've got more primitive nerves than humans do. Like fish. . . . The thing is, Ok, the creechies are lazy, they're dumb, they're treacherous, and they don't feel pain. You've got to be tough with 'em." (pp. 10–11)

The Athsheans can talk, they have their own language and they learn to speak the language of the humans. They dream, and their experiences in dreamtime serve as guides to non-dreamtime, as opposed to "waking" life. They actually pity the Earth people for being able to dream only while asleep. The Athsheans, in fact, seem not to sleep at all. They have a complex social structure, though seemingly a static one, until the day, that is, when they have had enough from the colonizers, especially those of Davidson's ilk. Lyubov's report to a visiting delegation from Tau-Ceti (called Cetians) reveals the logic of the dilemma at the heart of the novel:

> "Well, I wonder if they're not proving their adaptability now. By adapting their behavior to us. To the Earth Colony. For four years they've behaved to us as they do to one another. Despite the physical differences, they recognized us as members of their species, as men. However, we have not responded as members of their species should respond. We have ignored the responses, the rights and obligations of non-violence. We have killed, raped, dispersed, and enslaved the native humans, destroyed their communities, and cut down their forests. It wouldn't be surprising if they'd decided that we are not human." (p. 62)

Lyubov's commanding officer is quick to attempt to counteract this statement: "Captain Lyubov is expressing his personal opinions and theories," said Colonel Dongh, "which I should state I consider possibly to be erroneous . . . ." Interesting that this counter-statement turns on the *possibility* of error, as though this is a strong enough basis to justify the *possible* exploitation and oppression of creatures who are outwardly different, but not so different, from earth people. (The truly hard case, of course, would be radical difference in appearance.)

In response to the claim, made by both Lyubov and one of the visiting Cetians, that the Athsheans are human, a branch of the human species, Colonel Dongh says, "The fact is that these creechies are a meter tall, they're covered with green fur, they don't sleep, and they're not human beings in my frame of reference." What follows is one of the strongest passages in the novel:

> "Captain Davidson," said the Cetian, "do you consider the native hilfs human or not?"
> "I don't know."
> "But you had sexual intercourse with one . . . . Would you have sexual intercourse with a female animal? What about the rest of you?" He looked at the purple colonel, the flowering majors, the livid captains, the cringing specialists. Contempt came into his face. "You have not thought things through," he said. By his standards it was a brutal insult.

I will return to this connection between thinking—thinking things through—and what it means to be human.

Most who read this novel will agree that the behavior of the earth colonists toward the Athsheans is an example of gross injustice. I have used this novel several times in the classroom, and there is no question that every member of the class, without exception, is on the side of the Athsheans. I'm militantly on their side as well. But why? How can we say that there is injustice here? What standard of justice allows us to make this judgment? And what, we might ask, is our court of appeal?

Let's put ourselves into the novel. We, we Earth people, we humans, have no "material" connection to the Athsheans. That is, there is nothing that materially connects the fates of our two societies. LeGuin has created a most difficult example. New Tahiti, Athshea, could be hit by a giant meteor, a calamity that would destroy all of the people there. This would not affect the population of Earth. (Earth's people would have to find another planet to exploit for its wood, but that is not what is at issue here.) What difference does it make if destruction comes to Athshea's people from a conscious, purportedly rational source or a chance occurrence in the cosmos? Perhaps there is a difference to the people of Athshea, but what is the difference to *us*? For that matter, countless species of rational beings in far-flung corners of the universe have most likely come into being, passed their time, and passed away into oblivion without our having the slightest knowledge of their existence. Other than how these species might matter to us for what we might gain by knowing them, why should they matter to us for themselves?

Despite the fact that we seem to know injustice when we see it in the novel, arguments seem to fail us.

And what is the answer of Marxism, in the specific terms of Marxism, to these questions? The general question, of justice toward the other, is a limit question, of the sort that I worried Marxism with earlier in the discussion of the question of being. I may be accused, I suppose, of going to extreme lengths—to other planets, for heaven's sake!—to contrive this question. The positivist answer to the question of being is that the infinite "something" and the non-existent "nothing" cannot serve as proper referents in a logically and empirically well-formed sentence. I suppose that the postivist response to the limit question of justice toward the other might be something on the order of, "We'll deal with that when we get to other planets and meet these aliens." Until then this "question" also has no proper referent. (How thinking in such a frame could ever encounter the unprecedented I do not know.)

But of course there are limit questions of justice toward the other that confront "us" on this planet all the time. LeGuin's novel is an allegory of many different historical episodes, but I take it to be especially an allegory of the U.S. invasion of Vietnam. If memory serves, I first read this novel in 1981. When I read the passage, quoted above, in which the words "they don't feel pain like humans" appear, I was transported back in time to a course I had in college, on religious perspectives on war and peace. This would have been around 1977. One day the head of the university's ROTC department addressed our class. A colonel, he had fought in Vietnam. He referred to the people of Vietnam as "gooks" and "the Cong." Even more offensively, he remarked that "the people of Vietnam are Buddhists; it doesn't bother them to die, because they know they're just going to be reincarnated."

One thinks too of the use of "defoliants" in Vietnam, as though there weren't people under those trees. The discussion of Agent Orange was especially telling, organized as it was around what it did to the people who dropped it from aircraft. Telling, too, is the fact that there is still no accurate count of how many Vietnamese people were killed by the U.S. invaders; the figure still stands between one and three million.

The injustice of the U.S. war against the people of Vietnam was condemned by all Marxists, myself among them, and rightly so. But this condemnation was not, at least for those thinking solely in Marxist terms, a "moral" condemnation, nor could it be. Shifting to the present tense of a schematization of what must be the purely Marxist case for distinguishing justice from injustice, we must look for the material connection between the people of Vietnam and at least a significant part of the people of the United States. That is, we must ask how the peoples of the two countries could share a common fate. Marx's answer is that there is a class of people, defined by its relation to the mode of production, that has no country. This class has no interest in the existence of nation states in the long run. Lenin's contribution (this is more thumbnail sketching here, I realize; it should not serve as an excuse for the reader to avoid looking into Lenin's theory of imperialism) was to show that, in the age of monopoly capital, the world was (and is) divided into oppressor nations and oppressed nations.[7] As part of the long-range struggle to transcend the nation state as a social form, and to create an international communist society, the proletariat and oppressed of all nations have an interest, a material interest, in promoting the national liberation struggles of the oppressed nations and the defeats of the oppressor nations that these struggles, when successful, entail.[8]

Now, how is it that people know that the liberation of oppressed people is in their interest? This seems like a silly question in the case of people who are brutally oppressed and exploited themselves. Of course they know that liberation is in their interest. I do mean a little irony here. On the one hand, people who are involved in struggles for day-to-day survival, when things get to that point, know how to cut through a lot of crap (there's no nicer word for it), not to mention fatally blithe "deconstructions" of the language of liberation. On the other hand, Frantz Fanon (*Black Skin, White Masks*, pp. 83–108) was on to something with his analysis of the "colonial mentality. But, how is it that people who live in the oppressor countries, who most likely have a higher standard of living as a result of living in these countries, who may themselves have taken on the mentality of the oppressor, how is it that these people know that the liberation of oppressed people is in their interest?

In some cases the people (and I do mean "the people," as opposed to members of the oppressing classes, i.e., capitalists) may "feel" their interest, they may feel the material connection that they have with oppressed peoples. In other words, the consequences of the oppression "come home." The way this happened, with the war in Vietnam, in the first instance is that the Vietnamese people fought back. This did, as one might imagine, have an effect on the U.S. soldiers—a salutary effect. As the U.S. Government began more and more to define the whole of the Vietnamese people as the "enemy," many U.S. soldiers began to understand that they were fighting for an unjust cause. This is one aspect of the Vietnam syndrome that the U.S. Government has worked for two decades now to eradicate. The fierce resistance of "the enemy" brought this home to many soldiers.

While the effects of oppression will in general sooner or later come home, however, the warping of the world by imperialism, especially the creation of a world order that is fundamentally lopsided, means that there is no simple closing of the circuit. Two points are important here. First, the most powerful imperialist countries, such as the United States, can generally get away with tremendously destructive acts toward small, poor countries. Often the borders of these countries have been drawn by one or several imperialist powers, for the very purpose of fragmenting people. Think of the Contra war waged by the United States against the people of Nicaragua. This was a very dirty war, waged by a mercenary army of thugs, rapists, cocaine dealers, gun-runners, and former members of Somoza's National Guard (or all of the above), in the pay of the United States and for the purpose of projecting and protecting U.S. imperial interests in Central America. The effects on the people of Nicaragua were devastating. What were the "feedback" effects on the people of the United States? In a real sense, there was no direct feedback. Second, even when there is feedback, the lopsidedness of the world, combined with the fact that many people in the imperialist countries, particularly those among the middle classes and the better-off part of the working class, have been more or less bought off by the spoils of imperialism, combined with the fact that the capitalists of these countries have at their disposal various ideological apparatuses (state or otherwise) that allow capitalism to create public opinion, means that this feedback can often be channelled into reactionary responses ("The Mexicans are taking our jobs," "Iran is holding America hostage").

There was some debate (not enough) in left circles concerning the feedback strategy around the Gulf War. Some activists who worked in opposition to the war thought (and think) the best thing to do is to tell people something on the order of, "You may support this war now, when it's not really affecting you directly, but when those body bags start coming home, or when oil prices start going up, or when the economy generally starts to decline, then you'll question the war, and then you'll oppose it." Well, the body bags didn't come home.

The war was followed by Nuremburg-style, fascistic victory parades

to welcome home the troops (a major effort—announced by George
Bush as such—to "kick" the Vietnam syndrome). Oil prices did go up,
though mainly because of price-gouging by the major oil companies.
And the economy continued on its generally downward path. This
may have led many people to question the Gulf War, but on the grounds
of prudence, not ethics. There has not been an accompanying questioning
about what the war did to the people of Iraq or the Kurdish people,
who were encouraged by the United States to rise up, then abandoned.
(Bush later stated that the United States never intended to help the
Kurds, which is no surprise, but it is amazing that this could be
promulgated as the reason for saying that the actions of the United
States were acceptable.)

I suppose that the Marxists (I want to say "supposed" Marxists, but
I'm trying to point out a tendency in Marxism itself) who argued the
"when it comes back to you, then you'll think about what the U.S.
government is doing" line would find no insult in my claim. Prudence
is a perfectly valid standard, they would say. Furthermore, it's impractical
and "idealist" to condemn the Gulf War because it is/was "wrong."

In this view, the only way to solidarity is through a common material
condition of deprivation. I argued above that the development of
imperialism in this century has created an economic lopsidedness such
that this common material condition is not likely to come about, at
least not in any direct, straightforward way. Again, to be sure, the
awful things that the imperialist system is doing to this planet and its
people will undoubtedly affect the people in the imperialist countries.
But even when this "lonely hour of the economy" (as Althusser put it)
finally arrives (Althusser thought that it would never arrive in any
kind of deterministic sense, which is the point here), there still will
have to be an additional leap to solidarity.

There were Marxists who opposed the Gulf War because it was wrong
and because of what it would do and did do to the people of Iraq,
apart from whatever consequences might come back to the people of
the United States. I count myself in this group. But I wonder if this
Marxism can be based entirely on the works of Marx (or even Lenin),
and I wonder if this argument, which is basically about justice and
about a fundamental regard for the other, can be fully grounded in
classical historical materialism.

This, to my mind, is where deconstruction comes in.

I hope, frankly, that this discussion of the Gulf War and historical
materialism and "prudential Marxism" has served to shake up some
readers who might have expected a book on deconstruction and politics to be about something else and to employ a different kind of rhetoric

altogether. I am not entirely unsympathetic to work in deconstructive politics that uses different rhetorical strategies—I've learned a great deal from such works, and my *Matrix and line* is, in places, such a work itself. I realize that the analysis of imperialism presented above may seem fairly standard Marxist-Leninist fare to some, although most likely to some who have a standard way of claiming this without ever having studied the question. Fine. My point, however, is that there is a real problem with any deconstructive politics that could not take these kinds of analyses into account or, as stressed earlier, encounter some of the problems that these analyses have, problems that cannot be entirely avoided, or even serve to negate such analyses and facts. To my mind, deconstructive politics of this sort renders talk of "the other" and "the margins" completely empty.

Some Derrideans, too, attempt to quash any real engagement with politics, supposedly "deconstructing praxis" in order to show that praxis is impossible. Well, that is right, praxis is impossible, in the Derridean sense of impossible. But it is the impossibility that we must strive for; indeed, it is the impossibility that also makes ethics, this striving beyond prudence, possible. In a moment I will discuss how this Kantian scheme may be understood as describing a material structure. On one level, though, without getting into too much discussion of ontology, the point can be put quite simply. There are, in fact, two impossibilities of praxis. One applies to people who engage in praxis and who find that the tasks are infinite, that there is no end to revolution (as Mao argued). The other applies to intellectuals who avoid praxis and who use deconstruction as a sophisticated way of saying that people cannot change the world. Why we need deconstruction to articulate this kind of conservatism (the kind most often heard from liberals in recent years) and cynicism, I do not know. Frankly, I think it would be better if these sophisticates would just leave the whole political thing alone and write little essays on Proust and metonymy.

But I was discussing Marx . . . .

Marx and Engels were sometimes notorious for their disparagement of ethics. Indeed, discussions of morality sometimes evinced fits of laughter from Marx. To be sure, Marx and Engels could both employ the language of justice and injustice with great rhetorical force. When we look for the material basis of their language of justice, however, we find prudence, we find that what is just is that which furthers the unfolding of the class struggle and the development of modes of production toward communism. Imperialism, in Lenin's sense of a qualitative development in capitalism that brings the entire world into a single mode of production (centered around monopoly and finance capital), only emerged in the last years of Marx's life. Although Marx did not live long enough to see enough of this phenomenon in order to systematically analyze it, he did recognize that changes were taking place on a global scale, and at that point he began to condemn the actions of the great powers toward economically backward countries (the social, if not always geographical, East). Engels, who lived for twelve more years after the death of Marx (1883), not only did not systematically analyze the emergence of imperialism, he made some major errors around this question, errors that continue to underlie the great power nationalism of the Second International, social democratic parties—of course, these aren't "errors" anymore. But Marx's condemnation at this later point only underscores the prudential basis for his rhetoric of justice. And this later condemnation therefore complements those passages in the earlier works where Marx and Engels take an amoral stance toward the "progress" that is supposedly brought to "backward" countries by colonialism. In *Kantian Ethics and Socialism*, Harry Van der Linden sets out a number of these passages; here is a representative passage, framed by Van der Linden:

> [Marx] writes in an article on imperialism in India that although the destruction of the village system in India caused by British industry and trade is a bitter pill for our personal feelings, this is irrelevant, because England is "the unconscious tool of history" in creating a social revolution in India, sweeping away its backwardness and repressive social order. Marx argues that this social revolution with all its suffering will lead to the final revolution between capital and collective labor and that, therefore, "we have the right, in point of history, to exclaim with Goethe: Should this torture then torment us? Since it brings us greater pleasure? Were not through the rule of Timor, Souls devoured without measure?" (pp. 262–63)

As a Marxist I find this not only disturbing but sickening. There has got to be another Marx, even if this is a Marx who is "dangerously supplemented."

On one level, the material ground for prudential Marxism is set out in the critique of what neo-classical economics calls externalities. If I may be indulged a textbook definition, "Externalities are the costs that society bears by the actions of firms, individuals, and governments not reflected in prices" (Cochrane et al., *Macroeconomics*, p. 332). The type of externality that most people are familiar with is pollution. "For example, a firm that discharges pollution into a river is throwing off a cost onto society—the cost of a polluted river." In neo-classical economics the idea is that every cost can be measured in monetary terms; this is a positivist strategy for making economics a value-free domain. However, even pursuing the line of reasoning in its own terms—as Marx of course did—we see that: 1) there is a cost, even if not directly to those responsible for polluting the river, and 2) sooner or later, all humanity will be living downstream. We are beginning to see that "later" is now.[9]

Imperialism has managed to send the worst forms of exploitation (what Lenin in *Imperialism* calls super-exploitation), oppression, and outright plunder "downstream," to the Third World. In the uneven economic development that characterizes capitalism and imperialism generally, declining imperialist powers such as the United States also bring this exploitation and oppression to bear on parts of their own populations, often those who are not members of the dominant sex or ethnic group. For example, despite the publicity given to the myth of progress in race relations and in the position of Black people in society, the economic position of Black people has steadily declined since 1964. Poverty, too, seems to have a sex: female. This is not to say that white males have it easy, although middle-class white males have had a comparatively easy time of it. The working class, including that part of it that is white, has also seen its standard of living erode in recent years, including through the perverse "economic recovery" of the Reagan years. Economically, politically, socially, and culturally there are many people in the imperialist countries who find themselves "downstream."

Will this process, however, in which more and more of humanity finds itself downstream, ever result in a common condition of immiseration for the overwhelmingly greater part of the world's people? I do not believe so. I do not believe that there will ever come a point, on a world scale, where the proletariat, fused into a single class that is aware of its common condition and its common enemy, will square off with the capitalist classes of the world. My reason for not believing in this scenario is not that I am a pessimist. The problem is that the necessarily uneven development of imperialism, driven by the overproductivity of capital, means that imperialist powers will go to war with Third World countries and other imperialist powers before they reach a point where social polarization leads to the complete breakdown of internal social order. Social polarization will grow, undoubtedly, as will breakdown, disaffection, and other markers of general crisis. Indeed, this process is "progressing" in the United States at the time of this writing, and may be expected to develop further. But crisis is an endemic part of capitalism, and capitalism, if left to its own devices, has its own way of forging through crisis in the hope of generating a new circuit of capital accumulation. Capital works through crisis by clearing the ground, starting over. In other words, capitalism means war.

And its politics, as the crisis develops and looms ever larger, becomes more and more war by other means.

That capitalism means war is one reason, a major reason, not to leave it to its own devices. People do begin to question a social order driving toward war, especially if the war develops into a global conflict. But even here, people are not all at once brought into a common condition of immiseration or even of anomie. Lenin argued, in *What Is to Be Done?*, that people who apply dialectical and historical materialism systematically will see that the only way to keep capitalism from resorting to its own murderous devices is to overthrow capitalism and create a new social order. These people, the communists, need to group together in order to better disseminate their understanding and to strategically plan the application of their understanding. I believe that Lenin was and is right. But what would be a new social order? My belief, which is influenced by Derrida's framing of the issue in *The Other Heading*, is that it would have to break with capital's false ethic of calculation. This would also mean a break with fundamentally prudential forms of Marxism; prudence simply reinscribes the logic of capital within that which seeks to break with capital; capital is nothing if not cunning.

There is, incidentally, an important comparison to be made here between Stalin's approach to Marxism and Mao's. The former, in his *Economic Problems of Socialism in the USSR*, argues for a continuing, fundamental role for the law of value even under socialism. Responding to this argument, in his *Critique of Soviet Economics*, Mao says that, with this conception of socialism as our guide, capitalism will be invincible. (In other words, with friends like these, who needs enemies?)[10]

Communists, in Lenin's view, are people from the broad masses who are the most politically advanced. On this understanding, even though it is often intellectuals who are the first people to unite vision and dedication into an applied science of revolution, it is only on the basis of the practice of the masses that radical intellectuals can become dedicated communists. Looking at this conception in terms of what was just said about the need to transcend the prudential ethic of calculation if capitalism is to be transcended, what is it that the political avant-garde must be able to see from their advanced position? I believe that they must be able to see the possibility of justice. It is their job, their obligation, to disseminate this vision.

Not justice itself, but the possibility of justice. In framing the conception this way, I realize that I am linking, or re-linking, Lenin to the tradition of Plato and Kant. Indeed, Lenin argued that it is the duty of communists and all radical and progressive people in the imperialist countries to go against "their own" ruling class and the national interests of that class, especially when this class finds itself in crisis. Crises can take many forms, but, returning to the earlier analysis, the most acute form of capitalist crisis is war, the forcible redrawing of borders in an attempt to expand the productive base. Lenin argued that the proletariat must work for the defeat of the imperialist ruling classes in such wars, including the defeat of their own ruling class. In other words, communists must be traitors and they must lead the proletariat in betraying the national interests of the imperialist countries. Lenin did not expect the basic masses to be especially pleased, at first, to hear this idea set out by the communists. In fact, he said that the communists must expect to be attacked for saying these things, that "the people will tear the communists limb from limb." He was quoting, of course, Plato, the Allegory of the Cave from *Republic*, Book VI, where Socrates is attempting to explain that there are ideas that reside at the limit of our understanding and beyond. The highest and most difficult of these ideas is the good, justice itself.

There are many interpretations of Plato's theory of forms and conception of justice; although I am not entitled to enter this discussion as a Plato scholar, please allow me to offer my interpretation. Returning to themes already set out earlier in the Preface, I believe that *Republic* is an all-out attempt to show the possibility of the human project. Thrasymachus's definition of justice, while it seems to appeal to a certain cunning, a certain competency (Socrates forces him to see this early in the discussion), has no use for the idea of the good. Brute force is all that matters in the end. Power completely and exhaustively defines the good (and the true and the beautiful). In the absence of constraints, as with the Ring of Gyges story, it is not that one is free to act as unjustly as one wishes. For Thrasymachus, there is no further definition of justice that applies. Whatever the person who possesses the Ring of Gyges does is "just," by definition. The only way that some other justice might come to bear on the wearer of the Ring is if the wearer is caught trespassing against someone who has the power to assert their authority.

Both Plato and Kant have essentially the same answer to this cynical view of justice: there has to be a truth that is beyond power, otherwise there is no point to the human project. But there is no guarantee that this truth exists. Plato says that this good is "beyond being," beyond the forms. But then the good is beyond existence itself, and thus proof of its "existence" is impossible. Kant says that the categorical imperative is a law reflective of the moral order of the world, and that the law is logically derivable from this moral order, but that the logic of the law is beyond the ken of humanity. Plato and especially Kant are often said to have given transcendental arguments (and they are often called foundationalists). Derrida does not give transcendental arguments but what he calls "quasi-transcendental" arguments. The quasi-transcendental also describes what Plato and Kant are both after, for neither ever claims that their arguments, whether they concern the forms or the universal law, can be fully developed in terms accessible to limited creatures such as ourselves. Their questions are simply: How can one think otherwise and How can there be a human project otherwise? In both cases, returning to the phrase from LeGuin's novel, to "think things through" means to strive for a good that is impossible. Indeed, to think, or to be able to think, means to strive for the good, for justice, *because* this is an impossible task.

Lenin, the materialist, the philosophical revolutionary, said that his formulations of materialism would be regarded as "metaphysical" by professional philosophers. No matter, he said, in the opening pages of his *Materialism*, "I do not philosophize with their philosophy, I *practice* it." For Lenin, the ethical-political is not first of all a philosophical conception, it is a practice. This is the point where all who grapple with Marx's Eleventh Thesis must arrive. This is the point that Althusser was driving at with his essay, "Lenin and Philosophy." Academic philosophers will say that this is the cancellation of philosophy—in the case of Althusser's essay they did say this (and he was plenty academic!). But this is a cop-out. The point is not to deny the place of philosophy, but it is also not to believe in the illusion that the ethical is something that can be conceived of in purely philosophical terms. Most philosophers would be pleased to admit that the ethical must be enacted, in practical terms, in order to be true to what it is. Lenin's practice of philosophy aims at showing that the ethical must be practiced in order to be thought. This, I maintain, is the "beyond" of the good, the impossible, infinite praxis that must ground all thinking of the good. This is the same praxis that calls the philosopher back into the cave, where people may tear the philosopher from limb from limb. This is the same praxis that renders the first formulation of the categorical imperative meaningless without its integration with the second and third formulations.

The meaning of materiality implicit here is a praxis that strives toward the good within the open-ended structure of the infinite, the beyond. But the case for this materiality cannot be made in the terms of traditional materialism or classical historical materialism. The repressed element of idealism must be rethought in materialist terms. This is a question of the materialist rethinking of the structure of recognition.

The question is one of recognizing the priority of intersubjectivity to subjectivity, with this priority itself contextualized against the background of the impossibility, the unendingness, of responsibility.

There is no need to deny, in this scheme of things, the basic materiality of the subject and the psyche. But what is this basic materiality? Is it simply of bodies and their brains? Certainly one could not be a subject without a body and without a brain of a certain type (for example, the kind of brain found in human beings; perhaps there are other kinds of brains, but the human brain is the example we have). A solitary body with its brain will not become a subject. Human consciousness (and, I would argue, any consciousness) is and must be, at root, responsive. That is, consciousness is defined by the ability to respond. To say that one has not "thought things through" is to say that one has denied: 1) thinking itself, 2) responsibility, and 3) human being itself, the possibility of the human project.

Why say that what is being described here is a material structure? There are two reasons. First, the basis of subjectivity is the existence of: 1) human bodies and their brains, 2) the interaction of bodies in various possible social forms, and 3) the path to response that exists in and through language. While the second and third elements of subjectivity listed here are not captured by a reductive, mechanical materialism (rightly and necessarily so), it can be readily seen that they are, all the same, dependent on matter. No matter, no language. This last element of subjectivity, which could not, by definition, exist in the form of a divine soliloquy, must necessarily have a certain character. Language cannot be a rule-governed practice, it must necessarily be an open-ended practice; interpretation must necessarily be open-ended. Or else there is no interpretation, and, crucially, there is no responsibility, there is no response. If interpretation is a closed practice (in which case there is no interpretation), then the ethical is simply a matter of calculation. But calculation is not the ethical and it is not a thinking of the polis. There are many who see Derrida's arguments concerning the non-closure of interpretation as somehow irresponsible, as giving rise to the endless play of rhetorical tricks. Certainly there are deconstructionists who take up Derrida's arguments in an irresponsible way; the structure of their irresponsibility will be set out in a moment. Derrida's argument, however, is that if there could be closure to interpretation, there could not be responsibility, there could only be calculation.

The argument for the non-closure of interpretation is also a materialist argument because it is an argument for externality. This is the second reason why it is right to say that, despite the elements of this

argument taken over from what have traditionally been thought of as
"idealist" philosophers (Plato, Kant), responsibility can be described
in materialist terms and thereby reinscribed into a historical materialist conception of politics and struggle. This reinscription, a supplement
the danger of which should be taken up in political struggle, transforms
the terms of struggle in a way that is necessary. But this transformation is itself a practice, and the thinking of it must be an accomplish-
ment of practice. Indeed, I believe that the thinking here reflects what
was untheorized in the practice of Marxist revolutionaries such as Marx,
Lenin, and Mao. Lenin described matter as that which is ultimately
and infinitely external, not finally bound by consciousness. The infinity of the world (to say "the material world" would be redundant) is
the background against which interpretation is never complete. There
is no final meaning against this background. But final meaning (full-
ness of meaning, presence of meaning) would be the end of meaning
and the end of responsibility.

Philosophers who argue that language is a rule-governed behavior,
that the human brain is simply a very sophisticated thermostat, that
there can be, in theory at least, a fully worked-out scientific psychology
and philosophy of mind ("neurophilosophy") do not and cannot believe
in interpretation or responsibility, but only in the calculation of "meanings" and social interactions.

Is there a knock-down, drag-out argument that shows that these philosophers, reductive materialists, are wrong? I believe that there is not
and cannot be, in the final analysis, an argument that shows this. If
there were, it would become part of an enlarged calculation. There is
an aporia where the argument should be, the anomaly of human being, the anomaly of responsibility.[11]

Derrida writes of a "responsibility to responsibility"; I believe that
this is a responsibility to the anomaly of responsibility just described.
There are arguments and demonstrations right up to this point, right
up to this anomaly. Indeed, much of Derrida's work is such a demonstration of the non-closure of interpretation. Some of Derrida's texts
are more directly relevant to the thinking of the ethical and the polis
than others, and it does not hurt to make that distinction on one level
(though it is, to be sure, a very difficult, ultimately impossible, distinction to make). On another level, all of Derrida's work is about the
possibility of responsibility. His work must be seen in that light, and
I will go so far as to say that anyone who does not see Derrida's work
in that light is not reading Derrida. Not to see Derrida's work in that
light is not to keep responsibility with responsibility. Still further: all
of the Derrideans who claim to read Derrida in this way but who do

not situate Derrida's work in relation to a practice that is necessary for a "thinking through" are also not reading Derrida.

What allows the move from the "is" of response-ability, as a material structure regulative of consciousness (i.e., the material ground and context of consciousness), to the "ought" of responsibility? In other words, why throw oneself open to the unprecedented? Certainly there are material conditions that urge people in this direction. When Lenin argued that class-conscious proletarians, that is, communists, must be ready to betray "their" imperialist fatherlands, he knew that the crisis of capitalism would deepen in a way that would encourage the broad masses to question, challenge, resist, rebel against, and ultimately overthrow the oppressive social order. But there are other ways for imperialist countries to resolve things, there are other visions than the overthrow of capitalism that the imperialists put out for mass consumption. Some of these are: fascism, followed by war; a constitutional crisis resolved by renegotiation of the social contract, but purely within the confines of bourgeois right; and, more recently, a postmodern cynicism that itself generally masks the violent workings of the logic of the Same, either at "home" or "abroad." What is it that will create an opening for the unprecedented?

Before trying to answer this question, I have to say something that may seem particularly nasty, but it needs to be said nonetheless. Revolution is not necessarily the unprecedented. There has been too much chic theorizing lately that seems to think it a brilliant thing to say that there is no "guarantee" with revolution, no guarantee that something new, something other, will make its appearance, that the possibility of justice will be realized. This is not brilliant, regardless of what Heideggerian or Levinasian or Derridean or what-have-you terminology it is wrapped up in. To say that there are no guarantees with revolution, therefore people should not seek revolutionary solutions to the crisis of capitalism that they find themselves in, is at best uninformed and irresponsible. It is generally uninformed about the history of revolutions and attempted revolutions. Indeed, many Heideggerians seem mainly informed about the Nazi "revolution" of 1933, and then only because they are looking for some way to extricate Heidegger from his participation in fascism. It is irresponsible for many reasons, one of which is that people who discuss "the political" have a responsibility to be informed. At worst, this line of reasoning is stupid and cowardly. And, most damning of all to the addressees of these remarks, it is not Derridean. To ask for a revolution with guarantees, without dangers, a revolution that makes itself fully present so that one may know what one is in for before one commits to it, this has nothing in common with Derrida's language of the impossible and the unprecedented.[12]

To repeat: What is it that will create an opening for the unprecedented, an opening that must be created amid many false alternatives? That is to say, amid false alterity? And where is the calculus that allows us to know false alterity from true alterity and, what's more, good alterity from bad alterity? For there must be true others who are not good others. Programs and projects in and of themselves will not do this. A revolution, in the narrower sense of the seizure of power by an oppressed class, will not in and of itself do this. Neither will there be an opening without programs, without projects, and without revolution. For those who want guarantees, and for those who don't want programs, the following must be said. There will not be a revolution without a program, and without a revolution there is certainly at least one guarantee: that imperialism will continue to generate various and often horrible forms of oppression for the great majority of the world's people. That is the guarantee "on this side" of the revolution. On the other side there are no guarantees. Specifically, there is no guarantee that a space for the other will be opened, no guarantee other than the conscious activism of people working toward this end. What must they be conscious of? After all, hasn't the category of consciousness been "deconstructed"? Again there are two impossibilities of practice at work here. One leads into the apolitical aestheticism that I have been polemicizing against (yes, I want to make war on it). The other is a practical awareness that the deconstruction of consciousness by alterity must lead to a striving toward the alterity of consciousness, what is barely and impossibly perceptible at the margins of language and thought. To give a name to it: the possibility of justice itself. Without this, even if there is a revolution, there will be no revolution; even if there is a project, there will be no project.

In the face of the anomaly, the aporia, where arguments lead us and leave us, there must be a keeping faith with the project, with the revolution, with the possibility of justice. This faith transforms projects and revolutions; it makes them impossible as fully calculable material structures; it therefore makes them possible as uncalculable material contributions to the possibility of justice.

Looking in this direction we find another Marx and another revolution. All that I have tried to emphasize with this interweaving of deconstruction and revolutionary Marxism is that only by looking in the direction of the revolutionary strivings of the masses do we find a deconstruction that is a "truer" and more "just" one.

It is through working in this direction that the case will be made for deconstruction as a key concept in critical social theory.

Part 2

Transformations of humanism (current events)

> Human Reason is by nature architectonic . . . . It regards all knowledge as belonging to a possible system.
> —Immanuel Kant

> My thought is anthropomorphism ripped to shreds.
> —Georges Bataille

Humanism purports to be a universalistic ideology; it is only fair, then, that I form a multifaceted approach to the subject. In this regard, the series of discussions presented in this part will only congeal into a single analytic framework at some projected, hypothetical point beyond the end, in the ordinary sense, of this text. The main purpose of this part is to demonstrate the role that Derrida's work has played in some recent debates on or near the subject of humanism. In that respect, the discussions of Descartes, Kant, and other important figures of modern western philosophy, while important in their own right, are also the staging ground for demonstrations of significant disagreements between Derrida and others who are grappling with the problems of modernity: Nietzsche, Foucault, Susan Bordo, Habermas, Rorty, and various intellectuals and journalists involved in the debate around the philosophical and literary canon. To give a general characterization to these discussions is to violently rein in their excesses. It is through the operation of these excesses that Derrida enacts a transformation of humanism, by making that transformation legible. In other words, deconstruction happens, humanity is transforming itself. All the same, I will offer a general characterization that will serve as a guide when the excesses get out of hand (as they will and must). The following discussions are aimed at opening and articulating two questions. First, what is human, or, as Derrida puts it in "The Ends of Man," what is proper to humanity? What is it to participate in humanity? Second, what is universalism, and what are its possibilities, if any, today?

Circuits

The circuit of the argument presented in this text runs from Kant's "Idea for a Universal History" to Derrida's "The Ends of Man" and *The Other Heading*. It seems entirely appropriate to view Derrida's more recent text as an extension and updating of the 1968 essay. The idea of the circuit necessarily means that the argument will move from Kant to Derrida and back again, though this will be no simple return to the source.

But why this source to begin with? Even holding deconstructive arguments about origins at bay for a moment, there is no question that western humanism was already a vibrant current long before Kant, certainly with the Italian Renaissance, certainly with Descartes.

The single most important reason for beginning the discussion of humanism with Kant rather than with other figures or periods is that he is the figure most identified with the Enlightenment formulation of ethical universalism. Important precursors must be mentioned in this project as well, especially Vico, Voltaire, and Rousseau. As significant as these thinkers are, however, we do not see in them, as we do with Kant, a multi-dimensional, fully articulated, systematic body of work in which all of the classical branches of philosophy are set out in a matrix that has the ethical as its connecting thread. Before him, Kant is matched only by Aristotle in the scope and orientation of his project. Kant is to the modern western world what Aristotle was to antiquity.

Arguments can be made, however, that Kant's critical philosophy was not the beginning, but the beginning of the end, of humanism. These arguments, most associated with Nietzsche, are radicalizations of Kant's views. Michel Foucault summed up the thrust of this radicalization by arguing that the death of God leads inevitably to the death of the idea of humanity.

Why would this Nietzschean radicalization be associated with Kant in the first place? Because, despite the arguments of some to the contrary, Kant is not a Cartesian; rather, he represents the first real step beyond Cartesianism. Why is this honor not conferred upon Spinoza or Hume? Because the determinism of the former and the agnosticism of the latter make them skeptics where ethics is concerned. Kant himself has been called a skeptic, of course. Our direct knowledge must be of our experiences, primarily of that form of experience that is public, namely, sense experience. But we can have no direct or certain knowledge of the unity of our perceptions and thoughts, and, indeed, there is the possibility that there is no such unity. Hume's contribution to the history of western philosophy is mainly in demonstrating that possibility. This does not mean that he believed in the possibility, and that he was therefore a skeptic in that sense; on the other hand, Hume did not seem to take the further step of asking how, despite the possible disunity of experience, one might think otherwise. Kant, on the other hand, believed that metaphysics is a fundamental part of the human condition, that one can only think particular thoughts in so far as they belong to a possible system of thought.

Spinoza might be seen as a forerunner of Kant in this respect, for he certainly located the human prospect within a metaphysical framework. But, in his determinism, Spinoza is radically at odds with Kant's view that human reason is *of* nature but not determined by it.

Neither Spinoza nor Hume agree with Kant on a further, all-important point: that the center of the architectonic of human reason is the ethical. Indeed, we might go so far as to say that the resolution, for Kant, of metaphysical dilemmas must be found in the realm of the ethical. Quine once said, famously, that "the Humean dilemma is the human dilemma." The reason why this is not true may seem incidental for a study such as this, but it is not. There are many who argue, on both sides of philosophy's continental divide, that the unity of Kant's thought is to be found in his metaphysics (taking the latter term in the narrow sense). The Humean dilemma is the human dilemma only if the crucial human question is the unity of knowledge. For Kant the crucial human question is, How should any rational creature live? In other words, the question is one of discovering the universal moral law and applying it. Indeed, for Kant, the unity of knowledge itself is only a possibility—even if at the same time it is the only possibility—and this possibility must itself be guided by the moral law. The ethical is not first of all a "knowledge," and knowledge is only a good to the extent that it is guided by the ethical.

The incidental part of this discussion is that here one sees why Quine, for all that he has been pivotal in the transition to a post-positivist analytic philosophy, is still very much representative of positivism's banishment of ethics from philosophy. This is ironic, of course, given the admiration that the leading figures of the Vienna Circle had for Kant—an admiration not shared by their young disciples Quine and Ayer. More directly important for my discussion of humanism is the fact that the logical positivists stressed that knowing and caring are two qualitatively different things. Carnap, especially, argued that only the former has to do with truth. At the conclusion of his important essay, "The Elimination of Metaphysics through the Logical Analysis of Language," Carnap praises the work of Nietzsche, not as philosophy but instead as poetry. In fact, Carnap argues, it is to Nietzsche's credit that he presents his own work as such. (The problem with Heidegger, Carnap claims, is that his work is not real philosophy and, in addition, it is bad poetry.) Perhaps there has been an over-reaction to Carnap's distinction, for it is also in the realm of poetry that Carnap believes worldviews can be formed. A worldview cannot be validated by any philosophical or scientific procedure, it cannot be verified through empirical means or logical analysis, and it cannot make a truth-claim. Carnap's whole point seems to be that there is too much confusion generated in the conflation of truth with justice (or with beauty).

Despite the fact, however, that Carnap and the others were already "structuralists" in the sense that they sought to rethink Kant's architectonic without the language of consciousness, the missing element in all of this remains Kant's unification of thought under the auspices of the ethical. This unification remains a "possibility": Kant cannot and does not ignore Hume. But the possibility of knowledge fundamentally depends on the possibility of the ethical. There is no former possibility without the latter. There is no stronger formulation of the dependency of knowledge than Kant's view that there can be no theological argument for morality; rather there must be an ethical argument for the existence of God. (This is Kant's resolution of the dilemma that Plato sets out concerning the priority of God and the good.)

Every question here, every relation, comes down to one thing, one reason: ethics must exceed calculation.

This is the promise, almost entirely hidden, of humanism. The practice of humanism, however, is something else.

The ethical heart of Kant's philosophy beats to a different rhythm than Cartesian culture, the culture in which "I" am at the center of the universe. To be sure, then, there are two circuits of humanism. One circuit moves from Descartes to Hobbes to Mill to present-day individualists, libertarians, utilitarians, and other calculating thinkers of the ego. This circuit has every right to claim the mantle of humanism. Its highest aspiration is self-knowledge, though defined as self-assertion. The other circuit moves, in modernity, from Kant to some contemporary Kantian thinkers, Derrida among them. The highest aspiration here is the fundamental regard for the other. There are many thinkers, Marx being a very important one, who move between the two circuits. They are not merely confused in their thought, they are caught between two cultures, the one a dominant Cartesian culture that makes the other, the Kantian culture that we might better understand in the work of Jacques Derrida, barely visible—that is, marginal.

Of course, this way of setting out the problem, in terms of two worlds that are in fundamental conflict, is quite Marxist. However, even though I do not want to lose sight of the question of modes of production (especially in the larger, Althusserian sense), there is a clash of ideologies that should be set out as the framework for understanding the two humanisms, the one Cartesian, the other Kantian, that vie for the soul of the modern world. I now consider the Cartesian circuit further, followed by a discussion of the Nietzschean variant.

Cartesian culture

In her excellent book *The Flight to Objectivity: Essays on Cartesianism and Culture*, Susan Bordo calls a key moment in the development of Cartesian culture the "emergence of inwardness." This subjective turn in European philosophy and culture

> turned "genius" from a visiting spirit into a personal quality of mind. It transformed the idea of "authority" into the notion of inner "influence." And it created a new sense of experience as deeply *within* and bounded by a self. (p. 53)

What was displaced by this turn was the "participating consciousness," structured around interaction with nature rather than detachment from it. In providing what Bordo calls the "first real 'phenomenology' of the mind" (p. 55), Descartes both grounds the individualist notion of autonomy that will be developed in the political theories of Hobbes, Mill, and others and he discloses

> the deep epistemological alienation that attends the sense of mental interiority: the enormous gulf that must separate what is conceived as occurring "in here" from that which, correspondingly, must lay "out there."

The value of Bordo's study, which focuses on Cartesian culture rather than simply Cartesian philosophy, is that it demonstrates the way that inwardness comes to characterize the western form of life. Simply deconstructing the metaphysics of subjectivity will not address this culture, which comes to be insinuated in social institutions, patterns of social interaction, ways of speaking, and in speaking itself.

The path of Cartesian culture is always toward "purification." Alienation from the outside is not to be overcome, but instead strengthened.

What lies outside the mind can only contaminate the mind; Descartes' "entire system is devoted to circumscribing an intellectual arena which is pristinely immune to contamination, a mirror which is impossible to smudge" (p. 82). Bordo argues that the mind, in this conception, must remain essentially passive, it must only accept those ideas that themselves can command consent (pp. 82–88).

The larger parameters of this Cartesianism Bordo describes as the "masculinization of thought." The self-sufficient, non-corporeal mind must, in denying embodiment, first of all deny its mother.

> If the transition from Middle Ages to early modernity can be looked on as a kind of protracted birth, from which the human being emerges as a decisively separate entity, no longer continuous with the universe with which it had once shared a soul, so the possibility of objectivity, strikingly, is conceived by Descartes as a kind of *rebirth*, on one's own terms, this time. (p. 97)

This "flight to objectivity" is simultaneously a "flight from the feminine":

> The particular genius of Descartes was to have philosophically transformed what was first experienced as estrangement and loss—the sundering of the organic ties between the person and the world—into a requirement for the growth of human knowledge and progress. And, at this point, we are in a better position to flesh out the mechanism of *defense* involved here. Cartesian objectivism and mechanism, I will propose, should be understood as a *reaction-formation*—a denial of the "separation anxiety" described above, facilitated by an aggressive intellectual *flight* from the female cosmos and "feminine" orientation towards the world. That orientation (described so far in this study in the gender-neutral terminology of "participating consciousness") had still played a formidable role in medieval and Renaissance thought and culture. In the seventeenth century, it was decisively purged from the dominant intellectual culture, through the Cartesian "rebirthing" and restructuring of knowledge and world as *masculine*. (p. 100)

This flight from the feminine, as purification strategy, was at the same time a rejection of "dirt" (p. 82).

Such are the elements of the Cartesian political culture of modernity: the denial of the mother, of the feminine, of the body, and of dirty toil (of the labor of the mother and labor in general). Such are the Cartesian roots of the boot camp, where one is made over into a man. This last comment is not merely gratuitous; just as a society's politics are concentrated in war, so is its culture concentrated in its war-making machineries.

Not everything in Kant runs counter to this Cartesian conception. If nothing else, there is still plenty of masculinization at work in his philosophy. Insofar as Kant's ethical centering of philosophy represents a refounding, in modernity, of the participatory consciousness, however, perhaps one of the directions we can rightfully open up for the Kantian circuit is the reversal of the Cartesian reaction-formation, the memory of the mother.

At the same time, one cannot help but contrast the autonomous passivity and passive autonomy of the Cartesian mind to other possibilities. These would not be other possibilities of the polis, of the community, because there is no such thing in Descartes' "thinking." Of course, Descartes' thinking requires a community of dirty laborers, but the Cartesian mind, which is practically the mind of philosophy itself, cannot be a participant in this community. Indeed, the dirty community, the mothers, the workers, the dark-skinned, the people of unreason, must be purified from the mind.

Derrida has also written at length on Descartes' struggle for mental purity, in "Cogito and the History of Madness," (pp. 31–63). This text is a response to Michel Foucault's *Folie et deraison: Histoire de la folie a l'age classique*. (As reported by Didier Eribon, Derrida originally presented this work in a public lecture, with his former teacher, Foucault, in attendance.) Foucault's argument is that Descartes, by means of the *cogito*, sublates unreason (madness); this sublation is a turning point in history, it is the inaugural moment from which sense shall be sovereign over nonsense, reason over madness. Derrida's disagreement with Foucault might seem to concern an overly obscure point. Derrida does not disagree with Foucault that Descartes' strategy is to found reason on the suppression of unreason. Furthermore, as William Corlett puts it, "Derrida shows how insane the principle of sovereignty can be, because it guards the traces of violence which make unflinching stands possible" (p. 182). By "unflinching stands" Corlett means the univocity that is Derrida's prime target. (My entire analysis here is fundamentally indebted to Corlett, especially pp. 163–83.) But the disagreement between Derrida and Foucault is not over this insanity of reason but over the form in which the traces of violence are guarded. For Foucault, the moment of madness is temporally succeeded by the clarity and distinctness of the *cogito*. For all that this way of conceptualizing Descartes' flight from madness may be useful as a heuristic, Derrida finds Foucault's analysis naive (the word is Derrida's, used throughout the essay).

In the experiment in radical doubt, there can be no earlier moment of madness, followed by a later moment of clear and distinct reason.

There can be no "earlier" or "later" at all. Derrida's strategy is therefore to ask: 1) What is the motivation for Foucault's introduction of linear temporality into Descartes' atemporal frame? And 2) Is the suppression of unreason indeed a result of a temporal-dialectical sublation, what Foucault calls, in a Nietzschean gesture, "the Decision"? Or must the *cogito* itself stand above the dialectic of reason and unreason; in other words, in order for there to be a "decision" for reason, doesn't the *cogito* first have to initiate the temporal dialectic in which the decision can be made?

In pursuing the second question, Derrida turns the tables on Foucault. He refers to the "mad audacity" of the *cogito*, which consists in

> the return to an original point which no longer belongs to either a *determined* reason or a *determined* unreason, no longer belongs to them as opposition or alternative. Whether I am mad or not, *Cogito, sum*. Madness is therefore, in every sense of the word, only one *case* of thought (*within* thought). (p. 56)

What is the meaning, then, of Foucault's characterization of the Decision? As Corlett puts it, Derrida's argument is that

> madness must be silenced in order to open up the possibility of having the instants in time presupposed by . . . Foucault. The elapsing time continuum requires an inaugural moment which silences madness; but this silence can never in principle be enforced like a decision. Perpetual dispensation is most indecisive and ambiguous; it lives on like an open wound. (p. 174)

For Foucault, the *cogito* is the moment when the crisis of reason is held at bay. For Derrida, Foucault's conceptualization of the Decision is the moment when the possibility of different temporalities, different histories and historicities, is held at bay. As Corlett argues, both Descartes and Foucault *reassure* themselves in time. This denial of a different time, this reassurance, is, for Derrida, the silencing of historical excess; it is the banishment of the possibility of monstrosity.

On the most basic level we have here a critique of Foucault's genealogical method. This method, which takes the discourse as its most basic unit of measurement, is one of finding discontinuities in history, reading history backwards to decisive moments when new "regimes of discourse" are launched. There is no need to deny the fruitfulness of this method, which takes its inspiration from Nietzsche (see Foucault, "Nietzsche, Genealogy, History"), and which provides an important counterbalance to methodologies, typical in the social sciences, that stress continuity to the exclusion of breaks in history. Derrida is not interested in denying Foucault's positive contributions (neither am I). Indeed, in some ways their projects are similar in that both are interested in opening up the "crisis of reason," rather than in perpetuating the accepted philosophical practice of enforcing the truly violent insanity that supposedly keeps this crisis at a safe remove. But Derrida fears that Foucault has his own totalizing strategy for keeping reason-as-usual in business, the strategy of linear temporalization. On this point (as I shall argue, it is all about "the point"), it will be useful to quote Derrida at length:

> The extent to which doubt and the Cartesian Cogito are *punctuated* by this project of a singular and unprecedented excess—an excess in the direction of the nondetermined, Nothingness or Infinity, an excess which overflows the totality of that which can be thought, the totality of beings and determined meanings, the totality of factual history—is also the extent to which any effort to reduce this project, to enclose it within a determined historical structure, however comprehensive, risks missing the essential, risks dulling the *point* itself. Such an effort risks doing violence to this project in turn (for there is also a violence applicable to rationalists and to sense, to *good* sense; and this, perhaps, is what Foucault's book definitely demonstrates, for the victims of whom he speaks are always the bearers of sense, the *true* bearers of the *true* and *good* sense hidden and oppressed by the *determined* "good sense" of the "division"— the "good sense" that never divides itself enough and is always determined too quickly)—risks doing it violence in turn, and a violence of a totalitarian and historicist style which eludes meaning and the origin of meaning. [In an endnote Derrida adds: "It risks erasing the excess by which every philosophy (of meaning) is related, in some region of its discourse, to the nonfoundation of meaning."] I use "totalitarian" in the structuralist sense of the word, but I am not sure that the two meanings do not beckon each other historically. Structuralist totalitarianism here would be responsible for an internment of the Cogito similar to the violences of the classical age. I am not saying that Foucault's book is totalitarian, for at least at its outset it poses the question of the origin of historicity *in general*, thereby freeing itself of historicism; I am saying, however, that by virtue of the construction of his project he sometimes runs the risk of being totalitarian. Let me clarify: when I refer to the forced entry into the world of that which is not there and is supposed by the world, or when I state that the *compelle intrare* (epigraph of the chapter on "the great internment") becomes *violence itself* when it turns toward the hyperbole in order to make hyperbole reenter the world, or when I say that this reduction to intraworldliness is the origin and very meaning of what is called violence, making possible all straitjackets, I am not invoking an *other world*, an alibi or an evasive transcendence.

That would be yet another possibility of violence, a possibility that is, moreover, often the accomplice of the first one. (p. 57)

Ironically, the procedure that "dulls the point" the most, interning not only "madness" (or "the mad") but even the *cogito* itself, is Foucault's leap from the question of historicity and temporality in general to the straitjacket of a singular history. To what extent does humanism, in *all* of its manifestations, depend on this straitjacket? To break out of the straitjacket, to listen for the possibility of different histories, is this the end or the transformation of humanism and its subject, Man?

At the close of "Cogito and the History of Madness," Derrida thematizes the crisis of reason that Foucault has covered with his own "decision." Derrida argues that this crisis both logically precedes and underwrites all temporality; he is carrying through to its logical conclusion a Cartesian critique of Foucault:

> This crisis in which reason is madder than madness—for reason is non-meaning and oblivion—and in which madness is more rational than reason, for it is closer to the wellspring of sense, however silent or murmuring—this crisis has always begun and is interminable. (p. 62)

To be sure, the crisis of reason that is brought about by the culture of positivism, the crisis diagnosed in great detail by Husserl, is real enough. Derrida speaks of this crisis as "the danger menacing reason and meaning under the rubric of objectivism, of the forgetting of origins, of the blanketing of origins by the rationalist and transcendental unveiling itself." But there is another crisis, brought on by the straitjacket of reason, that is implicit in the very critique of the crisis brought on by all-pervasive positivism. Derrida concludes the "Cogito" essay by speaking to the presence of this crisis in Foucault's book.

> The crisis is also decision, the caesura of which Foucault speaks, in the sense of *krinein*, the choice and division between the two ways separated by Parmenides in his poem, the way of logos and the non-way, the labyrinth, the palintrope in which logos is lost; the way of meaning and the way of nonmeaning; of Being and of non-Being. A division on whose basis, after which, logos, in the necessary violence of its irruption, is separated from itself as madness, is exiled from itself, forgetting its origin and its own possibility. Is not what is called finitude possibility as crisis? A certain identity between the consciousness of crisis and the forgetting of it? Of the thinking of negativity and the reduction of negativity?
>
> Crisis of reason, finally, access to reason and attack of reason. For what Michel Foucault teaches us to think is that there are crises of reason in strange complicity with what the world calls crises of madness. (pp. 62–63)

Although Bordo's analysis might seem at first to have more in common with Foucault's, in that the flight to objectivity also seems to already assume the temporality that is only initiated with the *cogito*, I would suggest that the pathway to a different history, in which the reality of the mother and all who labor is found in its own time, is better sought through the argument offered by Derrida. This is not a pathway to a deeper or more fundamental reality, nor is it a promise of an organic "participatory consciousness." Instead, Derrida's argument is a listening for other present eras, other histories. And yet, it is true, the contents of these histories must be developed in their own right.

In describing a crisis that has "always begun and is interminable," has Derrida described a universal structure in which all who are human participate? Is this the very definition of human? And, is the form of participation, for humans or what-have-you, the same in all cases? Can there be different participations in this structure? Can there be different ways to be human? Then what is the meaning of humanism as a universalism? We are still a long way, necessarily, from answering these questions. However, the importance of attempting to think with both Derrida and Bordo, together if not simultaneously, is to insist that these questions cannot be answered in the abstract, through the mere discovery of an appropriate ontology.

The Nietzschean variation: Habermas and Derrida on the critique of pure reason

Habermas, as is well known, is interested in reestablishing the concept of normativity in social theory. His project, as he defines it, involves recognizing the groundlessness of the political project of modernity, on the one hand, but an avoidance of what he takes to be the Nietzschean response to this groundlessness on the other. Habermas identifies a number of French or French-language philosophers, such as Bataille, Foucault, Lyotard, and Derrida, as having fallen into what he takes to be the Nietzschean trap of believing that to give up on metaphysical foundations is to necessarily give up the concept of normativity.[1] My primary concern, here and elsewhere, is Habermas's critique of Derrida on this score. In *Matrix and line* I argued that it is the work of Derrida, not Habermas, that gives us the best philosophical basis for working through and out of the historical impasse of postmodernity. Accordingly, I argued that Derrida is neither a postmodernist nor a young conservative. Because Habermas's critique of Derrida (in *The Philosophical Discourse of Modernity*) was not very well formulated, it was not difficult for me (or whoever) to argue against. What was much harder was the task, a necessary one, of presenting a detailed and sustained confrontation between the fundamentally different understandings of language and communication held by Habermas and Derrida. Even though the longest chapter ("What is at the heart of language?") of the book was devoted to this task, much remains to be done.

Whatever the outcome of this debate that has hardly begun, however, I have lately wondered, partly in reaction to a certain "postmodern scene," if simply framing a confrontation between Habermas and Derrida is at all adequate to the many questions about modernity raised by the former. I have little doubt that Habermas is wrong and Derrida is right on the points of contention set out in *Matrix and line*. The long and the short of it is that Derrida's is not really the work that Habermas needs to demolish, though perhaps Baudrillard's is. (The Derrida Baudrillard conflation seems to be a common and all-too-convenient confusion by those who have not really read Derrida with care. On this point, see Christopher Norris, *Uncritical Theory*, pp. 15–25.) But perhaps this sort of talk has obscured an important point. Some of us, in our rush to defend Derrida, however justified we may have been, have perhaps missed the more crucial question, namely, What is it about postmodernism that Habermas was agitated by in the first place?

The reaction by some to Habermas's critique of Derrida in *The Philosophical Discourse of Modernity*, the move to make this simply a debate about Derrida, has unfortunate overtones of the typical reactions of the Heidegger cult. Not only is this cultic atmosphere disturbing and problematic in its own right, it has a way of obscuring important questions—things get too tangled up in webs of competing personalities. (I do not believe that Derrida has encouraged this, not in the way that the mandarin Heidegger did, but some Derrideans have.[2]) Habermas's real and valid concern about the transformation of philosophy after Nietzsche and Heidegger is not answered by playing out the battle of the proper names.

Now that I have said this, forgive me that the following discussion is wrapped around four names: Kant, Nietzsche, Habermas, and Derrida. Two main theses, I hope, will remain in the forefront of the discussion. First, there are two different ways of "deconstructing metaphysics," similar to the two forms of the impossibility of praxis discussed in the first part. Second, for all that Derrida does share an affinity with Nietzsche, in the final analysis he is closer to the heart of the critical project of Kant.

Some Habermasians, in particular Thomas McCarthy, have used the term Kantian as a kind of curseword to hurl at Derrida (see "The Politics of the Ineffable"). This is odd, given the clear affiliations that Habermas has with Kant (developed at length in Kenneth Baynes, *The Normative Grounds of Social Criticism: Kant, Rawls, and Habermas*). Indeed, it seems that the dispute between Habermas and the philosophers he calls postmodern, especially Foucault, Lyotard, and Derrida, might be characterized as a dispute over where to stand within the Kantian project. Certainly Nietzsche stands within this project when he takes the critique of pure reason to its natural, reflexive conclusion and initiates a critical theory that undermines itself. (See Mark Warren, *Nietzsche and Political Thought*, pp. 116–26, for a useful overview of Nietzsche's radicalization of Kant's metaphysics.) Habermas (*Philosophical Discourse of Modernity*, pp. 107–30) recognizes that there are strains of this Nietzschean critical theory in the work of the earlier Frankfurt School, especially in Adorno's work.[3] This Nietzschean critical theory involves one in a performative contradiction, Habermas argues, and therefore undermines reason itself by pointing to reason's aporias. In Habermas's view, this is all that Derrida and, among others, Paul de Man, are doing. They find the antinomies of reason in various texts, and that is the end of the story. (As discussed in Part I, I tend to think that Habermas is right in the case of de Man.)

Habermas takes the Kantian project seriously, and so he recognizes that it is not an adequate answer to this Nietzschean challenge to simply reinstate some authority or foundation. Habermas agrees with Kant that the philosophy of the Enlightenment must be a critical philosophy, that is, a self-reflexive philosophy. Critical philosophy must supply its own ground, and it must submit this ground to critical procedures. The point of critical philosophy, then, is to be radically anti-authoritarian. (Habermas's engagement with Kant is dispersed throughout his many works, but a useful guide to his overall approach to Kant is found in "The Unity of Reason in the Diversity of Its Voices," where he refers to "the humanism of those who continue the Kantian tradition by seeking to use the philosophy of language to save a concept of reason that is skeptical and postmetaphysical, yet not idealist" [*Postmetaphysical Thinking*, p. 116].)

Habermas's critique of the young conservatives, Derrida among them, is that they take up the Kantian project in a one-sided, Nietzschean way. For Kant, the critique of pure reason and the critique of judgment are tied together by the critique of practical reason and the ethical-political project as a whole. Remember that whenever Kant stood on the verge of speculation about the noumenal realm (which he always marked as speculation) he was always compelled in that direction by ethical, not primarily metaphysical, considerations. Readers of Derrida's essay on Levinas, "Violence and Metaphysics," will undoubtedly have trouble with this last distinction, between ethics and metaphysics. Kant was not interested in making the distinction "in philosophy" either. But he was interested in the practicality of ethics. To cancel that practicality, no matter how philosophically sophisticated the means, is to perform the kind of purely Nietzschean deconstruction of metaphysics that I will turn to in a moment. To shift this question of the phenomenal and the noumenal to a slightly different question: Kant is perhaps unique in providing not a theological argument for morality but an ethical argument for the *possibility* of God's existence. Again "possibility" must be underlined, because God in this argument is an example of Kant's famous concept of the "regulative ideal." The critique that remains on the level of pure reason, as Habermas charges that a certain Nietzscheanism does, then argues that this regulative ideal, this sense of possibility-but-not-necessity, permeates and undermines the entire Kantian project. (I will discuss Richard Rorty's variation on this theme, which goes under the name of contingency, in the next section.) On the level of pure reason, these Nietzscheans (whoever they might be, and rest assured they are out there) are of course correct. But what about on the level of practical reason or on the level of the Kantian project as a whole, as unified by the ethical-political?

The transition from focus on pure reason to practical reason must be made very carefully: Berkeley is not so easily refuted by the simple gesture of kicking a rock. Habermas makes the transition through an integration of some work in American pragmatism, especially the more socially oriented work of Mead and Dewey and work in analytic philosophy of language, into the Kantian project. In a formulation that sounds as though it could have come straight out of the work of Donald Davidson (unfortunately Habermas has not undertaken a systematic discussion of this work), Habermas says,

> My reflections point toward the thesis that the unity of reason only remains perceptible in the plurality of its voices—as the possibility in principle of passing from one language into another—a passage that, no matter how occasional, is still comprehensible. This possibility of mutual understanding, which is now guaranteed only procedurally and is realized only transitorily, forms the background for the existing diversity of those who encounter one another—even when they fail to understand each other. (*Postmetaphysical Thinking*, p. 117)[4]

In the act of speech communication, one depends on a universal principle: that truth-telling is the general aim, the *telos*, of communication. Even lying and miscommunication depend on this principle. I accept this argument, and I further accept Habermas's claim that this principle is as much pragmatic as it is transcendental. (I dispute, however, the supposed derivation of this "pragmatic transcendental" principle from Wittgenstein.)

The *telos* of communication, in Habermas's scheme of things, generally remains buried in the "lifeworld," that repository of lived experience that is generally covered over and colonized by the "system." Revealing this *telos* is one thing, most likely a good thing. But is it the same thing as grounding a particular social formation or set of norms? Is it the same thing as developing an emancipatory critical theory and practice? David Rasmussen argues that

> one can conclude that not only is the emancipatory thesis, as located in a reconstruction of the philosophy of language, uncertain, but that the very attempt to locate critique in the distinction between system and lifeworld undermines the rather insecure status claimed for emancipation. (p. 54)

Rasmussen goes on to argue that, "At best, the communicative thesis is grounded in a utopian assumption about the way society ought to be." Indeed, Habermas's famous "ideal speech situation" is evidence of a utopian impulse; it is, furthermore, an example of a regulative ideal. The part of Habermas's ideal that is eminently practical is the valid point that a society that has such an ideal is different from one that does not. For Habermas the humanist, western democratic societies can be characterized as having recognized this ideal formally but not materially. Perhaps Habermas needs to be saved from himself, for, as Rasmussen argues, his ideal of a society ruled by the "unforced force of reason" is often buried under a heap of philosophical machinery that is meant to ground the ideal but, instead, seems to undermine it:

> The distinction between system and lifeworld tends to rob even that [communicative] thesis of its [utopian] force, inasmuch as the utopian insight upon which critique rests is lost in the supposed scienticism of a biocybernetic insight regarding the primacy of ideas derived from systems theory. Hence, the project of modernity which is supposed to show how the emancipatory thesis, the brainchild of the enlightenment, can be sustained through an analysis of the progressive differentiation between system and lifeworld under the paradigm of the transition to the philosophy of language, resolves itself in a series of contradictions which echo the beliefs of their author but remain insecure in the world of desire. (pp. 54–55)

Would Habermas perhaps do better to listen first and foremost for the voice of desire?

Derrida writes, especially in earlier work (e.g., *Speech and Phenomena*), of the "quasi-transcendental" and of the character of language as promise. When I speak, I make a promise, if not of truth, then at least of meaning. This view does not seem so different from Habermas's. But, for Habermas, there is a big difference, that between the promise of meaning—and its possibility, which can then be seen as a regulative ideal in its own right—and the ability to make validity claims, which Habermas posits as the *telos* of communicative action. To undermine such claims, for Habermas, is to engage in a performative contradiction, ultimately to arrive in the aporia of "This sentence is false." This is a possibility of pure reason but not of practical reason, hence Habermas's focus, in his philosophy of language, on pragmatics rather than semantics. (All of this I discuss at length in *Matrix and line*, Chap. 3.) I would argue, however, that Derrida's point is also practical: that meaning is a possibility but not a necessity. It is in the space of this possibility that the fundamental regard for the other, which is the sine qua non of the Kantian project (in "ethics," but not only in ethics), can open up. In the final analysis this regard cannot be grounded—argument will not close the gap between I and thou. (Remember that, in the first part, I argued that material circumstances pure-and-simple would not do the trick either.)

It is important that the possibility of a convergence of Habermas and Derrida on at least some aspects of the political project of modernity not be given up on. The choice faced in the "West" (and where is the "not-West"?), the choice faced by humanists, is not between Marx and Locke (but then, I am writing this in the land of Locke, the United States) so much as it is between Kant and Hobbes. Hobbes has reality on his side, in more ways than one: practically and metaphysically speaking, Hobbes has everyone kicking that rock. Thankfully, neither Habermas nor Derrida take this path toward practical reason. However, Derrida's orientation toward practice, an orientation toward the possibility of the other in light of the other's impossibility, is, to say the least, rarely spelled out in programmatic terms. Where there is no program, no project, the aporias of a not-practical-enough reason can be seen. This is the mere deconstruction of metaphysics, of the "set 'em up and I'll shoot 'em down" variety. On the other hand, Habermas's orientation toward practice is centered primarily on the question of the public sphere, so that, while he has contributed extensively and impressively to the rethinking of Kantian intersubjectivity, the question of alterity does not seem present with all of the Kantian force that we find in Derrida's work.

I will now shift the scene of this comparison to a specific and somewhat narrowly defined aspect of the public sphere, though an aspect close to the heart of humanists, namely, the university. Both Habermas and Derrida have been much involved in the critique and formulation of educational policy.[5] I might usefully compare two of their theoretical interventions, "The Idea of the University—Learning Processes," by Habermas, and "The Principle of Reason: The University in the Eyes of Its Pupils," by Derrida.

In his essay, Habermas discusses the changes that have taken place in the German university system since the time of Kant. He is specifically concerned to compare the classical notion of a university education with more recent developments that seem guided by purely economic and technocratic impulses. At the beginning of the essay, Habermas characterizes the ideal university, one that "vitally embodies its inherent idea":

> The functions the university fulfills for society must preserve an inner connection with the goals, motives and actions of its members. In this sense the university should institutionally embody, and at the same time motivationally anchor, a life form which is intersubjectively shared by its members, and which even bears an exemplary character. What since Humboldt has been called "the idea of the university" is the project of embodying an ideal life form. Moreover, this idea does not limit itself to one of the many particularized life forms of early bourgeois society, but—thanks to its intimate connection with science and truth—to something universal, something prior to the pluralism of social life forms. The idea of the university points to principles of formation according to which *all* forms of objective spirit are structured. (p. 3)

One purpose of the essay is to mark the distance traveled from this idea of the university to a university that has no idea. In terms taken from Max Weber, Habermas raises the possibility that the contemporary university in the western world can neither have nor embody such an idea:

> The organizational reality into which the functionally specified subsystems of a highly differentiated society imbed themselves rests on wholly different premises[.] The functional capability of such institutions depends precisely on a *detachment* of their members' motivations from the goals and functions of the organization. Organizations no longer embody ideas. (p. 4)

And yet, Habermas wonders if the university must necessarily become just another brick in the wall, just another bar of the iron cage.

Must the university, on its way towards functional specialization within an ever more swiftly differentiating system of knowledges, discard like an empty shell what once had been called its "idea"? Or does the frame which universities provide for scientific learning processes still account for a bundle of integrated functions which, while perhaps not in need of a normative self-image, nevertheless requires a somehow shared self-understanding of the university's members—traces of a corporative consciousness? (p. 5)

Anyone who is familiar with Habermas's work will recognize that he is asking, on one level, whether there might still be a lifeworld to the university that can be liberated from the crushing, monological-yet-fragmenting domination of the system. A reading of Derrida's essay shows that he is not unsympathetic to this line of reasoning, despite significant differences. It should be noted that both are concerned with the politics of speed. However, there are at least two important differences.

First, Habermas's essay, as with all of his work concerning specifically German or western social institutions, has no international dimension. This is not surprising; Habermas's work in general is extraordinarily Eurocentric. He ends the essay on an optimistic note: despite the incursions of the military-industrial complex into the university, the spirit of scientific investigation remains egalitarian and universalistic. Indeed, Habermas invokes

the stimulating and productive power of discursive disputes that carry the promissory note of generating surprising arguments. The doors stand open, and at any moment a new face can suddenly appear, a new idea can unexpectedly arrive. (p. 21)

These norms of scientific discourse may not yet apply to society as a whole (meaning western society), "But they share in a pronounced way that communicative rationality, the forms of which modern societies ... must employ to understand themselves" (p. 22). It is clear that "new faces" and "new ideas" can only arrive, unexpectedly or otherwise, from within western societies themselves. Furthermore, even the connection with these societies that Habermas sets out at the beginning of the essay, in which the idea of the university must be rooted "to something universal, something prior to the pluralism of social life forms," is significantly narrowed in subsequent formulations, so that Habermas comes to speak of "a somehow shared self-understanding of the university's members." Here Habermas has succumbed again to a favorite dream of many academy-bound intellectuals: the university as the locus of social reform, the university as the main institution that needs reforming, the world of the university as the world, period. This can be, after all, a comfortable world.

Contrast Habermas's approach to that of the young conservative, Derrida, who speaks not only of the military-industrial complex as imposing "system" from the outside. (I will turn to this outside-system/ inside-lifeword distinction in a moment.) Derrida, the impractical thinker, turns more explicitly to "a certain concrete actuality in the problems that assail us in the university," raising specifically the question of the "orientation of research." The problem with this "contrast," of course, is that the following passages from Derrida's essay are only matched by absences or, more accurately, aporias that are points of repression, in Habermas's essay.

> A major debate is under way today on the subject of the politics of research and teaching, and on the role that the university may play in this arena: whether this role is central or marginal, progressive or decadent, collaborative with or independent of that of other research institutions sometimes considered better suited to certain ends. The terms of this debate tend to be analogous—I am not saying that they are identical—in all the highly industrialized countries, whatever their political regime, whatever role the State traditionally plays in this arena (and, as we all know, even the Western democracies vary considerably in this respect). In the so-called "developing countries," the problem takes shape according to models that are certainly different but in all events inseparable from the preceding ones.
>
> Such a problem cannot always—cannot any longer—be reduced to problematics centered on the nation-state; it is now centered instead on multinational military-industrial complexes or techno-economic networks, or rather international technomilitary networks that are apparently multi- or trans-national in form. (p. 11)

One may dispute the terms of Derrida's political economy (I will dispute the idea of the "multinational complex" in Part 3), but it is not hard to see that he sets the stage of the discussion in a much different way than Habermas. That is, Derrida sets the discussion of the work and idea of the university in an international frame. This is a crucial point for the consideration of what the "inside" and the "outside" of the university's idea, its "principle of reason," might be. What are some of the effects of this work outside the university, beyond the "barrier" which protects the principle of reason? (I will turn to the question of this barrier in a moment.) I quote a passage on this issue from the young conservative:

> At the service of war, of national and international security, research programs have to encompass the entire field of information, the stock-piling of knowledge, the workings and thus also the essence of language and of all semiotic systems, translation, coding and decoding,

the play of presence and absence, hermeneutics, semantics, structural and generative linguistics, pragmatics, rhetoric. I am accumulating all these disciplines in a haphazard way, on purpose, but I shall end with literature, poetry, the arts and fiction in general: The theory that has these disciplines as its object may be just as useful in ideological warfare as it is in experimentation with variables in all-too-familiar perversions of the referential function. Such a theory may always be put to work in communications strategy, the theory of commands, the most refined military pragmatics of jussive utterances (by what token, for example, will it be clear that an utterance is to be taken as a command in the new technology of telecommunications? How are the new resources of simulation and simulacrum to be controlled? And so on . . .). One can just as easily seek to use the theoretical formulations of sociology, psychology, even psychoanalysis in order to refine what was called in France during the Indochinese or Algerian wars the powers of "psychological action"—alternating with torture. (p. 13)

This discussion, too, Habermas seems to cordon off from the discourse of the idea of the university; these things are outside.

The walls of Habermas's university, then, mark the second area of basic disagreement with Derrida, the sort of disagreement for which the latter is branded a mere Nietzschean, concerned only with the critique of pure reason (i.e., the mere deconstruction of metaphysics). For Habermas, the attack on the principle of reason (communicative or otherwise) and the idea of the university must necessarily come from the outside. That there is such an attack, such a mere deconstruction of the university's lifeworld by the systemic mechanisms of money and power, is undeniable. The original "conflict of the faculties," of which Kant wrote, has certainly been displaced. No longer is it a matter of establishing priority among the faculties of philosophy, theology, law, and medicine, for all have been pushed to the periphery of the university. In their formerly central place we now find departments of commerce. We find departments carrying out military-oriented research—although, as Derrida notes, *that* could be practically anything. However, as he further argues, the key research has to do with "information" and "informations systems." Significantly, the U.S. Department of Defense has first right of access to all computer technologies developed at U.S. universities. This right is obtained—and enforced—not through openly authoritarian measures but through seemingly innocent funding mechanisms: the Department of Defense is not suppressing research but "enabling" it. Enablement is not limited to the "hard" sciences but extends to such diverse fields as anthropology, language study (both of these are useful to the CIA), and even philosophy. Kant placed philosophy at the center of the faculties.

Now, the organizing role of philosophy has been marginalized, in the United States at any rate, by the more recently minted academic specializations of marketing and advertising. These "disciplines," I would argue, have no place in the university at all, for they do not value the idea of truth. Indeed, study in these fields makes many university students both cocky and fundamentally unteachable; when the university is organized around these fields the ideal is what sells. And while it never hurts to have some performative skill in the classroom, these fields have made charisma of the glitziest sort the standard that university teachers must aspire to, because, after all, everything comes down to a good promotion.

These are real problems facing universities today, and no one would deny that insidious pressures placed on the university from a certain "outside" have given rise to these problems. What are we to make of Derrida's essay, which challenges this idea of the outside? Derrida speaks of a "gorge" in the midst of the university, one that is both inside and outside. His literal example is of the gorge that runs through the middle of Cornell University. Ezra Cornell associated this landscape with the Romantic sublime, and he chose the land thinking that "a cultivated man" in the presence of the gorge

> would find his thoughts drifting metonymically through a series of topics—solitude, ambition, melancholy, death, spirituality, "classical inspiration"—which could lead, by an easy extension, to questions of culture and pedagogy.[6]

Derrida notes that these questions of "life and death" were further sharpened on the Cornell campus in 1977,

> when the university administration proposed to erect protective railings on the Collegetown Bridge and the Fall Creek suspension bridge to check thoughts of suicide inspired by the view of the gorge. "Barriers" was the term used . . . . Beneath the bridges linking the university to its surroundings, connecting its inside to its outside, lies the abyss. In testimony before the Campus Council, one member of the faculty did not hesitate to express his opposition to the barriers. . . . on the grounds that blocking the view would mean, to use his words, "destroying the essence of the university." What did he mean? What *is* the essence of the university? (p. 6)

In leading up to this passage Derrida describes the reasons given by Ezra Cornell for the choice of the site with the gorge (the metonymic chain leading to classical inspiration) and says that "the Board of Trustees, reasonably enough, concurred with them [it is difficult to be sure who 'them' refers to], reason won out." "But in this case was reason quite simply on the side of life?" (p. 6).

Derrida's presentation of the topos, a geographical setting for a discussion of the principle of reason, is not the least gratuitous, for he is concerned to seek out the ground of reason and its purported locatedness in the university. Furthermore, like Habermas he strives to locate this discussion historically, in the discourse of the classical German university and in the conceptions of Kant, including the latter's conception of the sublime.

Here is Derrida's description of what would seem to be the fundamental characteristic of the university, a description that can be contrasted to the one Habermas gives at the beginning of his essay:

> As far as I know, nobody has ever founded a university *against* reason. So we may reasonably suppose that the University's reason for being has always been reason itself, and some essential connection of reason to being. (p. 7)

I am trying to account for the "invasion" of the university by forces opposed to reason. The question, again, is whether these forces simply come from the outside. Derrida proposes, in a formulation that Habermas could hardly dispute, that "A responsibility is involved here . . . . We have to respond to the call of reason" (p. 8). What is it to respond, and to respond reasonably, to reason? Citing Leibniz, Derrida argues that this responsibility consists in "rendering reason": "for any true proposition . . . a reasoned account is possible" (p. 7). Derrida articulates the question further:

> Are we obeying the principle of reason when we ask what grounds this principle which is itself a principle of grounding? We are not— which does not mean that we are disobeying it, either. Are we dealing here with a circle or with an abyss? The circle would consist in seeking to account for reason by reason, to render reason to the principle of reason, in appealing to the principle in order to make it speak of itself at the very point where, according to Heidegger, the principle of reason says nothing about reason itself. The abyss, the hole, the *Abgrund*, the empty "gorge" would be the impossibility for a principle of grounding to ground itself. This very grounding, then, like the university, would have to hold itself suspended above a most peculiar void. (p. 9)[7]

Interestingly enough, Derrida presents these considerations, of the reasonableness of reason, before turning to the questions of the "orientation of research" with which I opened this comparison with Habermas. Derrida introduces this turning to "certain concrete actualities"—problems that have "invaded" (my word) the university, problems that are not entirely dissimilar to those raised by Habermas—by saying that he would prefer to turn to these concrete actualities "instead of meditating at the edge of the abyss—even if on a bridge protected by 'barriers'" (p. 11).

The discussion of the principle of reason, with its inability to ground itself, and the discussion of certain concrete actualities comprise the first two parts of Derrida's essay. He opens the third and final part by saying, "What, then, is my topic?" (There's nothing wrong with seeing the humor in this.) But, of course, Derrida has already introduced two topoi, the gorge of reason and the university, with its concrete actualities, suspended above the gorge. This is Derrida's topic: to think the university, the campus, on the heights and in the abyss:

> There is a double gesture here, a double postulation: to ensure professional competence and the most serious tradition of the university even while going as far as possible, theoretically and practically, in the most directly underground thinking about the abyss beneath the university, to think at one and the same time the entire "Cornellian" landscape—the campus on the heights, the bridges, and if necessary the barriers above the abyss—and the abyss itself. (p. 17)

Habermas, I think it safe to say, thinks neither the abyss nor the barrier(s), in the sense that Derrida locates them as topoi. But this double-gesture must indeed be practiced, by what can appropriately be called a new kind of intellectual, despite how dangerous, and how trivial, this sort of appellation has sometimes come to be. Derrida is describing a complex responsibility that "implies multiple sites, a stratified terrain, postulations that are undergoing continual displacement, a sort of strategic rhythm" (p. 17). While certain divisions of labor may operate to an extent within this responsibility, within this new intellectual terrain, the division cannot be between those who practice "professional competence and the most serious tradition of the university," on the one hand, and those who practice "directly underground thinking," on the other. Simply to stand for the former, in a defensive gesture against the commodification of knowledge by outside forces, is to ignore the coappearance of the modern university and commodity production in general. This gesture may, out of the desire "to remove the university from 'useful' programs and professional ends," end up "serving unrecognized ends, reconstituting powers of caste, class, or corporation" (p. 18). In a passage that speaks well to the critique of "project" discussed in the first part, Derrida says:

> "Thought" requires *both* the principle of reason *and* what is beyond

the principle of reason, the *arkhe* and an-archy. Between the two, the difference of a breath or an accent, only the *enactment* of this thought can decide. That decision is always risky, it always risks the worst. To claim to eliminate that risk by an institutional program is quite simply to erect a barricade against a future. The decision of thought cannot be an intra-institutional event, an academic moment.

All this does not define politics, nor even a responsibility. Only, at best, some negative conditions, a "negative wisdom," as the Kant of *The Conflict of the Faculties* would say: preliminary cautions, protocols of vigilance for a new *Aufklarung*, what must be seen and kept in sight in a modern re-elaboration of that old problematics. Beware of the abysses and the gorges, but also of the bridges and the barriers. Beware of what opens the university to the outside and the bottomless, but also of what, closing in on itself, would create only an illusion of closure, would make the university available to any sort of interest, or else render it perfectly useless. Beware of ends; but what would a university be without ends? (p. 19)

Let me return to concrete actualities. When the space for the reason of the university to interrogate itself is opened up, the institutional space of the university, its topos, is criss-crossed by relations of power. Is this to say that the principle of reason *is* power? Any Habermasian would expect any Nietzschean to say as much. Furthermore, it would seem that, precisely at the point when advertising has displaced philosophy (and history and literature, etc.) from the center of the university, the university has admitted openly that it is indeed "founded against reason." The fine Latin mottoes might as well come down at this point, and the university can simply inscribe on its entranceways, "Money talks, bullshit walks." But then, I am not talking about a university that has been founded against reason, but rather one that has seemingly been eroded by the antithesis of reason. The question would be, Has this antithesis come from the outside or the inside of the university? I believe that Habermas would answer the former, while Derrida forces us to consider that it could be the latter. Derrida is not so far here from the argument of Adorno and Horkheimer, in *Dialectic of Enlightenment*, that Enlightenment can be totalitarian, especially if it is blind to its own suspension above the gorge of circular foundations. That Derrida and Adorno and Horkheimer are looking to the possibility of a radicalized Enlightenment, of a double-gesture that fractures the logic of the Same of blind Englightenment, does not seem enough to make them Nietzscheans, even by Habermas's standards. There is certainly some Nietzschean inspiration to their arguments; I do not see what is wrong with that. Isn't it a matter of the uses, theoretical and practical, to which this inspiration is put? In Derrida's arguments in "The Principle of Reason," it is recognized that there is, and always has been, unreason at the heart of reason. (The argument parallels Derrida's argument in the essay on Foucault and Descartes.) Furthermore, this unreason is a place of power—but the larger point is that the negotiation between reason and unreason is also inseparable from the workings of power. To theorize some pure reason that can be freed from power relations, decolonized as it were, is perhaps the greatest blindness of Enlightenment insight. None of this can be considered apart from Habermas's consistent failure to really come to terms with the network of power in which the modern university finds itself.

But the fact that truth and power are inextricable from one another does not mean, despite Habermas's charges and somewhat legitimate fears, that there is no possibility of speaking truth to power. It is true, there is no possibility of speaking some "pure" metaphysical truth to power, but the former is simply a mask of power. Furthermore, speaking truth to power is only a possibility at the limit of possibility, it is the "impossible possibility." Adorno and Derrida are very close on this point. The intersection of truth and power is not simply the place where Socrates' wisdom is simply shown to have Thracymachus's interest of the stronger at its heart. It is not simply the place where Socrates' dialectic has Gorgias's rhetoric at its heart. It is the place where these things are possible, to be sure, with all sorts of possible effects, some good, some bad. For Habermas, only bad effects could arise, for example, from a reason that allows poetry into its heart. (Thus he is concerned about the letting down of "genre distinctions"; see *Philosophical Discourse of Modernity*, pp. 185–210, and *Postmetaphysical Thinking*, pp. 205–27.) But not all that is not reason is anti-reason; furthermore, to repeat, to be concerned only with the barrier that will supposedly keep one from having to look into the abyss is perhaps the greatest unreason, and the most dangerous.

Because reason cannot be fully separated from unreason, it must be recognized that there is a place proper to reason that is also the place of unreason. This is a place where, it is true, anti-reason can grow and conceivably displace reason. Derrida's argument, however, is that this happens precisely when reason itself cannot be interrogated. In Habermas's view, such interrogation consists in the free expression of the "unforced force of reason." For Derrida, this is not broad enough: we must also be willing to ask how reason is constituted as such in particular institutional settings. That seems to be a practical question and one that can be acted upon practically.

That this is not the question, in any practical sense, for some of the people whom Habermas labels postmodern, and for many people who are writing in or on deconstruction, is something that should be recognized. To put forward as the main argument against Habermas that he has not done a very scholarly job of analyzing and criticizing Derrida is often a smokescreen. Derrida himself is certainly entitled to be upset about Habermas's treatment—or non-treatment—of his work, but Derrida's work, if it is not defended as part of a larger effort to both theoretically and practically create an ongoing transformation of the world toward respect for the other, cannot be defended at all.

To the extent that some postmodern thinkers (whether they accept the tag or not) and their epigones are simply saying that underneath all claims to truth is a will to power, and that, in the final analysis, this will to power is all there is to truth, I agree with Habermas's concerns. Even more so do I agree in the case of societies that are moving in the direction of openly taking the will to power as their guiding and, indeed, only principle. I would even go beyond Habermas in asserting that there can be forms of such societies that do not appear, at least outwardly, to be fascist (even though they may be fascistic in some respects—and obviously I am thinking of the United States) but that can exemplify an insidious and brutal logic of the Same. In their analysis of the culture industry, Adorno and Horkheimer gave the best initial analysis of this phenomenon, at least in the form of social theory, and of course they drew on Nietzsche and Weber. Fredric Jameson has done a good job of updating aspects of that analysis in the context of a society (rather than a theory) that has become more and more postmodern.[8] If the project of modernity is to be completed, it must be completed under the conditions of the possibility, but not the necessity, of a Kantian regulative ideal. Those conditions are in danger of disappearing. I am not sure that they will reappear in the west per se; rather, the scene of modernity's possibility must now be international, it must now develop that side of Kant's project that stresses not only the *telos* of intersubjectivity but also the fundamental role of alterity. Here I think Habermas needs Derrida, and then everything changes.

Possibility and contingency (Rorty)

The key part of "everything," however, might be the question, What changes about the classical program of the Enlightenment? To be more specific, What changes about the idea of having a universalist ethics and politics? Even without the foregoing analysis, most people who have at least a passing familiarity with the work of Habermas and Derrida know that they do not agree on these issues. However,

Habermas's position is better understood, in part because it is framed in the terms of social theory, whereas Derrida's position is generally framed in terms of, for want of a better term, philosophical principles. One reason that I discussed Derrida's "Principle of Reason" essay at length is because it is concerned with practices and how they need to be changed. The essay is somewhat akin to the work of Paulo Freire in two respects. First, Derrida and Freire are not simply concerned with "literacy" or "learning" pure and simple, as if such things existed. Both break with the model of literacy as "either a functional perspective tied to narrowly conceived economic interests or a logic designed to initiate the poor, the underprivileged, and minorities into the ideology of a unitary, dominant cultural tradition."[9] By contrast, those excluded by the university system do not make any kind of appearance in Habermas's essay. Second, and relatedly, both are concerned with how a different kind of literacy, a different reading, could lead to the empowerment of the excluded and marginalized. I will return to these issues in the final section of this part, when I consider not Derrida the young conservative but Derrida the wild-eyed radical who wants to blow up the walls of the university so that the politically correct hordes of multiculturalism can take over. May I reach now, however, for a provisional conclusion? That is, in providing the philosophical principles of a reading of the margins and an empowerment of the excluded, Derrida may be searching for a different kind of universalism than the kind Habermas wants, but he is indeed trying (theoretically, practically, and, as Althusser used to say, in "theoretical practice") to open a space for this differential universalism.

This point may now be emphasized through an initial encounter with the theme of anti-humanism. This theme, as the reader probably already knows, is most often associated with Martin Heidegger, on the one hand, and Louis Althusser, on the other. Rather than pursue this rather interesting combination (which certainly has its presence in Derrida's work) at this point, however, I want to turn to a discussion of the work of a philosopher who came out of analytic philosophy and who has done a great deal to initiate what is often called post-analytic philosophy, namely, Richard Rorty. In discussions that are generally quite a bit too fast and loose, his work is often linked to Derrida's, as though Rorty's work is a kind of analytic equivalent to the emergence of deconstruction in "continental" philosophy. There are more important reasons than that to compare the two, however. Indeed, linking Rorty and Derrida is more the result of a careless reading (I won't say misreading) of both, and no matter how bothered more straitlaced analytic philosophers might be, Rorty's work is still in the tradition and style of analytic philosophy. (Not that there is anything wrong with that.) Still, there are two points that are central to the concerns of the present chapter where a useful comparison might be made. First, where Derrida might be called a philosopher of possibility, Rorty has certainly marked out a space as the philosopher of contingency. What is the difference? Second, Rorty and Derrida are often taken both to be working toward the fragmentation of the ideals of political modernity. In broad terms, this characterization may even be accurate, but the two are very different when it comes to spelling out the meaning of this fragmentation, and it will be useful to set out the difference. In making this comparison I will focus mostly on Rorty's 1989 *Contingency, irony, and solidarity*.

I hope that this section will be useful even for the reader who already knows that Rorty and Derrida are quite different, because, with the help of others who have taken up this question I hope to thematize the meaning of these differences for politics, for political practice, and for thinking the polis. In other words, I do not want to leave these differences simply at the level of differing philosophical problematics.

The general layout of *Contingency, irony, and solidarity* is meant to convey the overall direction of Rorty's thought. The book begins with discussions of important nineteenth- and twentieth-century philosophers, such as Kant, Hegel, Nietzsche, Wittgenstein, Quine, Goodman, Sellars, Davidson, Putnam, Heidegger, and Derrida, and works their arguments into a general framework for the articulation of three contingencies: of language, of selfhood, and of liberal community. In the second part Rorty moves to a discussion of literary works, including in this category Derrida's text, *The Post Card*. Rorty also shifts from "public" concerns to private ones, in particular the concern with self-creation. Indeed, Rorty takes *The Post Card* to be a demonstration of such concern. Nietzsche plays a key role here also, as someone who purportedly lived his life as a work of art. In the third and final part of the book Rorty returns to what he takes to be the one unifying theme of a liberal society: concern with cruelty and its prevention. That is, this concern, and the solidarity that is generated by it, is the one "public" theme of a liberal society; apart from this concern, and whatever time and effort one might devote to it, liberal society is, in Rorty's view, primarily about "freedom," the freedom to pursue one's own private heaven or hell.

Rorty draws a sharp distinction between these two spheres, basically in the manner of John Stuart Mill. (Incidentally, Rorty's debt to Mill, and his general critique of Kant, makes problematic his use of the work of Derrida, Davidson, and Rawls—three outstanding Kantians.)

His argument is interesting, very much worth thinking about, not easily answered. Basically Rorty's public/private distinction is between two kinds of vocabularies. He associates one kind of vocabulary, "private irony," with

> authors like Kierkegaard, Nietzsche, Baudelaire, Proust, Heidegger, and Nabokov [who] are useful as exemplars, as illustrations of what private perfection—a self-created, autonomous, human life—can be like. (p. xiv)

Rorty associates the other kind of vocabulary, "social hope" and "justice," with

> authors such as Marx, Mill, Dewey, Habermas, and Rawls [who] are fellow citizens rather than exemplars. They are engaged in a shared, social effort—the effort to make our institutions and practices more just and less cruel. (p. xiv)

Rorty places the development of these vocabularies within a historical framework that one is tempted to call a grand narrative. The earlier form of the tension between the private and the public, Rorty claims, is in the opposition between metaphysicians and theologians, on the one hand, and skeptics, on the other. The former try "to unite a striving for perfection with a sense of community [that] requires us to acknowledge a common human nature" (p. xiii). Rorty cites Plato as exemplary of this way of thinking. "Skeptics like Nietzsche," on the other hand, "have urged that metaphysics and theology are transparent attempts to make altruism look more reasonable than it is." Of course, lurking behind this skepticism, Rorty argues, is another theory of human nature, in which the will to power, libidinal impulses, or something of this sort is what is common to all human beings.

> Their point is that at the "deepest" level of the self there is *no* sense of human solidarity, that this sense is a "mere" artifact of human socialization. So such skeptics become antisocial. They turn their backs on the very idea of a community larger than a tiny circle of initiates. (p. xiv)

Rorty argues that this opposition of metaphysicians and skeptics seems to undergo a transformation with Hegel's philosophy and the emergence of historicist thinking. Historicism, in Rorty's view, holds that "there is no such thing as 'human nature' or the 'deepest level of the self'"; instead, "socialization, and thus historical circumstance, goes all the way down ... there is nothing 'beneath' socialization or prior to history which is definatory of the human" (p. xiv). Furthermore, this historicist turn has helped free us, gradually but steadily, from theology and metaphysics—from the temptation to look for an escape from time and chance. It has helped us to substitute Freedom for Truth as the goal of thinking and of social progress. (p. xiv)

Interestingly, Rorty does not say that historicism has helped free us from skepticism and its preoccupation with "private autonomy" (as Rorty puts it). This is a point I will return to.

Indeed, the classical tension is modified by historicism, but "the old tension between the private and the public remains."

Historicists in whom the desire for self-creation, for private autonomy, dominates (e.g., Heidegger and Foucault) still tend to see socialization as Nietzsche did—as antithetical to something deep within us. Historicists in whom the desire for a more just and free human community dominates (e.g., Dewey and Habermas) are still inclined to see the desire for private perfection as infected with "irrationalism" and "aestheticism." (pp. xiii–xiv)

Rorty, however, wants to "do justice to both groups of historicist writers." He argues that not only should we not attempt to choose between these two categories of writers, but, further, there is no basis for such a choice. This argument, to the effect that we are dealing with a case of apples and oranges, or, better, "paintbrushes and crowbars," must be set out at length:

We shall only think of these two kinds of writers as *opposed* if we think that a more comprehensive philosophical outlook would let us hold self-creation and justice, private perfection and human solidarity, in a single vision.

There is no way in which philosophy, or any other theoretical discipline, will ever let us do that. The closest we will come to joining these two quests is to see the aim of a just and free society as letting its citizens be as privatistic, "irrationalist," and aestheticist as they please so long as they do it on their own time—causing no harm to others and using no resources needed by those less advantaged. There are practical measures to be taken to accomplish this practical goal. But there is no way to bring self-creation together with justice at the level of theory. The vocabulary of self-creation is necessarily private, unshared, unsuited to argument. The vocabulary of justice is necessarily public and shared, a medium for argumentative exchange.

If we could bring ourselves to accept the fact that no theory about the nature of Man or Society or Rationality, or anything else, is going to synthesize Nietzsche with Marx or Heidegger with Habermas, we could begin to think of the relation between writers on autonomy and writers on justice as being like the relation between two kinds of tools—as little in need of synthesis as are paintbrushes and crow-bars. (p. xiv)

But, one might argue, surely there is a question of priorities. Rorty agrees that there is such a question, and he has said something about this in the passage I just quoted. Indeed, I think that he may have said more than he meant to say, but I will turn to that point in the argument in due course. Rorty agrees that there is a question of priorities, but he does not believe that answers to that question can be given in the form of arguments. Thus he says that there is no "answer," that is, no "noncircular theoretical backup" to the question, "How do you decide when to struggle against injustice and when to devote yourself to private projects of self-creation?" (p. xv). Furthermore:

Anybody who thinks there are well-grounded theoretical answers to this sort of question—algorithms for resolving moral dilemmas of this sort—is still, in his heart, a theologian or a metaphysician. He believes in an order beyond time and change which both determines the point of human existence and establishes a hierarchy of responsibilities. (p. xiv)

The vocabularies of social justice and private fulfillment mark out two forms of life. This line of thinking Rorty takes, of course, from Wittgenstein. The fact that a single individual might partake of both of these forms does not mean that the vocabularies are reducible or translatable one into the other. Although the tension between the vocabularies goes back at least to the time of Plato, the possibility of framing this tension in the way that Rorty does emerges in a specific social-historical context, that of the modern, liberal, western democracies—societies that Rorty also refers to as "lucky, rich, [and] literate" (p. xiv).

Rorty argues that liberal societies may claim to be rooted in Kantian principle,—at least, their politicians, ideologues, judges, and constitutional lawyers may make this claim—in particular the distinction between morality and prudence, but, as a matter of fact, the legitimacy of such societies is based in the same thing that the legitimacy of all other societies must be based in: the "mere solidarity" of particular communities. "Hegelians," that is, historicists, recognize this fact. Furthermore, this is a reality that Rorty is happy to defend—the Kantian vocabulary is representative of a "world well lost," to use an expression from *Philosophy and the Mirror of Nature*. In "Postmodern Bourgeois Liberalism" Rorty expands on this:

I shall call the Hegelian attempt to defend the institutions and practices of the rich North Atlantic democracies without using such [Kantian] buttresses [e.g., an account of 'rationality' and 'morality' as transcultural and ahistorical] "postmodernist bourgeois liberalism." I call it "bourgeois" to emphasize that most of the people I am talking about would have no quarrel with the Marxist claim that a lot of those institutions and practices are possible and justifiable only in certain historical, and especially economic, conditions. I want to contrast bourgeois liberalism, the attempt to fulfill the hopes of the North Atlantic bourgeoisie, with philosophical liberalism, a collection of Kantian principles thought to justify us in having those hopes. Hegelians think that these principles are useful for *summarizing* these hopes, but not for justifying them. I use "postmodernist" in a sense given to this term by Jean-Francois Lyotard, who says that the postmodern attitude is that of "distrust of metanarratives," narratives which describe or predict the activities of such entities as the noumenal self or the Absolute Spirit or the Proletariat. These metanarratives are stories which purport to justify loyalty to, or breaks with, certain contemporary communities, but which are neither historical narratives about what these or other communities have done in the past nor scenarios about what they might do in the future. (pp. 198–99)

Again it is an interesting point that, just as the historicist turn seems to put the metaphysician/theologian out of business but not the skeptic, it would also deny the "moral principles" side of Kant's distinction but not his prudence.

Indeed, even prudence is given a somewhat reductive interpretation, with appeal to Quine's behaviorism. Rorty accomplishes this reduction in two moves, the first of which does not seem to necessarily lead to the second. (However, at this stage I am primarily concerned with explicating Rorty's argument.) First, Rorty argues that the "moral self" should be conceived

not as one of Rawls's original choosers, somebody who can distinguish her *self* from her talents and interests and views about the good, but as a network of beliefs, desires, and emotions with nothing behind it—no substrate behind the attributes. (p. 199)

This is an argument, of course, against what Rorty thinks of as the Kantian conception of the noumenal self. Second, Rorty moves to his positive conception:

For purposes of moral and political deliberation and conversation, a person just *is* that network, as for purposes of ballistics she is a point-mass, or for purposes of chemistry a linkage of molecules. She is a network that is constantly reweaving itself in the usual Quinean manner—that is to say, not by reference to general criteria (e.g., "rules of meaning" or "moral principles") but in the hit-or-miss way in which cells readjust themselves to meet the pressures of the environment. (p. 199)

Reweavings of the moral self, on *this* historicist view, occur not on the basis of transcendental principles (even if some agents claim to be reflecting upon such principles) but on the basis of loyalties and narratives.

Thus, Rorty argues elsewhere ("On Ethnocentrism: A Reply to Clifford Geertz"), postmodern bourgeois liberals are "ethnocentric," in the sense that they acknowledge their loyalty to a particular form of society, they acknowledge that there is no "deeper" basis for their loyalty than the fact of their historical situatedness in the narrative of the emergence and development of western liberal democracies, and, finally, they acknowledge that the search for some "deeper" basis for their loyalty is simply evidence of a metaphysics well abandoned.[10]

And yet, in Rorty's view, the postmodern bourgeois liberal does have a social mission. One could not call the pursuit of this mission an obligation, I suppose, but, all the same, Rorty wants to "suggest the possibility of a liberal utopia" (*Contingency*, p. xv), in which "ironism" is universal. In Rorty's argot, ironism means facing up to contingency— accepting that even one's "most central beliefs and desires" are contingent; an ironist is "someone sufficiently historicist and nominalist to have abandoned the idea that those central beliefs and desires refer back to something beyond the reach of time and chance" (p. xv). Not all ironists are liberals—witness Nietzsche. But Rorty's particular pet project is the joining of liberalism and ironism:

> Liberal ironists are people who include among these ungroundable desires their own hope that suffering will be diminished, that the humiliation of human beings by other human beings may cease. (p. xv)

There does seem to be a point, in Rorty's framework, where liberalism and ironism necessarily intersect. Turning Engels's formulation on its head, Rorty suggests that the culture of the liberal utopia would be one "in which recognition of contingency rather than of necessity" would be "the accepted definition of freedom" (p. 40).

A few more passages may be quoted to give a better flavor of Rorty's use of "contingency."

> The important philosophers of our own century are those who have tried to follow through on the Romantic poets by breaking with Plato

and seeing freedom as the recognition of contingency. These are the philosophers who try to detach Hegel's insistence on historicity from his pantheistic idealism. They accept Nietzsche's identification of the strong poet, the maker, as humanity's hero—rather than the scientist, who is traditionally pictured as a finder. More generally, they have tried to avoid anything that smacks of philosophy as contemplation, as the attempt to see life steadily and see it whole, in order to insist on the sheer contingency of human existence. (pp. 25–26)

Rorty develops the idea of the "quarrel between poetry and philosophy" in terms of

> the tension between an effort to achieve self-creation by the recognition of contingency and an effort to achieve universality by the transcendence of contingency. (p. 25)

The "pre-Nietzschean" philosopher (Rorty does not say "non-Nietzschean," which seems to indicate that the post-Nietzschean philosopher is the more developed thinker) maintains that, measured by universal and transcendental standards,

> the particular contingencies of individual lives are unimportant. The mistake of the poets is to waste words on idiosyncrasies, on contingencies—to tell us about accidental appearance rather than essential reality. (p. 26)

Quintessential post-Nietzschean philosophers, such as Wittgenstein and Heidegger, in contrast, "write philosophy in order to exhibit the universality and necessity of the individual and contingent." The culture of the liberal utopia would be a post-Nietzschean culture, "in which poetry [has] publicly and explicitly triumphed over philosophy" (p. 40). The effort to make post-Nietzschean philosophy into an ethical and political program is, for Rorty, a non-starter and a big mistake. Thinkers such as Erich Fromm and Herbert Marcuse who attempted to integrate Freud into their social theories were barking up the wrong vocabulary, for Freud's

> *only* utility lies in his ability to turn us away from the universal to the concrete, from the attempt to find necessary truths, ineliminable beliefs, to the idiosyncratic contingencies of our individual pasts, to the blind impress all our behavings bear.... Freudian moral psychology cannot be used to define social goals, goals for humanity as opposed to goals for individuals. (p. 34)

Does the possibility even exist, then, for the systematic development of a social program or a social project? Appealing to Freud, Rorty argues that there can be no social "program" that is developed in a standardly understood "programmatic" way. How, then, can it come to pass that social programs and projects are developed and embraced? By accident: "Poetic, artistic, philosophical, scientific, or political progress results from the accidental coincidence of a private obsession with a public need" (p. 37). Contingency is the mother of invention and all else besides.

Rorty devotes a chapter to the argument that "the later" Derrida "privatizes his philosophical thinking, and thereby breaks down the tension between ironism and theorizing." Derrida

> simply drops theory—the attempt to see his predecessors steadily and whole—in favor of fantasizing about those predecessors, playing with them, giving free rein to the trains of associations they produce. There is no moral to these fantasies, nor any public (pedagogic or political) use to be made of them; but, for Derrida's readers, they may nevertheless be exemplary—suggestions of the sort of thing one might do, a sort of thing rarely done before.
>
> Such fantasizing is, in my view, the end product of ironist theorizing. (p. 125)

In other words, such fantasizing is the end product, the aim, of Rorty's theorizing. In what sounds like a Derridean formulation, Rorty argues that the importance of Derrida's later work is that it has found a way to be creative and to avoid repetition. Rorty's argument, however, moves a further step in setting out the stakes—I would say the costs—of inventiveness in post-Nietzschean philosophy. Here is the complete formulation, which follows the final sentence in the passage just quoted.

> Falling back on private fantasy is the only solution to the self-referential problem which such theorizing encounters, the problem of how to distance one's predecessors without doing exactly what one has repudiated them for doing. So I take Derrida's importance to lie in his having had the courage to give up the attempt to unite the private and the public, to stop trying to bring together a quest for private autonomy and an attempt at public resonance and utility. He privatizes the sublime, having learned from the fate of his predecessors that the public can never be more than beautiful. (p. 125)

Derrida, Rorty argues, does not even attempt to bring together his "private allusions" with the public existence of the western philosophical canon: "*All* that connects him with the philosophical tradition is that past philosophers are the topics of his most vivid fantasies" (p. 126).

Other than Plato, the philosopher whom Rorty most wants to distance his conception of post-Nietzschean philosophy from is Kant.

Perhaps the reader will especially see now, and in the pages to come, why I opened this text with a discussion of Plato, and why I have situated the Kantian ethical project at the heart of this text. This project is at the heart of every text, and of textuality, even if it is also a kind of absent, because impossible, center. In other words, in taking Plato and especially Kant as predecessors to Derrida in a non-Rortyan sense, I am attempting to steal Derrida's work back from Rorty and others who believe that the point of "important" (and purportedly "post-Nietzschean") philosophy is to concoct vivid fantasies. If all that I am going to get from Derrida is a fantasy narrative that uses this or that traditional philosophical figure as a character, then, frankly, I'd rather watch Monty Python reruns. That doesn't mean that I don't enjoy a good fantasy—certainly the idea of Jean-Paul and Muriel Sartre is really funny—and it doesn't mean that I am only interested in a Derrida who can be rendered humorless. I'll happily watch the reruns and enjoy Derrida's sense of humor, but I will also persist in wanting a good deal more from philosophy. In the pages to come I hope to show that it is right and necessary to want more.

I turn, once more, to that arch(e)-pre-Nietzschean, Kant, in particular to Rorty's description of the Kant well lost. In Rorty's scheme, the idea of a society in which the poet is paradigmatic is liberating and inspiring. Instead, Kant "sees the unselfish, unselfconscious, unimaginative, decent, honest, dutiful person as paradigmatic." Furthermore,

> It was for the sake of such persons that Kant distinguished practical from pure reason, and rational religion from enthusiasm. It was for their sake that he invented the idea of a single imperative under which morality could be subsumed. For, he thought, the glory of such people is that they recognize themselves as under an unconditional obligation—an obligation which can be carried out without recourse to prudential calculation, imaginative projection, or metaphoric redescription. So Kant developed not only a novel and imaginative moral psychology but a sweeping metaphoric redescription of every facet of life and culture, precisely in order to make the intellectual world safe for such people. In his words, he denied knowledge in order to make room for faith, the faith of such people that in doing their duty they are doing all they need do, that they are paradigmatic human beings. (pp. 34–35)

For Rorty, Kant's universal moral law faces the same basic stricture that any proposal for social improvement does: the only universality the categorical imperative can conceivably claim is that which might contingently be bestowed upon it in the weave of time and chance, that is, through the accidental coincidence of Kant's private obsession with a public need.

For Rorty, the announcement of one's obsessions is all that there is to social theory. In Rorty's view, even when compelled by need, people are not likely to set out upon the road to moral and political improvement because of their having read or heard about some writing in philosophy or social theory. Rorty recommends "a general turn against theory and toward narrative" (p. xvi). For the liberal ironist, the point of such a turn as a replacement for social theorizing would be to eliminate cruelty and humiliation through the work of creating solidarity. In articulating this idea Rorty comes closest to an engagement with the question of alterity: solidarity

> is created by increasing our sensitivity to the particular details of the pain and humiliation of other, unfamiliar sorts of people. Such increased sensitivity makes it more difficult to marginalize people different from ourselves by thinking, "They do not feel it as *we* would," or "There must always be suffering, so why not let *them* suffer?" (p. xvi)

Social theory engages too much in the violence of abstraction; instead,

> this process of coming to see other human beings as "one of us" rather than "them" is a matter of detailed description of what unfamiliar people are like and of redescription of what we ourselves are like. This is a task not for theory but for genres such as ethnography, the journalist's report, the comic book, the docudrama, and, especially, the novel. Fiction like that of Dickens, Olive Schreiner, or Richard Wright gives us the details about kinds of suffering being endured by people to whom we had previously not attended. Fiction like that of Choderlos de Laclos, Henry James, or Nabokov gives us the details about what sorts of cruelty we ourselves are capable of, and thereby lets us redescribe ourselves. That is why the novel, the movie, and the TV program have, gradually but steadily, replaced the sermon and the treatise as the principal vehicles of moral change and progress.
>
> In my liberal utopia, this replacement would receive a kind of recognition which it still lacks. (p. xvi)

Finally, the turn toward narrative by the larger society, in the liberal utopia, would signal the abandonment of "the attempt to hold all the sides of our life in a single vision, to describe them with a single vocabulary." Positively,

> a historicist and nominalist culture of the sort I envisage would settle instead for narratives which connect the present with the past, on the one hand, and with utopian futures, on the other. More important, it would regard the realization of utopias, and the envisaging of still further utopias, as an endless process—an endless,

proliferating realization of Freedom, rather than a convergence toward an already existing Truth. (p. xvi)

I propose to make a strategic pause between this somewhat belabored
exposition of Rorty's arguments and the critique that will come soon
enough. A pause would be useful for the purpose of settling down to
honest work, without leaping into the sort of hatchet job on Rorty that
is typical of some "left" critiques.[11] I have pursued this lengthy expli-
cation, burdened by lengthy quotations, because it is necessary to be
fair to Rorty. Sometimes, I must admit, I find it hard to want to be
fair, for example, when he tosses off phrases about "dumping Marx"
(or other gratuitous slurs about "Hitler and Mao" or "Hitler and Lenin"),
or when he actually sets out to describe some aspect of liberal society.
In my critique I will discuss the example of Rorty's description of a
particular "them," namely, indigenous peoples of South and North
America. Sample for now, however, a typical description of an important aspect of the liberal polity of the United States, "free discussion":

> "Free discussion" here does not mean "free from ideology," but simply
> the sort which goes on when the press, the judiciary, the elections,
> and the universities are free, social mobility is frequent and rapid,
> literacy is universal, higher education is common, and peace and
> wealth have made possible the leisure necessary to listen to lots of
> different people and think about what they say. (p. 84)

My first, gut reaction is to ask, "Any suggestions on how to get to this
point?" John McCumber asks,

> Is this intended as a description of the conditions of contemporary
> American life? Are the press and elections free in America today?
> Only if "free" means "already paid for." After ten years of Reaganite
> litmus testing, do we have a free judiciary? Only if "free" means
> "never having smoked marijuana or supported abortion." Is literacy
> universal in our Republic? We seem to have more *institutions* of higher
> education than *instances* of it. If peace and wealth have enhanced
> leisure, why are so many privileged yuppies grinding out 80-hour
> weeks under bi-career marriages? Rorty's redescription of American
> social realities, like his rereadings of philosophical texts, is enticing.
> But one wishes both were—well, truer. (p. 10)

McCumber is only being fair in holding Rorty to his own principles,
but my own, more developed reaction would be to question Rorty's
terms. (I don't mean "more developed" than McCumber's, necessarily,
but rather more developed than my initial reaction.) For example, What
can he mean by "peace"? But I will turn to such questions soon enough.
There is a side of Rorty's work that I find truly insidious, and per-

haps it is best to say this in the space of this brief pause. I do not think it coincidence that Rorty and Reagan encouraged U.S. citizens to "feel good about America" in roughly the same timeframe—or perhaps this was the coincidence of Rorty's private obsession with a public need. Where did this need come from? I would say that it came from the same place that Rorty's definition of peace comes from—but again, that is to get too far ahead, too quickly.

And yet, despite worries that there is a large dose of willful naivete and pragmatist know-nothingism in Rorty's work, I think that it would be foolish not to show appreciation for two aspects of his work.

First, as part of his recasting of analytic philosophy, Rorty has provided an interesting and provocative argument about the irreducibility of vocabularies. Any attempt to situate the vocabulary of private irony within the vocabulary of social justice must confront the question, Are the possibilities and dimensions of human life thereby enriched or restricted, and, if the latter, what is the justification for this? I am not entirely sure that Rorty would accept even this question, as there may be, in his view, no argumentative justification for restricting the preoccupations of the poet. If there is no argument, then, on Rorty's J.S. Mill-influenced view, there can be no justification, period. Although I believe that there is an answer to this line of reasoning, a justified answer, I think that it is important to answer in a way that is responsible to the way that Rorty has set up the problem. For reasons that will be developed further, I believe that this responsibility exists even though I do not believe that Rorty himself has always articulated the key questions in a responsible fashion.

As a postscript to this first reason for attempting to be fair in criticizing Rorty, I might add that his work in reconceptualizing analytic philosophy has on the whole been a good thing, has created openings for good discussions that may not have otherwise taken place.

Second, I believe that, whatever the problems with some of Rorty's other arguments, his claims about narrative are valid. Frankly, I'm quite skeptical about the idea that Nabokov's novels encourage solidarity, and I'm not too sure about the comic book or the TV docudrama, even though I'm an avid reader of comic books and I've also been known to watch some TV. Still, the point is well taken, and the argument leads to a provocative question. Only some aspects of this question will be set out now, for the question leads into a more general discussion of "metanarratives" and their supposed problems. But even the first approximation of the question will clue the reader into its larger framework.

The question is, Why can't there be, and why hasn't there been, a narrative of the proletariat? After all, even though all of us may join Rorty and Lyotard in their skepticism about the noumenal self or Absolute Spirit, why do we have to doubt the existence of a class of people called proletarians? Is the existence of such a class not simply a matter of empirical verification? In other words, does Rorty doubt that there are people who are characterized by 1) their position in the mode of production, as wage laborers (when they can find work, that is), and 2) their position in the overall social framework, as people who have no stake in the status quo, who have nothing to lose?

It would be silly to doubt that there are such people, and I would not attribute such a position to Rorty. But perhaps Rorty is skeptical about two other points that generally accompany a discussion of the proletariat. Perhaps Rorty doubts that people in the position just described form a class. Perhaps Rorty doubts that there is some *telos* to be found by looking at this class in relation to the society and mode of production. The question then might be framed, Is the reason why there has been no narrative of the proletariat simply that no such narrative is possible, because such a narrative could only be a groundless metanarrative, something that could not really give rise to the sort of solidarity that Marx was hoping would emerge? Why should we worry that such a narrative could only be a metanarrative? Perhaps because it is difficult to imagine a story line that draws the diversity of an unmanageable plurality of peoples together into a common account of past, present, and possible future simply on the basis of an underlying analysis of the development of modes of production.

The difficulties faced by any proposal of a proletarian narrative may be framed in a way that is more provocative still. There are, of course, narratives that are based on the potential solidarity of marginalized people: narratives that encourage these people to come together, to make a break with the society that oppresses them, and to build a new society. These narratives are most commonly associated with religious movements, which typically have as their goal, at least in the language of the west, the establishment of a "new Zion." There is no better example of such a movement in recent times than the Mormons (the Church of Jesus Christ of Latter Day Saints). Why is it that the Mormons achieved a coherence and power in their movement, not to mention sheer numbers of converts, that the other new religious movements—Christian Scientists, Jehovah's Witnesses, Seventh Day Adventists—of the nineteenth century did not? After all, the Mormons did establish their new Zion in the western part of the United States (the kingdom of Deseret, which originally extended far beyond Utah); despite the downsizing of this kingdom by the U.S. government—through military force—the Mormons still maintain the state of Utah as a quasi-theocratic kingdom, and Mormon power extends far, and ever farther, beyond Utah.[12] This new Zion, which the Mormons originally attempted to establish in Missouri and Illinois before being driven out of the (then) United States, was originally a communitarian experiment. My own belief, which I've argued for elsewhere, is that communists need to learn from historical communitarian experiments (and historical communities; this is to say, among other things, that communist theory needs to get beyond the rationalism characteristic of much Marxism, as well as Nancy, Blanchot, etc.), even ones that contain reactionary elements or that end up as reactionary communities.[13] In the case of the Mormon movement and experiment I state this partly for the sheer provocation of it, but let me return to the earlier question. One very important thing that distinguished the Mormons from other religious movements that sprang up about the same time and that had a similar social basis (especially among poor and dispossessed farmers in the northeastern United States, at a time when class differentiation was beginning to take hold and move at a fast pace) was the *Book of Mormon*. This narrative united marginalized people. (For better or for worse is not my concern here.) The narrative gave these people a sense of historical and spiritual past, present, and their future. Furthermore, it seemed inclusive, in the sense that anyone who read and believed the *Book of Mormon* could join the movement (except that women and Black people could not become full members; in this respect, the Mormon movement was no different from all universalisms in the period of the rise of liberalism and political modernity).

Now, the ambition of this movement was (and is) to turn not only Utah but indeed the whole world into the new Zion. I realize that I may have taken Rorty's concerns a great distance away from where he would see them going. (I take great pleasure in this post-secular poke at Rorty and other secular thinkers.) But then, on the other hand, I'm not sure that Rorty really has a conception of what narratives might do to encourage and forge solidarity (his examples do not, after all, have grand pretensions). In the light of the example I am pursuing, then, I want to ask: Is the proletariat awaiting its *Book of Mormon*? Could there be such a thing? The Mormons, despite universalist claims, have basically forged an American movement, and they have even put forward that aspect of Mormonism (including the appeal of American wealth) as part of their appeal to would-be converts outside of the United States. One might see the Mormon narrative as existing primarily within a larger narrative, that of the "promise" of "America." To be sure, that narrative does have a theoretical basis, of sorts, in

Jeffersonian views of a democratic, somewhat egalitarian, basically rural society, and perhaps also in the larger tradition, going back to Aristotle, of civic virtue and civic republicanism (on these points, see Kenneth H. Winn, *Exiles in a Land of Liberty*). Must narratives and their movements—the Mormon narrative is hardly the only example that can be given; another narrative and movement is the obvious subtext of these remarks—lead not to a universal new Zion but to an exclusionary Zionism? (We are in the vicinity of Stalin's interpretation of Marxism.) To repeat the first formulation of the question, Is there no hope for a universal human narrative? If there is no such hope, if there can be no such *narrative*, does that mean all attempts at a universalistic description of the human project amount to no more than silly, even if sophisticated, pretentious, metaphysical-theological babbling?

These are damned hard questions, good questions, I believe, and we should credit Rorty with raising them and framing them in such a way that they have to be confronted. Although, in the critique that I am finally about to enter, I think it important to go toe-to-toe with Rorty on every aspect of his position, and to call him out when he has not been responsible to the larger implications of some of his own arguments, these questions just now framed will remain and they will have to be answered one way or another.

Taking stock of the discussion up to this point, I now seem to have four questions.

The two questions just set out are obviously the result of a reworking of Rorty's line of thought. Although Rorty would most likely not frame the question about narrative in the way that I do, I believe that, on the other hand, he would either have to accept this kind of reframing or be guilty of mere arbitrariness. It can hardly be said, in any case, that the question of narrative has been made less complex or less difficult in the reworking. It may be useful to say something about the motivations behind this reworking. Many of the left critiques of Rorty raise objections to his work that are true but that conveniently let themselves off without this sort of reframing. It is simple enough to see how the ideals of a rich, North Atlantic democracy might appeal to a rich, North Atlantic democrat. I suppose that it doesn't hurt to point out that Rorty's philosophy is a convenient one for someone in his position to hold. (Rorty probably would not take that as a criticism, however.) The work of radical social theory, however, is not primarily to hold a trial for Richard Rorty. Radical social theorists should seek out hard questions wherever they might be found, and be grateful for them. Furthermore, extending the principle of philosophical charity to Rorty, to ask what he is saying that could be a challenge to the project of radical social theory, is also a way to get beyond the kind of comparison between thinkers (in this case Rorty and Derrida) that is not just a battle of the proper names (or of the strong poets, as Rorty would have it).

In the analysis that follows, I hope to show that the four questions are actually the two questions with which this section began, that of contingency and possibility and that of humanism and fragmentation. Then I hope to show that these two questions are closely related, actually two parks of one question. However, in the aftermath of both Rorty and Derrida, my aim is not a monological reduction, in which all questions become one question, but instead the discovery of a question that opens up, in a way that will have strategic import, a principle of questioning. In other words, there may be one question, but that does not mean that there are not many answers.

Two epigraphs will serve as regulative principles for the critique of Rorty that will now begin.[14] The first consists in two passages from Max Horkheimer, *The Eclipse of Reason*:

> As soon as a thought or a word becomes a tool, one can dispense with actually "thinking" it, that is, with going through the logical acts involved in verbal formulation of it. As has been pointed out, often and correctly, the advantage of mathematics—the model of all neo-positivistic thinking—lies in just this "intellectual economy." Complicated logical operations are carried out without actual performance of all the intellectual acts upon which the mathematic and logical symbols are based. Such mechanization is indeed essential to the expansion of industry; but if it becomes the characteristic feature of minds, if reason itself is instrumentalized, it takes on a kind of materiality and blindness, becomes a fetish, a magic entity that is accepted rather than intellectually experienced. . . . (p. 23)
>
> The neutralization of reason that deprives it of any relation to objective content and of its power of judging the latter, and that degrades it to an executive agency concerned with the how rather than with the what, transforms it to an ever-increasing extent into a mere dull apparatus for registering facts. Subjective reason loses all spontanaety, productivity, power to discover and assert new kinds of content—it loses its very subjectivity. Like a too frequently sharpened razor blade, this "instrument" becomes too thin and in the end is even inadequate for mastering the purely formalistic tasks to which it is limited. This parallels the general social tendency to destruction of productive forces, precisely in a period of tremendous growth of these forces. (p. 55)

I will have recourse to this text as the critique develops. The second epigraph is from an unsigned article in the French journal *Internationale Situationniste* (no. 8, 1963), entitled "All the King's Men":

It is a matter not of putting poetry at the service of the revolution, but rather of putting the revolution at the service of poetry. It is only in this way that the revolution does not betray its own project. . . .

Every revolution has been born in poetry, has first of all been made with the force of poetry. This is a phenomenon which continues to escape theorists of revolution—indeed, it cannot be understood if one clings to the old conception of revolution or of poetry—but which has generally been sensed by counterrevolutionaries. Poetry, whenever it appears, frightens them; they do their best to get rid of it by means of every kind of exorcism, from auto-da-fe to pure stylistic research. The moment of real poetry, which has "all the time in the world before it," invariably wants to reorient the entire world and the entire future to its own ends. As long as it lasts its demands admit of no compromises. . . .

Poetry is becoming more and more clearly the empty space, the antimatter of consumer society, since it is not consumable (in terms of the modern criteria for a consumable object: an object that is of equivalent value for each of a mass of isolated passive consumers). Poetry is nothing when it is quoted, it can only be *detourned*, brought back into play. Otherwise the study of poetry of the past is nothing but an academic exercise. The history of poetry is only a way of running away from the poetry of history, if we understand by that phrase not the spectacular history of the rulers but rather the history of everyday life and its possible liberation; the history of each individual life and its realization. (Ken Knabb, ed. and trans. [p. 116])[15]

Richard Rorty does credit thinkers such as Marx and even Kant with having made innovations in the vocabulary of social justice. They have accomplished this through what Rorty calls "redescription" (or even "radical redescription"). Nietzsche, Proust, and Derrida, similarly, are innovative wordsmiths on the other side of Rorty's divide. Because the form that innovation must take in either the work of social justice or the work of "private autonomy" is that of redescription, the recreation and reweaving of vocabularies, Rorty is fond of calling these innovators "writers." Whether a writer will catch on, in either public or private life, is contingent upon the felt needs and desires of people in the society at large. An individual will seize upon the words of a writer if she or he finds these words useful, either as a citizen or as a person seeking private autonomy. If a vocabulary of social justice proves useful to a large or demographically significant number of people, it may foster a social movement. If a vocabulary of private autonomy proves useful to people—here the numbers do not have to be so large—then an artistic trend may be launched.

The distinction between the private and the public must itself be made on pragmatic grounds. There are no markers in language itself that tell people when they are working with the social vocabulary and when they are working with the private vocabulary. (Rorty's adoption of Davidson's theory of metaphor ensures that there can be no such division in language; see *Contingency* pp. 11–20.) The poet may have keen insight into the forms that human cruelty takes, but when the poet attempts to move from this insight, as expressed in some textual form, to a social program, Rorty sees romanticism run amok. What the poet *is* able to do is to make vocabularies *available*, and Rorty argues that the best hope for a postmodern liberal society is the "redescription of liberalism as the hope that the culture as a whole can be 'poeticized' rather than as the Enlightenment hope that it can be 'rationalized' or 'scientized'" (ibid. p. 53).

Thus the development of liberal society will depend on making society safe for poets. "Poeticized culture" is good, in the postmodern liberal view, for two reasons. First, in Rorty's view, the development of society *just is* the development of vocabularies. A stagnant society must be an "authoritarian" society in the sense that there must be some "author" or "author-function" at work, attempting to contain the dynamism of language. A society safe for poets is one in which the poets are continually able to offer up linguistic innovations. This does not mean that people will necessarily always take up these innovations. Indeed, romanticism run amok is simply an authoritarianism of particular poets (but not of poeticizing as such). Second, not only would a poeticized culture be a dynamic one, but that dynamism would aim at the elimination of cruelty and humiliation (among other things).

That is, a poeticized culture will develop in this direction if it is also a liberal culture. In Rorty's view, although the thoughtful ironist would seemingly desire to expand her or his vocabulary by coming into contact with the vocabularies of others, there is no built-in requirement in ironism that requires it to actually encounter other vocabularies, much less to respect them. Indeed, Rorty recognizes that ironism is likely to arouse suspicion:

> Ironism, as I have defined it, results from awareness of the power of redescription. But most people do not want to be redescribed. They want to be taken on their own terms—taken seriously just as they are and just as they talk. The ironist tells them that the language they speak is up for grabs by her and her kind. There is something potentially very cruel about that claim. For the best way to cause people long-lasting pain is to humiliate them by making the things that seemed most important to them look futile, obsolete, and powerless. (p. 89)

At best, then, the alliance between ironism and liberalism is uneasy. The ironist, especially the poet, expresses an alienation in personal terms which may all the same resonate with someone else's feelings. This resonation, however, remains "private"; no matter how many others have the same or similar feelings, these remain private, not "shared." And yet, Rorty argues, societies that are not safe for the poet are not safe for private autonomy, either. In actuality, Rorty maintains, "the only societies that give [the ironist] the freedom to articulate her alienation are liberal ones" (p. 89).

Without poetry, or "poeticization," liberal culture remains trapped in the search for metaphysical foundations, or, worse, liberal society may convince itself that it has actually found these foundations. We may safely conclude that a "liberal" society that has discovered the real foundations and has therefore embarked on an anti-poetic course is also a society on the road to fascism. (I take the policing of rap music, especially of Ice-T's "Cop Killer," as an important example here.)

While this is a real danger for liberalism, and while the poet may see that the creation of a liberal society *sans* foundations is in his or her best interest, there is, again, no guarantee. The ironist recognizes contingency, first of all in his or her own life. This means that the ironist has

> radical and continuing doubts about the final vocabulary ["the words in which" the ironist tells, "sometimes prospectively and sometimes retrospectively, the story of" his or her life] she currently uses, because she has been impressed by other vocabularies, vocabularies taken as final by people or books she has encountered. (p. 73)

While the ironist would seem to be someone who would work to preserve bourgeois liberties, in order to ensure his or her own space for experimentation, the private nature of the ironist enterprise means that this is not necessarily the case. As Nancy Fraser (p. 308) puts the relevant question: "Is to say goodbye to objectivity really to say hello to solidarity?" (In a moment I will discuss the important question, What kind of solidarity?) "Ironically," the ironist may make peace with fascism and even serve it. While Rorty has put forward the idea that there is no necessary connection between Heidegger's philosophy and fascism, for instance, his theory also serves to show that there is no necessary repulsion between these two either. This is a telling point. Rorty's imaginary story about the contingency of Heidegger's life, which aims to show that Heidegger could have just as easily ended up living with Hannah Arendt in Chicago, is interesting and instructive. It does show that, under the model of Heidegger's philosophy as a vehicle for creating private fantasies with no relevance to conceptions of society or justice, Heidegger's engagement with Nazism is a purely contingent matter in relation to that philosophy. But then, are we not entitled to ask why Heidegger's philosophy did not contain the elements that would have urged him toward a principled opposition to Nazism? Of course, one might then maintain that there is nothing about a private fantasy that should or could either support or resist fascism (or liberalism, for that matter). But then, we would be just as entitled to our own fantasies in which Heidegger did not go to Chicago with Hannah Arendt but was offered the position of official ideologue of the Nazi Party that he demonstratively craved, so that he could have been in a better position to hold the "revolution" to its ideals, etc. That the national revolution did not live up to its supposed ideals was the only regret that Heidegger expressed during and after the war. It is not hard to see that Heidegger carried an entire universe inside his head, and that he must have spent a good deal of time there. A story told by a well-known Italian philosopher brings this out especially well. This philosopher had been a student of Heidegger's in the early thirties, but broke with him over his involvement with Nazism, after which the two were not on speaking terms. During one of the most intense periods of World War II, the philosopher happened to see Heidegger walking down the other side of the street. When Heidegger saw him he walked toward him, muttering, "It's terrible, it's just terrible." The Italian thought that Heidegger had finally understood something about the war and about his own political engagement. But when he said to Heidegger, "What is it, what is so terrible?" Heidegger's response was, "It is terrible, they have locked me out of the Nietzsche archive!"

Now, most people would say, I think, that Heidegger's private fantasy—or, at any rate, to be wrapped up in it—at that point was fantastically, almost unthinkably irresponsible. Rorty might agree. But his rejoinder would be that, although most people would not want to cross the street to hear such words from Heidegger (or anyone—though here the idea that Heidegger was not "just anyone" takes on a special twist for those who are always looking for special dispensation for Herr Heidegger, as opposed to your average, run-of-the-mill Nazi), that is not the same thing as saying that they could provide an argument that proves that Heidegger was irresponsible. In other words, people might use words such as irresponsible and irrational, but all that they can mean, on Rorty's view, is that there does not exist a common vocabulary that serves to bring Heidegger within the pale of an anti-Nazi sensibility. I will return to the general principle behind this point.

On Rorty's view, then, even the coming together of liberalism and ironism must be the result of a happy accident. Liberalism and ironism were not looking for each other, and, now that they have been thrown together through historical contingency, they may not always appreciate one another.

In any case, the marriage of liberalism and ironism provides the basis for only a minimal solidarity. This is best brought out by Rorty's comparison of the liberal ironist and the liberal metaphysician:

> The ironist thinks that the *only* redescriptions which serve liberal purposes are those which answer the question, "What humiliates?" whereas the metaphysician also wants to answer the question "Why should I avoid humiliating?" The liberal metaphysician wants our *wish to be kind* to be bolstered by an argument, one which entails a self-redescription which will highlight a common human essence, an essence which is something more than our shared ability to suffer humiliation. The liberal ironist just wants our *chances of being kind*, of avoiding the humiliation of others, to be expanded by redescription. She thinks that recognition of a common susceptibility to humiliation is the *only* social bond that is needed. Whereas the metaphysician takes the morally relevant feature of other human beings to be their relation to a larger shared power—rationality, God, truth, or history, for example—the ironist takes the morally relevant definition of a person, a moral subject, to be "something that can be humiliated." Her sense of human solidarity is based on a sense of a common danger, not on a common possession or a shared power. (p. 91)

This minimal sense of solidarity is not without its appeal. It seems to me that Rorty does have a good framework here for rejecting a form of monolithic solidarity that crushes difference.

I must ask, however, if the form in which Rorty seems to draw difference out of this framework is really a recognition of difference or an avoidance of it. If the latter, I must also ask what the consequences of such an avoidance might be. If I am reading Rorty correctly (which means?), the whole point of solidarity is to create a world in which each of us may privatize his or her difference. Immediately following the passage just quoted, Rorty asks about the relationship between minimal solidarity and the fact (at least in existing liberal society) "that people want to be described in their own terms." Rorty's answer is that

> the liberal ironist meets this point by saying that we need to distinguish between redescription for private and for public purposes. For my private purposes, I may redescribe you and everybody else in terms which have nothing to do with my attitude toward your ac-

tual or possible suffering. My private purposes, and the part of my
final vocabulary which is not relevant to my public actions, are none
of your business. But as I am a liberal, the part of my final vocabulary which is relevant to such actions requires me to become aware
of all the various ways in which other human beings whom I might
act upon can be humiliated. So the liberal ironist needs as much
imaginative acquaintance with alternative final vocabularies as possible, not just for her own edification, but in order to understand
the actual and possible humiliation of the people who use these alternative final vocabularies. (pp. 91–92)

The liberal ironist, then, does not make the mistake that the liberal
metaphysician does, of wanting a final vocabulary that is not just a
"patchwork." The liberal metaphysician

> thinks that acknowledging that everybody wants to be taken on their
> own terms commits us to finding a least common denominator of
> those terms, a single description which will suffice for both public
> and private purposes, for self-definition and for one's relations with
> others. (p. 92)

In contrast, the liberal ironist's conception of minimal solidarity applies only to a person's "public persona." In the pursuit of one's own
conception of private perfection—which is the realm where, in Rorty's
view, philosophy is important—it matters not at all whether or not
"kindness" or something of that order is a value. In this "patchwork"
conception, a person might conceivably fantasize about rape or torture in his "private life" and yet be a regular choirboy in his public
persona. Furthermore, with the private/public distinction firmly in place,
there are no more worries about troublesome Marxist notions such as
"false consciousness." There is simply no such thing—nor is there, of
course, such a thing as "true consciousness" either. Finally, because
"pain is nonlinguistic," there is nothing more to solidarity than the
recognition of pain, there is no "language" of solidarity in which the
"voice of the oppressed" might be expressed (p. 94).

There may be a kind of ethical and political universalism here, but
it now seems to come down to one minimal principle, with no metaphysical backing: live and let live. You do your thing, I'll do my thing,
and let's try to stay out of one another's way. Such is life, at its best,
in the realm of contingency: we, you and I, happen to find ourselves
on this planet at the same time, so we might as well make the best of
it. Fortunately, we just happen to live in a rich society, so there are
plenty of opportunities for the privatization of desire. The only real
"social" problems are ones of clearing a space, not for the other to

speak but to stay out of my way. There is no need for struggle here, only social engineering. After all, there are no fundamental social antagonisms in Rorty's scheme of things, because such antagonisms could only exist between "we liberals," we who already share a vocabulary of expanding, through redescription, our chances of avoiding the humiliation of others and some supposed "other" who/that is beyond the pale of this "we." But this other has no voice that we might hear. Nancy Fraser brings these points together:

> Rorty homogenizes social space, assuming, tendentiously, that there are no deep social cleavages capable of generating conflicting solidarities and opposing 'we's.' It follows from this assumed absence of fundamental social antagonisms that politics is a matter of everyone pulling together to solve a common set of problems. Thus social engineering can replace political struggle. Disconnected tinkerings with a succession of allegedly discrete social problems can replace transformation of the basic social structure. And the expert social-problem-solver and top-down reformer can replace the organized social movement of people collectively articulating their own interests and aspirations. (p. 315)

Fraser is right on the mark with her point about homogenization, in two respects. Ironically, pursuing this issue shows that Rorty, at least on some levels, subverts his own project; that is, as Rebecca Comay puts it,

> precisely where Rorty's hermeneutic pragmatism, if pursued rigorously, could and should have led philosophy in the direction of a general social and political critical project, Rorty shrinks back from the potentially subversive or utopian implications of his own understanding and retreats to safer ground. (p. 125)

The argument about homogenization applies to both the social and the historical.

Taking the question of history first, and again quoting Comay, "What is most striking . . . is the way in which a concrete historical undertaking has been neutralized and deflected *in the name of history itself.*" Rorty's pursuit of a "historicized" philosophy might be called "Heidegger without depth." (Not that Rorty would take this as an insult.) Just as Heidegger is interested in historicity, but not the details of history per se, so Rorty has no deeper or broader conception of the historicality of thought, truth, conceptions of the good, and so forth than that these things are contingent. History is the new and the now. After all, what is history for Rorty other than an analytic framework that allows him to make statements about contingency? What is contingency other than the idea that "anything can happen" and "things could be otherwise"?

This move to contingency, which in a different framework could be liberatory, is simply a way to valorize difference without getting into difficult questions about values, about what is good. The play of this difference has a great deal in common with the production of "difference," that is, new products, in postmodern capitalist society. One pole of the circuit is history defined as no more than contingency, or, as Comay puts it, "a flickering succession of instants, without sequence, without end." She goes on to say that this is "the logic of sheer obsolescence, the eternal repetition of the same." The other pole of Rorty's history is the conception of freedom as the ability of "human beings to adopt any of the competing discursive practices, to interpret any way we like, to choose one of the optional vocabularies, as long as *it gets us what we want*" (Rick Roderick, "Reading Derrida Politically [Contra Rorty]," p. 444). To be sure, this ability is itself contingent, in Rorty's view, upon being a member of a "rich" and "lucky" liberal society. Because "we liberals" simply find ourselves contingently in this historical situation, there is seemingly no reason why we might have to take responsibility for this situation.[16]

Is it unfair to link Rorty—his rise to fame and fortune—with his own historical moment, his moment of accidental coincidence of private obsession with public need? It almost seems unfair because the task is so simple. Rorty has risen to intellectual stardom at a time when cynical ideologues of the western democracies have also gone postmodern. They also see no need to justify the actions of their governments in terms of a meta-vocabulary. George Bush's cynical maneuverings around justifying the war against Iraq is a very good demonstration of this point, as was the lack of any substantive debate about this action, as is the lack of any substantive forum for carrying out such a debate. For the great powers, power *is* the justification.

I would not want to accuse Professor Rorty of supporting any particular action of the government of the United States or of any other western liberal society. I do not know what his position on the Gulf War was. But it is clear from his statements vis-à-vis cold war liberalism and Soviet imperialism that the range of political possibilities that he is willing to consider is exceedingly narrow. For instance, in an essay titled "Thugs and Theorists," aimed especially at some of his critics on the left, Rorty says:

I do not think that old-fashioned cold war liberalism needs any apologies. It will need them only if new evidence shows that Soviet Imperialism never existed, or no longer exists, or if somebody comes up with a better alternative for dealing with it than the Cold War. (Cited in Alan Malachowski, ed., *Reading Rorty*, p. 324.)

This is somewhat typical liberal-speak. Would Rorty consider that the "luck" involved in being a citizen of one of the rich North Atlantic democracies has anything to do with imperialism? And what kind of luck is this that depends on the exploitation and oppression, often under extremely brutal circumstances, of people in the Third World, or of some (ever more) people in these rich countries themselves, who do not share in this "luck"?

The further point is that this is a typically narrow liberal view, the kind, again, that represents one of the most intransigent strains of conservatism, in which there is no higher goal than to stand on the side of one's nation. Too bad if, because the United States and the Soviet Union were systematically driven to contend on a global scale, this meant that the whole world had to be held hostage in the process—at least "we liberals" should thank our lucky stars that we're able to pursue our private fantasies in a rich country.

What is especially amusing about the present example is that, if one were to speak of imperialism with regard to the United States, Rorty would immediately jump to the all-encompassing accusation of metanarrative. In his earlier book, *The Consequences of Pragmatism*, Rorty claims that "we should be more willing than we are to celebrate bourgeois capitalist society as the best polity actualized so far, while regretting that it is irrelevant to most of the problems of most of the population of this planet" (p. 210, n. 16). I would like to see Professor Rorty explain to peasant laborers in Latin America how the U.S. polity is irrelevant to the fact that they must grow crops for export rather than consumption. I would like him to explain to them the "contingent" presence of U.S. corporations, business executives and bankers, and military advisors. The U.S. polity is quite relevant to the problems of most of the population of this planet.

The larger point is that Rorty's conception of society is as narrow as his conception of history is thin. The majority of the population of this planet is very much a part of the polities of the great powers (especially the rich North Atlantic democracies and Japan), but they have no voice in the questions that determine the shapes of their lives. Another mere contingency, I suppose.

Jo Burrows brings out the homogenization of social space that Nancy Fraser thematized:

If we were to end [this critique] on a "Rorty-is-peddling-liberal-ideology" note, [Rorty] could simply admit to the charge, and then

argue, in a "fair-minded," pragmatic, sort of way, that perhaps liberalism is not such a bad system to be peddling ideology for. Then
we would be at stalemate. If, however, we take up the perspective
of someone who has good reason to contend for (say) a new political set-up, then irrespective of the merits, or otherwise, of liberalism *in situ*, it begins to look as if Rorty is surreptitiously narrowing
down the options, and doing this in a way which belies the even-
handed gloss of his ideology. (p. 332)

In other words, as Fraser puts it, "what was supposed to be a political
polylogue comes increasingly to resemble a monologue":

Consider that Rorty makes non-liberal, oppositional discourses non-
political by definition. Such discourses are associated by him with
Romanticism, the quest for the uncharted. They are made the pre-
rogative of free-floating intellectuals who are "bored" with widely
disseminated vocabularies and who crave "the new" and "the interesting." Radical discourses, then, are inflected as a turning-away from
the concerns of collective life. Thus Rorty casts the motive for
oppositional discourse as aesthetic and apolitical. He casts the subject of such discourses as the lone, alienated, heroic individual. And
he casts the object or topic of radical discourses as something other
than the needs and problems of the social collectivity. (p. 315)

What lies at the end of this "road which we liberal intellectuals have
been travelling since the Enlightenment" (Rorty, "Theories and Thugs,"
p. 18, n. 25; cited in Malachowski, ed., *Reading Rorty*, p. 324) does not
seem to me to be a vibrant, experimental society where people take
up responsibility for overcoming all forms of exploitation, oppression,
and domination (themes which never really appear in Rorty's work),
but instead an extension of the junk society that we already live in,
the society of William Gibson's *Neuromancer* or Stanislaw Lem's *The
Futurological Congress*, where self-seeking individuals are each free to
jack into the matrices of their private fantasies.

We need an argument against this sort of thing that is not mere
moralizing. For instance, consider Rorty's claim (quoted earlier as part
of a longer passage) that,

For my private purposes, I may redescribe you and everybody else
in terms which have nothing to do with my attitude toward your
actual or possible suffering. My private purposes, and the part of
my final vocabulary which is not relevant to my public actions, are
none of your business. (*Contingency*, p. 91)

Apart from the exceedingly narrow conception of what it means to be
a person, a conception that I would call metaphysical insofar as it is

deeply implicated in a metaphysics of selfhood and individualism, we must consider the argument that not only do our descriptions of others have an effect that is "public," but further, our descriptions and fantasies of others are of a piece with conceptions dominant in the culture. Clearly the example that is crying out for treatment here is pornography.

Without even invoking the idea of false consciousness (or getting into questions of pornography versus erotica, etc.) we can see the limitations of Rorty's framework. Pornographic fantasies that simply objectify people, mainly women, are not simply private fantasies, they are of a piece with a multi-billion dollar pornography industry, with a social formation that continually encourages women to view themselves and their possibilities in a certain way (and their self-conception is hemmed in, of course, by the "other-conception" of patriarchal society at large), and an economic set-up that leaves many women little choice but to become playthings for patriarchy. Is it an adequate answer to this social matrix, which is hardly "contingent," to say, "That's not my worry, and my fantasies are none of your business"? Of course, Rorty might say that the thing that needs changing is the element of force in all of this. My question, then, is: Who has the responsibility to make these changes, along this royal road that "we liberals" are traveling? What is "force," exactly, especially when one is operating within a metaphysics of individualism where consenting adults may play out their contingencies?

There seems little room in Rorty's scheme to speak of responsibility. Rorty is smart to stay away from this concept, especially because of its association with Kant.

Incidentally, although Rorty has established the practice more than anyone of using names such as Plato, Kant, and Hume as ideal types, he does not quote Kant directly. I raise this point only because, while it is true that Kant distinguished practical from pure reason "for the sake of such persons" who are "unselfish, unselfconscious, decent, honest, and dutiful" (though this last not in the merely obedient way that Rorty is obviously inferring), it seems completely unfair to say, as Rorty does, that Kant was aiming his ethical arguments at the "unimaginative." This seems to be a roundabout way of inferring that the Nietzschean poet is simply too imaginative to have to submit to the morality of the herd.

Kant is often misread on the question of responsibility and, therefore, on the distinction between pure and practical reason. For Kant, responsibility is not first of all something that one has, but rather what one is. The distinction between pure and practical reason is, therefore, an analytic distinction that is grounded in the fundamental responsiveness of reason.

Rorty, of course, will not be any more pleased with this reading of Kant, issuing as it does a description of a fundamental characteristic of rational beings. And yet, this is where the difference between Rorty and Derrida begins, and where it is simply not the case that Rorty's ironist theorizing represents a parallel to Derrida's work in analytic philosophy. (I am making no judgment about analytic philosophy itself in putting forward this argument. My point is simply that, whether or not there could or should be "analytic Derrida," Rorty isn't it.)

Individuals are tied up with their final vocabularies to the extent that they are individuals. The development of the individual of liberalism is a historically situated reality which exists alongside other possible realities that are excluded by certain contingencies of political modernity. The only point to discussing contingencies is to open possibilities that may be better than the existing situation. In this setting, the idea of contingency could have a liberatory use; that is, if the idea of contingency is used to show that things may be determined by the present historical and social situation, but they are not so determined that things could not be different. Derrida reads the canon of western intellectual culture not simply to have fun with some ideal types but rather to read, in the margins, those possibilities that cannot appear in logocentric orders of discourse or the societies founded upon these discourses.

Reading Rorty, one would think that individuals invent vocabularies. Rorty is really arguing that people put their vocabularies together out of what is available. But in his instrumentalist conception of language, in which words are tools, there is a strong sense of the individual as a kind of metaphysical center or foundation. This sense is itself a contingent historical fact, an achievement of modernity. Rorty's argument would then seem to be that: 1) this is an achievement that we can be happy about, 2) this is an achievement that makes us who we are (as western liberals), and 3) this is not something that we can get "outside" of in any case.

Derrida would agree with some of this. In *of Grammatology* Derrida criticizes the idea of easy journeys to other (non-western) civilizations. What we can do is to attempt to read in the margins of our own civilization and culture. Furthermore, the realization of our contingent individuality, from a deconstructive standpoint, especially as constructed around the vocabulary of political modernity, should make us wary of an instrumental view of language. Do we make our final vocabularies individually, or do they make us? Taking stock of the dynamic weave that, under certain historical conditions, results in the individuals of political modernity, should make us aware of both the good and the not-so-good side of any notion of "private autonomy." The good side is the possibility of ease of mind, the possibility for reflection and experimental thinking. This is truly an achievement of modern secular society. The not-very-good side of this notion is its denial of responsibility, of the fundamentally responsive nature of rational being.

Why hasn't political modernity lived up to its promise? This question is the motivation behind Habermas's critical theory. Rorty seems to answer that we do not need all of the machinery of Habermas's theoretical work to answer the question or to get things on the right track; indeed, as the project of modernity and Enlightenment has matured, it sees that it does not need any such machinery. For Rorty, the problem is not how reason in modernity can ground itself (which is how Habermas sees the problem), but rather how can liberal society keep to the road of casting off metaphysical pretensions or quests. Such a postmodern liberal culture would supposedly be an experimental culture, and yet, considering the narrow horizons of Rorty's comments about politics, and looking at the anti-participatory nature of the present social formation, it is hard to see how an exciting, dynamic, participatory and responsible society will emerge.

In one sense, whatever will emerge, for better or for worse, will emerge from these parameters. Derrida's work is about reading participation and responsibility in the language that we already speak, but through a critical reading that is attentive to the suppression of these things. This is a thinking of the polis. This thinking springs from "liberalism" if by that is meant a reading of the possibilities of political modernity, the possibilities that remain unrealized and even unthought in present practices. But it is not a liberalism in which the highest goal is for everyone to be able to be left alone, nor is it one in which the vocabulary of the other simply exists as a kind of smorgasbord for the logic of the Same to feed at when the latter becomes bored.

In his engagements with the western intellectual canon, Derrida does not seem to be only or mainly interested in constructing a "usable past" that can be fragmented into grist for the mill of his personal fantasies. Rorty's concentration on *The Post Card* ignores many other texts from the same period by Derrida that continue to speak of a fundamental responsibility toward the other. Is Derrida simply backsliding in these texts, into his earlier phases as a "transcendental philosopher" (as Rorty describes the Derrida of *Speech and Phenomena* and *of Grammatology*)? Let me stay with *The Post Card* for a moment. What is this text about if not communication, its possibilities and its impossibility, and the demonstration that the latter is integral to the possibility of possibility? Socrates does not write; this is a message across time, one that has had a great effect on western culture, that Derrida offers can be read another way: Socrates writes. How does the fact that Derrida weaves this idea into a narrative that may or may not be about his "personal life" somehow make this a text without "public" import? The fact that this "may or may not" is a major theme of the text—or one that is not "in" the text but therefore more assuredly in the text—seems to run counter to Rorty's strict private/public distinction. How could *The Post Card not* be about Derrida's personal life and fantasies? But then, how could it *only* be about these things?

When I turn to a text such as *Glas*, this point is even more glaring. Certainly, I could read *Glas* as simply about Derrida's personal fantasy of intertwining the texts of Hegel and Genet. I take the point to be instead that there is no simple answer to the question "Who, he?" put to Hegel or Genet, and that, when discussions of these two figures are put alongside each other (along with discussion of many other figures, e.g., Kant, Feuerbach, Marx) the very idea of their "personal autonomy" unravels. The separation of two different kinds of vocabulary, one public, the other private, seems to come unstuck as well.

Again, responsibility is the key term, and, even more, as Derrida puts it in *The Other Heading* (the discussion of which I am working toward), "responsibility to responsibility." My answer to the person who says that he is not interested in the vocabulary of justice because he is too involved in getting his private autonomy together, pursuing private perfection, is that that person has abdicated responsibility, that person is irresponsible, and that person has abdicated his humanity along with his responsibility. Indeed I am thinking of a certain well-documented side of Nietzsche (and even more so some of his epigones, who launch their never-ending search for self-involvement from that side). Such people are takers. I do not believe that Nietzsche was only a taker, but I do see a good many people justifying their own self-seeking pursuits in quasi-Nietzschean terms. Where do they think they get the terms and criteria of their supposedly private autonomy and perfection? For someone who is supposedly concerned to historicize philosophy and to show its social roots, Rorty's claims about self-invention come awfully close to being a species of the private-language argument. Rorty's conceptions of history and society must necessarily be thin and superficial.

There is no private autonomy. Rorty argues that the notion of private autonomy only makes sense in a postmodern liberal culture, which is possible solely in the lucky and rich countries. He takes it as no criticism that the notion of private autonomy would be difficult to explain to people in the Third World who are struggling to survive. That's very convenient, but I think that such people would understand the rich American's conception quite well; after all, they see rich Americans and Europeans exercising their private autonomy in Third World countries all the time (or they see the effects of this exercising).

Now, again, there is no point in being unfair. Rorty does say that "the aim of a just and free society" is to let "its citizens be as privatistic, irrationalist, and aestheticist as they please as long as they do it on their own time—causing no harm to others and using no resources needed by those less advantaged" (*Contingency*, p. xiv). The question might be just how far Rorty is ready to go with this principle. The unfortunate thing is that nowhere in the rest of *Contingency* does Rorty talk about the systemic dimensions of "causing no harm to others" and "using no resources needed by those less advantaged," and nowhere does he speak of a responsibility to fight and break down systemic violence. At best, he speaks of the "hope that suffering will be diminished, that the humiliation of human beings by other human beings may cease" (p. xv). Given the contingent historical moment of this text, one wonders why Rorty didn't say that we could also pray and rub crystals if necessary. But the fact is that Rorty did well to stay away from the idea of responsibility, for it would have led to a different kind of analysis. Furthermore, even though it would be a good thing if a conception of systemic violence were to be integrated into Rorty's framework, the principle enunciated above, "Do what you want as long as it doesn't hurt anybody," is not one of respect for difference but rather denial of it.

Denial is at the root of the pragmatist liberal's conception of politics; it is the civil libertarian's conception that, in principle, a panoply of voices might be heard, but there is no point in attempting to find the true or the good. The liberal, in any case, sets himself above this great confusion (generally in the same "above" and "neutral" position that the bourgeois state occupies), and the postmodern liberal especially has better things to do in any case, such as to pursue private autonomy and perfection. This is not a thinking of the polis but instead the idea that it is fruitless to engage in any such thinking. In other words, this is a radically anti-participatory conception of politics, which in the name of respecting difference simply drones on with the monologue of telling people who would pursue the thinking of the polis how naive and impractical they are.

Instead of considering how writers such as Nabokov might help us understand cruelty toward others, let me turn to one of Rorty's own descriptions of "unfamiliar people." In the essay "On Ethnocentrism," Rorty takes up Clifford Geertz's example of the "drunken Indian and the kidney machine." As Rorty explains, this example involves

> an alcoholic American Indian in the southwestern United States [who],
> having taken his place in line, was permitted to begin and continue
> treatment on a kidney machine even though he refused to heed the
> doctors' orders to stop his drinking. He died after a few years on
> the machine, presumably in part because of his drinking. Geertz used
> the case to illustrate the moral dilemma of the doctors—and by ex-
> tension "enlightened" society—confronted by values and behaviors
> hostile to their own "liberal" ones. (p. 203)

Rorty is concerned to make the point that there is a kind of "anti-
ethnocentrism" that does not enhance, but rather undermines, the ca-
pacity to make ethical judgments. Rorty argues that, for example,
contempt for and indignation toward the intolerance shown by Nazis
and fundamentalists may be legitimately considered a form of bourgeois liberal ethnocentrism or cultural bias. Under the rubric of what
he calls anti-anti-ethnocentrism, Rorty argues that we ("we liberals"
again) should not worry so much over our liberal ethnocentrism, that
in fact it is a good thing

> we begin to wonder whether our attempts to get other parts of the
> world to adopt our culture are different in kind from the efforts of
> fundamentalist missionaries. If we continue this line of thought too
> long we become what are sometimes called "wet" liberals. We be-
> gin to lose any capacity for moral indignation, any capacity to feel
> contempt. Our sense of selfhood dissolves. We can no longer feel
> pride in being bourgeois liberals, in being part of a great tradition,
> a citizen of no mean culture. We have become so open-minded that
> our brains have fallen out. (p. 203)

Geertz wonders if this line of reasoning is "destined merely toward
making the world safe for condescension." Further (quoting Rorty),
"Geertz fears that if the anti-anti-ethnocentrist reaction goes too far
we shall become content to think of human communities as 'semantic
monads, nearly windowless'" (p. 204). Here is Rorty's response to that
concern:

> Some human communities are such monads, some not. Our bour-
> geois liberal culture is not. On the contrary, it is a culture which
> prides itself on constantly adding more windows, constantly enlarging
> its sympathies. (p. 204)

Although the details of Rorty's disagreement with Geertz over the
"Case of the Drunken Indian and the Kidney Machine" are interesting, I want to move ahead to the part of the story where Rorty explains

how "our bourgeois liberal culture" has enlarged its sympathies to encompass the American Indian. This is where the reader may judge whether Rorty's conception of liberal culture respects and appreciates the other and the other's difference or simply amalgamates that difference to the logic of the Same.

It is the signal glory of our liberal society that it entrusts power to people like Geertz and his fellow anthropologists as well as to people like the doctors. Anthropologists, and Geertz's other connoisseurs of diversity, are the people who are expected and empowered to extend the range of society's imagination, thereby opening the doors of procedural justice to people on whom they had been closed. Why is it, after all, that the Indian was ever allowed into the clinic? Why are drunken Indians, in Geertz' words, "as much a part of contemporary America" as yuppie doctors? Roughly, because anthropologists have made them so. Drunken Indians were more common in America a hundred years ago, but anthropologists less common. Because of the absence of sympathetic interpreters who could place their behavior in the context of an unfamiliar set of beliefs and desires, drunken Indians were not part of nineteenth-century America: that is, the vast majority of nineteenth-century Americans took no more notice of them than they did of criminal psychopaths or village idiots. The Indians, whether drunk or sober, were nonpersons, without human dignity, means to our grandparents' ends. The anthropologists made it hard for us to continue thinking of them that way, and thereby made them into "part of contemporary America." To be a part of a society is, in the relative sense, to be taken as a possible conversation partner by those who shape that society's self-image. The media, prodded by the intellectuals in general and the anthropologists in particular, have been making such partners of the Indians. But if the anthropologists had not sympathized with, learned from, even sometimes loved, the Indians, Indians would have remained invisible to the agents of social justice. They would never have gotten into the queue in the first place. . . .
Our society's device for resolving what Geertz calls "wrenching social issues centered around cultural diversity" is simply to keep lots of agents of love, lots of connoisseurs of diversity, on hand. (p. 206)

Because this characterization of how the indigenous peoples of North America have now been "welcomed" into the U.S. polity—now that these peoples have been in large part killed off and their cultures destroyed—literally boggles my mind, I would prefer to leave this passage simply as a monument to the Rortyan sense of what it means to appreciate difference. The word "connoisseur" here speaks volumes.
Rorty, the anti-rationalist, the anti-foundationalist, the ruiner of meta-

vocabularies, presents here the most rationalistic scheme possible for understanding the discipline of anthropology and its role simply in not appreciating other cultures but more in dominating, assimilating, and (if these functions cannot be carried out) destroying other cultures. The power relations in which anthropology participates is what Geertz and other dissident anthropologists (e.g., James Clifford) are attempting to thematize and challenge. Rorty, the anti-foundationalist, paints a pretty picture of how the other has been welcomed into the society of "us liberals," never once thematizing or questioning the foundation of violence upon which this welcome has been based, never questioning once that a vocabulary with an army can serve just as well as a meta-vocabulary.

The philosophical answer to Rorty—on top of the political exposure of willful naivete that is also necessary—is to read the Kant who Rorty never reads, for whom responsibility is not a foundation or a meta-vocabulary but that which makes vocabularies and talk of foundations possible. The basis for "having" a vocabulary is, first of all, the socially generated ability to respond. It is in this context that I develop "my" vocabulary (final or otherwise) and, simultaneously and inextricably, "my" values. (On this point, the most helpful source is one that Rorty himself purportedly relies on; see Donald Davidson, "Expressing Evaluations.") Whether I choose to pretend that I can take this vocabulary, which society gives me, and go off to my room to play a little game with myself or whether I attempt to enter into a relationship with others, I must choose in the context of a relationship and a relationality that always already exists (at least insofar as "my" vocabulary, "my" choices, and my "my" are concerned). There is a great deal in Rorty's work that recognizes this point, especially in the first chapter of *Contingency*, "The contingency of language." But he denies these arguments when he turns to the task of making them square with the priority of a particular social formation's politics, that is, liberal democracy.

In setting up this priority (Rorty elaborates his argument in a Deweyan frame in "The priority of democracy to philosophy"), Rorty is apparently, and in good faith, attempting to stick closely to the materialist, naturalist, and contextualist arguments that he has articulated in all of his post-analytic work, from *Philosophy and the Mirror of Nature* forward. Well and good, but his exclusive focus on "what is" leaves no room for what can and should be. No wonder, then, that there can also be no room for Kant, for responsibility, for the unprecedented, and for the other.

The difference between Rorty and Derrida on this point is as follows.

Both Rorty and Derrida recognize that there is no pure "leap" to the other "as such." Furthermore, if the other is going to be recognized at all, it must be in the terms, first of all, that we already know. But, for Derrida, everything hinges on the impossible attempt to recognize the other despite these limitations. Otherwise, there can be no real responsibility, no real ethics, no real rethinking of the polis, and therefore no real thinking of the polis in the first place. For both Rorty and Derrida, context only changes through the actions of people within that context; for both, the vocabulary is in some sense the locus of change. But, for Derrida, there is the question of what calls us to change. Returning to my earlier discussion of Marx, it is true that one thing, a very important thing, that could encourage us to change our society would be if this society becomes unliveable. This is a possibility that never seems to occur to Rorty, and perhaps he is right to think that things will not get so bad for the conservatives who call themselves liberals (as opposed to ordinary people who call themselves conservative because they hate to see consumer society tear up the landscape just to put up another shopping mall). For these liberals, I suppose it is good that things won't get so bad, so that they can continue their wonderful work of being connoisseurs of difference and diversity. I'm sure that those who are being further marginalized and who are then taking up arms to fight back will remember to send a note of thanks to these magnanimous liberals. (In any case, for Rorty, as for many followers of the Habermasian wing of Critical Theory, the idea that capitalism could go into a deep and destructive crisis is *passé*.) For Derrida, for things to change there has to be something beyond the material crisis of the system, there has to be responsibility, and "responsibility to responsibility."

As Ron Scapp puts it, for Rorty, "it is not the ear of the other, but instead simply my other ear"; furthermore, Scapp writes in a discussion of *Contingency*,

> liberals may pride themselves in their ability to tolerate others but it is only after the other has been redescribed as oneself that the liberal is able to be "sensitive" to the question of cruelty and humiliation. This act of redescription is still an attempt to appropriate others, only here it is made to sound as if it were a generous act. It is an attempt to make an act of consumption appear to be an act of acknowledgment.[17]

The question might be, If one cannot empathize, then what can one do? In Rorty's view, there is nothing beyond empathy, nothing beyond finding the common description (meaning the description in "my"

terms) that allows the other to appear to me as a conversation partner. There is nothing, in other words, that allows the appearance of
the unprecedented, and, therefore, there is no reason to speak of changes
in society that might create a space for the other.

Rorty, of course, does not want change, or at least he does not want
a change from the road that western liberal society is already on. What
will he tell the majority of people in these societies when they find
that they can no longer tolerate their lives on this road? What does he
have to say right now to the people in the Third World who are oppressed and exploited so that western society can stay on the liberal
road? Is it simply that their concerns are irrelevant? "Go away, I'm
busy with my private fantasies!" My point is that the possibilities that
are represented by these concerns will lead more and more people to
question the contingencies of liberal society, and at that point it will
be the liberals' problem if they cannot find too many conversation
partners in the larger society. The liberals will, in this case, most likely
hear the noises made by the other simply as the inarticulate ravings of
criminal psychopaths or village idiots, and one can easily see the liberals and liberal society responding accordingly, as they always have
done, with violence.

It is true, and this is a lesson that we might take from Rorty, that,
even to the others of the others, that is, even to those among the diversity of others, the first sounds of resistance and rebellion may seem
incoherent. There are many different kinds of marginalization, and there
are many, diverse others. How will a conversation among the others
be organized such that this conversation can appear as a somewhat
coherent, articulate alternative to the liberal conversation? Rorty's example of the drunken Indian provides a clue. The liberal conversation
was and is itself a displacement of other conversations. Rorty's story
is a prime example of such displacement. The beginnings of the new
conversation, the new voices that must be heard, may be found in the
rearticulation and refunctioning of the marginalized voices.

This does not mean, however, that the emergent voices will recognize one another, much less that they will be speaking the same language or telling the same story. It almost seems that Rorty has "got
them there," that he is raising the idea that there is a need for a common story if other voices will be heard, but also the idea that a common story of difference must necessarily obliterate difference.

This is not an idle question. It is vitally important that the experience of different marginalized peoples not be made into the kind of
narrative that speaks with a single narrative voice (the sort of voice
that "we liberals" speak in). And yet, at the same time, there is a need

for a common response to marginalization, to those social forces that would "disappear" the marginalized, perhaps by extending to them the same sort of "welcome" that the U.S. and Canadian polities have extended to indigenous Americans.

Marx thought that theory could provide the glue for such a common response: "When the inner connections are grasped, theory becomes a material force." I do not believe that Marx's conception of social theory gets people into the sort of vicious metaphysical traps that Rorty seems to think all totalizing theories do. The question to ask, instead, is more concerned with the effectiveness of Marxist theory in really bringing the great majority of humankind together to fight an oppressive present and create an opening to a liberated future. In other words, when I raised the example of the *Book of Mormon*, I was not kidding, although obviously I chose a difficult and provocative, even outlandish and possibly even *unheimlische*, narrative.

Obviously, the revolution of the marginalized has not been waiting for a new kind of novel to be written. Rorty, with his focus on the novel as a literary form, has chosen his example well. Not only is the novel a form whose appearance and development parallels that of bourgeois society more generally, but, furthermore, the novel is generally a form for telling the story of an individual or a group of individuals. Novels simply do not seem to be the place where the story of a collectivity can be told.

There are, of course, other kinds of narratives, namely, the sort that historians write. Marx was a historian, though often of his own present, who attempted to write a new kind of history, infused with dialectical political economy. As a historian of his own present, and as someone who did not believe (Rorty and other non-readers of Marx to the contrary) in a collective historical subject in any trans-subjective sense, Marx wrote about those subjects who actually emerged in the course of struggle. (The *struggle* to be a subject, rather than an object, of history, of property relations, etc., seems to have little to do with Rorty's quintessential subject, "we liberals.") Following Marx, it would be premature, in the sense of a Hegelian hyper-idealism, to attempt to write the history of what might emerge in the future; even more to the point, such an attempt would be preemptive. Could such a narrative even be possible? There is no harm in the sort of speculation that has taken the form of the utopian novel, and there might be a great deal of good. I think of *Woman on the Edge of Time* by Marge Piercy and *The Dispossessed* by Ursula K. LeGuin as wonderful examples that have done me a great deal of good. In fact, to revive a label from the old days of the analytic/continental split in philosophy, it might be just the task of deconstructive "speculative" philosophy and theory to imagine a world in which the other can speak. But there is also the work, at least as important, of creating new histories of the present, in which we take stock of what else, what new things, what new people, have emerged through struggle.

Two points must be emphasized here. First, these new histories of the present will take their inspiration from Marx's effort and at the same time will come from places different from those Marx emphasized and perhaps even imagined, from new subjects who were not known to Marx. Second, the speculative work, whether it is of Derrida or LeGuin or whomever, of imagining a world in which the other can speak, rethinking the polis and therefore thinking it in the only way that it can be thought, this work must be intertwined with and motivate the work of the historian of the present. This does not mean that the historian of the present must already imagine the other, for, as I argued, that would be preemptive. It means, rather, that the new history of the present must actively prepare for the advent of the unprecedented.

Questions raised earlier, then, might be transmogrified as follows: Can there be a general strategy for listening for the other and for the other to tell its story to itself? Rorty, in a comment clearly aimed at Kant, charges that the attempt to find "algorithms for resolving moral dilemmas" remains bogged down in metaphysics and theology (*Contingency* p. xv). Although I believe that there is a great deal more to be said for metaphysics and theology than Rorty gives them credit for, there is a side to Rorty's formulation that seems a genuine attempt to avoid a false universalism. And yet, to maintain that there can be no unity, even strategic unity, to the struggle of the marginalized seems a liberal self-fulfilling fantasy: there can be no true universalism because the world must be divided up into "we liberals" and the hordes outside who cannot be "our" conversation partners. And yet, it is true that the attempt to find an ethical-political algorithm has generally resulted in the sort of universalism that denies difference. Could there be a "universalism" in which the other is always "beyond the law"— and what kind of thinking of the polis might take place with this illegal universalism as its guide? Finally, what does it mean to speak of strategies rather than principles of algorithms or laws? In working toward a society in which the other can speak, are we simply deceiving ourselves, are we simply plotting our course in Newtonian space when the trajectory of the other is indeterminate? If we attempt to determine this trajectory, have we fundamentally interfered with it, perhaps even created this seeming other out of our own projects? And yet, keeping with the language of quantum mechanics, how else might we encounter the other?

This question is common to Rorty and Derrida. The difference is that Derrida goes to great length to thematize the risks involved in encountering the "invention of the other," and he also urges that these risks must be taken, of necessity. This necessity is our possibility and the possibility of the other.

Derrida, barbarian

This as a mere postscript . . . .

I have purposely not lined up a series of counter-quotations by Derrida as a response to Rorty (despite having done this in the earlier section on Habermas). Rather, I have presented in schematic fashion a possibility, the deconstructive possibility, that I will further articulate in Part 3.

In the end, this encounter with Rorty proves quite frustrating. Habermas, a thinker with a good deal of depth to go along with his tremendous breadth, is dealt with in only a few pages, while Rorty, who makes a virtue out of superficiality, is discussed at great length. (Habermas was, however, discussed in much detail in *Matrix and line*.) What's going on here? As I said before, a vocabulary with a powerful army doesn't need metaphysics; liberalism with a nuclear arsenal and a world-dominating economy does not need metaphysics. As unfortunate as it is from a purely intellectual standpoint, it is the material foundation of postmodern liberalism that causes us to take up so much time with Rorty.

Liberals and other neo-conservatives take up your time, that's for sure. Sometimes I think that all they are saying is that, People cannot change society because "we liberals" are standing in your way. One interesting thing about the debate around Rorty is that those of us who have engaged in it have probably spent an inordinate amount of time simply speculating on whether Rorty has good intentions or not. He seems to be—no, he is—after all, a nice and generous person, and he does seem genuinely concerned about the question of a just society. Despite everything said above, I have no qualms about giving him that. Furthermore, it does seem that, despite my deep disagreement with Rorty over his conception of what Derrida is up to, one might also credit Rorty with seeing Derrida's experimental writing as aiming at new ways to be human. Perhaps I agree with Rorty, up to a point: what one sees in Derrida's work is the transformation of humanism. Further, I would say, but I do not think that Rorty would, that this transformation is in the direction of the other and must issue in a new thinking of the polis, a thinking that can only be fully accomplished (or fully begun, for it is never fully accomplished) in practice.

The larger story that needs to be told would be a close reading of key texts of humanism, from the post-critical work of Kant (and especially the "Universal History" essay), through Hegel's *Lectures on the Philosophy of World History*, Marx and Engels's *The German Ideology*, Nietzsche's *Twilight of the Idols*, and so forth, while keeping closer to the texts of Derrida in this reading. The aim would be to find, against Rorty's conception of "history," an "unusable past." But this will have to be a project for another day.

In closing this part, I turn for a moment to the gossip column, where one reads of Derrida, not the young conservative but the barabarian. Gossip can also take up a lot of time, it can wear one down; that seems the intention of certain forms of vicious gossip. The gossip I want to examine briefly, vicious indeed, is another example of a vocabulary with a powerful army and state apparatus. The central item in this gossip column is the claim that Derrida is simultaneously opening the canon and the academy to the clamoring hordes of multiculturalism and that (indeed, therefore) he is an ardent anti-humanist. The people making these claims in the pages of *Newsweek*, the *New York Times*, and in artificially hyped-up bestsellers, it is true, are basically moronic miscreants, though they may be credited with a certain amount of entrepreneural acumen (up there with the inventors of the pet rock). Unfortunately, intellectuals cannot afford to turn their backs on morons with guns. The Dinesh D'Souzas, Roger Kimballs, and George Willses of the world may appear harmless enough, but don't be fooled. They are spokespersons for money and power. They are well funded in their "research," which means that they must have a lot of money left over, because their research consists largely in fabricating anecdotes.[18] They seem to be afforded endless amounts of space in the media to put forward arguments that, if they weren't so vicious, would be seen as silly. And they have sanction from high government officials and politicians, including recent U.S. presidents.

As wild as it may seem, many of these ideologues have taken aim at Jacques Derrida. The opening shot was fired by Allan Bloom, who in *The Closing of the American Mind* referred to "deconstructionism" as

> the last, predictable, stage in the suppression of reason and the denial of the possibility of truth in the name of philosophy. The interpreter's creative activity is more important than the text; there is no text, only interpretation. Thus the one thing most necessary for us, the knowledge of what these texts have to tell us, is turned over to

the subjective, creative selves of these interpreters, who say that there is both no text and no reality to which the texts refer. A cheapened interpretation of Nietzsche liberates us from the objective impera- tives of the texts that might have liberated us from our increasingly low and narrow horizon. Everything has tended to soften the de- mands made on us by the tradition; this simply dissolves it. (p. 379)

This characterization, which, typical of the character who conceived it and of the characters who follow in his wake, depends for its own interpretation on no textual evidence whatsoever (Bloom condemns not only Derrida but Foucault, Barthes, and other "Parisian Heideggerians" as well), sets the tone for the journalistic hack work of D'Souza, Kimball, and Lehman. Unlike these three (and leaving aside the question of their opportunistic entrepreneurial genius), Bloom is certainly no mo- ron, although, to read his account, the rest of us are—especially the rest of us who do not attend the handful of colleges and universities that Bloom is concerned with. The title of Bloom's book is doubly a lie. He identifies the "closing of the American mind," in part, with the upheavals of the sixties. When, I ask the reader, was the American mind any more open? The second lie, which makes Bloom's book, in Paul Bove's terms, "unreadable," is in the fact that Bloom is not espe- cially interested in "opening" the American mind in general, but only the minds of students at elite universities; in other words, only the minds of the next generation of Guardians.

How open might even these minds become under Bloom's model? After all, in the name of faithfulness to the references of texts he closes off all questions of interpretation, all questions concerning problems of referentiality ("textual" or otherwise), and all questions of responsi- bility for one's claims. After all, if "deconstructionism" (the "ism," often added by neo-conservative commentators, has a McCarthyite ring to it) really does say that there is no text and no reality to which texts refer, then surely Bloom could produce some statements from Derrida or others to this effect. One would think that some sort of responsibil- ity to truth, which Bloom accuses deconstruction of abandoning, might impel Bloom to substantiate his claims.

Similar statements can be found in the works by Bloom's anti- multicultural, anti-Political Correctness epigones. For example, after "reviewing" in little more than a page such diverse critical approaches as formalism, hermeneutics, psychoanalytic theory, semiotics, structur- alism, and Marxism, Dinesh D'Souza comments,

Finally, there is deconstructionism. Inspired by Jacques Derrida and Paul de Man, deconstructionists hold that all literature is empty of meaning. Whereas structuralists try to find linguistic parallels and contrasts in texts, deconstructionists labor to discover ingenious, and sometimes bizarre, contradictions which render the work "radically incoherent." Focusing on the distance between word and subject—"signifier" and "signified"—Derrida and de Man demonstrate that literary reality is an illusion, that fact dissolves into fiction, that literal meaning cannot be divorced from metaphorical meaning. Critics have maintained, however, that the spectacular oppositions—between male and female, noun and verb, and so on—that the deconstructionists have identified are more in the heads of the critics than in the texts themselves. (pp. 178–79)

I do not know where D'Souza is quoting the epithet "radically incoherent" from (Barbara Johnson, perhaps), but it certainly applies to his own description of deconstruction. I must have been confused: I thought that it was the anti-deconstruction people who wanted to convince the deconstructionists that "literary reality *is* an illusion," that literal meaning *can* be divorced from metaphorical meaning.

One thing that is glaring about both Bloom's and D'Souza's description of "deconstructionism" is that one would never know from reading them that there is a debate in philosophy about reference. One would never know that Derrida's position on this question is not so different from the positions of Wittgenstein, Quine, and Davidson (positions that may be described by Davidson's formula, "reality without reference"). But then, one learns little about anything from Bloom or his epigones, except that there are some who call themselves deconstructionists out there who might be accused of shoddy scholarship. And so what?

"Spectacular oppositions," such as that between male and female, are "in the heads of the critics"? And not in the heads (and texts, if one were so bold as to check them) of the canonical philosophers of the western tradition? Really, it boggles the mind what these people will write.

I especially love the expression "the demands made by the tradition," when applied to Derrida. Having heard Professor Derrida lecture for many hours on such canonical and clearly significant thinkers as Heraclitus, Aristotle, Montaigne, Spinoza, Heidegger, Walter Benjamin, Franz Rosenzweig—lectures painstakingly prepared and delivered without the slightest trace of showmanship—there is no question in my mind that Derrida is responding to the demands of the tradition.[19] Anyone who actually reads Derrida's work will also see his response, his responsibility.

There is an amazing line in David Lehman's book, where the author says something to the effect of, "Before I immersed myself in the study of deconstructive theory . . . ," implying, of course, that this immersion has now taken place.[20] There is no evidence of this in *Signs of the Times*. The proper response to this sort of claim is to call these people out for their vicious lies. And yet, because this is not, in the final analysis, really an "academic" debate, the purely academic response to Bloom and his epigones is not adequate.

I will not quote further from these works. The only purpose of such quotations can be to get the blood boiling. The "demand" of Bloom's "tradition" is that people not be critical or questioning. One would think, on the contrary, that anything aspiring to the name humanism, or serious study of the humanities, would *require* the consideration of alternative interpretations and investigation into the sources (especially in material culture) of these interpretations. As Bove puts it, "It is a sign of the crisis under which Bloom writes that he so profoundly contradicts some of the deepest tenets of the position he claims to espouse" (p. 70). My purpose in quoting characterizations of deconstruction that are at once silly, uninformed, incoherent, and insidious, my purpose in getting your blood to boil, is to lead up to the point that it is the work of a deconstruction that is not confined to the academy to *deepen* this crisis, to make the worst nightmares of Bloom and company come true.

To return to the essay discussed earlier in this part, "The Principle of Reason," here is the way Derrida describes the project of education:

It is possible to speak of this new responsibility that I have invoked only by sounding a call to practice it. It would be the responsibility of a community of thought for which the frontier between basic and oriented research would no longer be secured, or in any event not under the same conditions as before. I call it a community of thought in the broad sense—"at large"—rather than a community of research, of science or philosophy, since these values are most often subjected to the unquestioned authority of a principle of reason. Now reason is only one species of thought—which does not mean that thought is "irrational." Such a community would interrogate the essence of reason and of the principle of reason, the values of the basic, of the principial, of radicality, of the *arkhe* in general, and it would attempt to draw out all the possible consequences of this questioning. It is not certain that such thinking can bring together a community or found an institution in the traditional sense of these words. What is meant by community and institution must be rethought. This thinking must also unmask—an infinite task—all the ruses of end-orienting reason, the paths by which apparently disinterested research can find itself indirectly reappropriated, reinvested by programs of all sorts. That does not mean that "orientation" is bad in itself and that it must be combatted, far from it. Rather, I am defining the necessity for a new way of educating students that will prepare them to undertake new analyses in order to evaluate these ends and to choose, when possible, among them all. (p. 16)

Now, why would Bloom and company find the philosophy of a person who can say this sort of thing dangerous? Is it because Bloom is afraid that Derrida's arguments about the meaning of education might lead to more "closing" of minds? I challenge anyone to derive that meaning from the passage just quoted, even if they are working within the loose canons of careless interpretation preferred by D'Souza and the other epigones.

The demands of Bloom's tradition, which, as Bove demonstrates, is the tradition of Bloom's own supposedly self-sufficient authority (Bove, pp. 70–79), is not that we open the texts of Plato, Aristotle, Kant, Nietzsche, etc. (Of course, we, if we are not at Harvard, the University of Chicago, or a few other schools, are not the addressees of Bloom's diatribe anyway.) On the contrary, what we must do instead is to read *The Closing of the American Mind* and to accept the fact that only specially anointed interpreters (mainly students of Leo Strauss, who was also, to be sure, no dummy) can present the thoughts of the great philosophers to people in positions of authority. (Witness the Straussians who served Ronald Reagan and J. Danforth Quayle, two of the stupidest political figures to ever be coughed up by the U.S. political system. The idea of hermeneuticists with special, secret knowledge advising men of great power and minimal intellect surely conjures images of Rasputin and the last days of a desperate empire.)

Reading the passage from Derrida, and placing it within the context of "The Principle of Reason" as a whole, it is clear that Derrida is not interested in destroying the canons of western intellectual culture but instead opening them and reading them in a different way, and finding ways to open these texts to their others. It is amazing, and yet, to use Bloom's word, predictable, that this argument about what education should be is threatening to the crusaders against multiculturalism and Political Correctness. I would challenge any of them to give even the beginning of an argument against Derrida's position.

In concluding this chapter, I would like to present a manifesto of sorts concerning the need to deepen the crisis in which Bloom and company find themselves, and the need for progressive and radical intellectuals to take the offensive against neo-conservative attacks on deconstruction and other critical schools of thought, multiculturalism, and Political Correctness.

The right to question is itself under attack. The specific questions in question concern patriarchy, ideologies of racial (especially white) superiority, capitalism, and other oppressive hierarchies. These are questions that were given especially powerful expression by the social movements of the sixties. In the past twenty years these questions were taken into the colleges and universities and developed in theoretical terms.

For this entire period, people who have structured their lives around fundamentally questioning the social formation that we inhabit have also questioned the efficacy of sophisticated "theory" in substantially questioning oppressive social structures. In *The Last Intellectuals*, Russell Jacoby legitimately worries that the move to the academy has become a mere retreat and a recuperation of Marxism, feminism, and other progressive and radical forms of analysis. To the extent that this retreat and recuperation are a reality (and they most certainly are a reality to some extent), we must ask if sophistication conceals mere sophistry.

Now we will find out, now we will have the chance to see what we "theorists," deconstructive or otherwise, are made of. On the one side, the crisis of an empire in decline calls forth neo-conservative demands for subservience to authority. The language of these demands is not first of all academic or argumentative. The question we face is whether, on the other side, the new discursive spaces that we have attempted to open up in the academy for marginalized voices will also have a real impact on creating a society that can be inhabited and fundamentally transformed by real, marginalized people.

There is no general, abstract "right to question." Bloom and company, in the name of a neo-conservative humanism, are reminding us of this every day now. Rights exist as part of social systems, and the European and North American social systems that gave rise to rights-discourse have never, and will never, allow the "right" to fundamentally question these systems themselves. Indeed, when people begin to raise fundamental questions anyway, regardless of whether they have been given permission by the authorities or not, the authorities are compelled to suspend questioning in general on all manner of subjects. They grow fearful and reactionary, as everything solid melts into air.

That rights and attendant notions, such as autonomy, are always situated does not mean that progressives and radicals should eschew all talk of rights, but rather that we should understand both the limitations of such talk and that this is a question *in motion*. This point has been made dramatically and painfully clear with regard to women's reproductive rights and basic civil rights for Blacks and other people of color.

If we cannot raise the question, to take one crucial example, of the oppression of women in the context of a transformative movement toward ending that oppression, we cannot truly raise the question.

In the aftermath of the U.S.-led war on the people of Iraq, a war that literally laid waste to the cradle of western civilization, and with the declaration of a New World Order, the distance between raising questions "in theory" and raising questions with an eye toward theory-informed radical practice is, paradoxically, both growing wider and narrowing.

At the same time as the New World Order is proclaiming, "Don't even think about fundamental change," it is also demanding, "Don't even *think*, period." (Figures such as Reagan and Quayle are role-models here.) The question itself is being ruled out of bounds. In resistance we must do many things, including the exposure of this politics of ignorance and stupidity that seeks to continually make suckers out of people. We must also resist 25-words-or-less solutions to problems that oppressive social systems themselves raise, even as we seek ways to popularize new ways of thinking. If journalists and ideologues have trouble understanding what we are talking about, let them speak for themselves, without excusing their own ignorance by blaming the basic masses. Let's answer every real quest for understanding, let's struggle, with radical patience and impatience, toward an understanding of the real questions and substantive answers; but let's not ourselves be suckers for the numbing simplifications of what passes for political rhetoric in the corporate media.

The attack on multiculturalism and Political Correctness has come first as an attack on such diverse trends as feminism, Afro-American literary studies, deconstruction, Marxism, gay studies, and other critical approaches. In all of these trends there has been an attempt to listen for the voice of the other. What a wonderful thing it would be if these trends were to find their social base—what a powerful and empowering thing. Amid the crisis of the giant with feet of clay that is the New World Order, critical intellectuals are faced with both the possibility and the necessity of taking these critical approaches beyond the academy.

George Bush announced the conclusion of the war against the people of Iraq with the words, "By God, we've finally kicked the Vietnam syndrome." The U.S. victory was celebrated with festivals of cruelty across the nation. Such festivals are indeed the only way that this system can relieve itself of the memory of mass carnage in Vietnam.

A war against memory: what better way to move the agenda of a social system that is compelled to intervene globally, with tremendous violence, on many fronts. This is a war on thought itself.

One of the more insidious forms of the war on thought is the strategy of "just mentioning." Dinesh D'Souza is especially fond of this strategy. Here it is apparently enough to just mention that scholars have been studying lesbian writers or writing Marxist analyses of the incarceration of Black men, in order to discredit these analyses and the theorists who perform them. In other words, no arguments are needed.

This destruction of discursivity has the intended effect of straightforward gay-bashing, red-baiting, etc. The "just mentioning" strategy is a call to the media and to the more backward among the masses to "get 'em," as in, "there's a communist, or there's a lesbian, or there's a Black person—get 'em!"

This turn in recent attitudes toward critical intellectuals represents something that has never been absent from this social system: there has never been a real space for truly questioning the system except for that space which has been created by determined resistance to and rebellion against the system. Until recently, the powers that be and their ideologues have been satisfied with keeping critical intellectuals confined to the university. In return we have lived in a kind of sanctuary (some more than others, of course), but these generally pleasant and privileged spaces can also be a kind of padded cell, where we realize that we are only permitted to raise relevant questions in irrelevant circumstances and irrelevant questions in relevant circumstances. However, some of us have not played by these rules, and, in combination with other social factors, this has resulted in some trouble for the cell-keepers.

In addition to taking full measure of the ugly and stupid attacks on the work of Jacques Derrida, we might also be heartened at the way that the powers that be seem to be freaking out over work of this sort. Professor Derrida must be doing something right! There seems to be a parallel, perhaps one of some significance, between the attacks on Jean-Paul Sartre in the fifties and sixties and the attacks on the work and person of Derrida that one reads more and more in the corporate media in the last few years. It must be added that even those who are not enthusiastic about deconstruction should think long and hard about what the attacks on it mean (in articles in *The Wall Street Journal*, *National Review*, etc.). These attacks, on a thinker whose works are indeed difficult, attack critical thought more generally. It is especially troubling to see professors and deans and university administrators and presidents taking these tabloid-style attacks at face value—there is a politics here, though actually a non-thinking against the polis, a desire for a non-thinking polis—that must be challenged.

On the one hand, the attacks on Derrida are meant as an opening to attack all forms of thought that challenge the existing order. This leads me to wonder if Derrida's work is not the most vulnerable of these to attack. But, on the other hand, there is something about Derrida's work, its opening toward the possibility of the other, that also makes it one of the more powerful forms of oppositional thought—or at least potentially so—and this is the other reason why the opening shots in the war on critical thought in the academy have been fired at Derrida.

The international context of the attack on critical thought is a United States that must face a changing world, one that is not for the time being driven by the struggle between two somewhat coherent, competing economic-political blocs. The New World Order, in some respects a kind of global military dictatorship with the United States at the top, is being forged through actions such as the Persian Gulf War, in which many tens of thousands died (the estimates, even by U.S. government sources, are between 150,000 and 200,000 deaths) or will die from the effects of the war. And yet, this war is not fundamentally a demonstration of U.S. strength. In the war, the United States sought to control a key resource of the industrial world, oil, but it no longer has the economic or political strength to compete with Japan, Germany, or other nations that are now emerging as top players in the international market. Therefore, the United States did militarily what it can no longer do economically. So much for capitalists playing by their own rules; so much for the wonders of the market. Marx talked about the essential anarchy of the market: the Gulf War provided an example of this in its most violent form. This bespeaks fundamental weakness, not fundamental strength. Domestically—nowhere more than here is there a need for the deconstruction of the inside/outside distinction—the powers that be are clearly rattled and deeply worried about the fact that, like it or not, a multicultural society is emerging. A world is emerging in which people of color, women, gay people, people who are downtrodden by their work and economic conditions of life, and indeed anyone who is "deviant" and different, and perhaps finally anyone who wants to use their brain to think rather than simply as a receptacle for the mind-rot of "Why ask why?" are refusing to sit quietly in the corner or to be beaten down into the asphalt by cops.

"The demand of tradition" in the Bloomian frame is little different than the demand, "America—love it or leave it!" or "Support our troops!"—or else; these are the demands of a society that has room only for those who will complacently accept their lot. The demand of these demands (against the question of the question) is a society of brown-nosers and ass-kissers. (Bove, incidentally, demonstrates the peculiarly American quality of Bloom's book; see p. 74.) Why are the powers that be afraid of having certain questions raised in the colleges and universities? Because they are afraid that, the supposed end of the Vietnam syndrome notwithstanding, some of these questions might leak out. Again, it is up to everyone who takes deconstruction and critical theory in general seriously to see that the worst fears of the establishment's well-paid "scholars" come to life.

Books such as *Illiberal Education*, *Tenured Radicals* (whose target is really untenured radicals), *Signs of the Times*, and *Profscam*, not to mention the articles that have appeared in *Time*, *Newsweek*, and other house organs of corporate capitalism put those of us who would propose a radical political deconstruction in a difficult position. On the one hand, how can we respond to such ridiculous demagoguery? Would Martina Navratilova seriously engage in a tennis match with Nancy Reagan? Would Michael Jordan accept a serious game of one-on-one with Dinesh D'Souza? Only if there was enough money and force behind the challenge. We know that major publishing companies, which are more than ever part of giant media conglomerates, do not print the words of D'Souza et al. because of their intellectual force or merits. Indeed, there is every reason to believe that the ball got rolling when William Bennett, Norman Podhoretz, and other powerful neo-conservatives bought up and sent out a large number of copies of Bloom's book, enough to put it on the *New York Times* bestseller list. Ironic, isn't it, that a book that attacks the MTV ethos is itself the beneficiary of so much hype. We are not dealing here with the unforced force of reason. On the other hand, how can we *not* respond to the absurd claims of the anti-PC/ anti-multiculturalism camp? The fact is that we are forced to respond: the writings and other pronouncements of this camp are backed not by intellectual force or the force of reason and argument but by power of a cruder sort.

This means, however, that our response also cannot be merely "argumentative," even though we should never, ever abandon our critical abilities—we will need them more than ever before. George Will, in an article in *Newsweek*, linked the tasks, international and domestic, of Dick Cheney (Secretary of Defense under Bush) and Lynn Cheney (chair of the National Endowment for the Humanities), claiming that each was fighting a war: Dick Cheney against enemies abroad, countries that do not snap to attention when Washington barks an order; and Lynn Cheney here in the United States, against progressive and radical intellectuals and artists. The force behind, rather than the force of, these attacks, coupled with the sheer ugliness and mean-spiritedness of much that is said by the anti-PC/anti-multiculturalism camp, often with fascistic overtones, is explicitly set out as a declaration of war.

What is declared in these attacks is the end of civility, the end of the intellectual sanctuary. This end has long been declared for people of color, women, gays, and others who experience violent attacks under the banner of the "war on drugs," the culture of rape that now wishes to deny basic reproductive rights, and proposals for measures such as the quarantine of gay men because of AIDS (a proposal made by Christian fascist Pat Robertson in the 1988 presidential campaign and given serious consideration by the corporate media), as well as more "traditional" forms of violence against gay people. The aftermath of the Gulf War, in which even the most transparently false justifications of the Bush administration and the complicitous U.S. Congress and other politicians (such as the Democratic Party candidates) gave way to a sickening festival of cruelty, coupled with the ongoing breakdown of civility and the attack on the question, has the feel of a period between the disintegration of society and its reconstitution through an intense struggle. The question, which again is itself being attacked, is: Which way from here?

Consider some words written by the poet Hölderlin, which I quote in part to show that there is on our side none of the desire to simply trash the past, western or otherwise, even when we believe that all the cultures of humanity should be open to critical discussion. Only in a society dominated by the commodity principle, more and more to the exclusion of all other values, is there time only for a single, dominant, canonical culture. Even then, time is available only to students in elite universities. Furthermore, the Dinesh D'Souzas of the world themselves have no time for Hölderlin or, for that matter, Plato, Wittgenstein, or Virginia Woolf—all homosexual writers, by the way—except as bludgeons to bash brains.[21] Hölderlin wrote, "Where the danger is greatest, there the possibilities are greatest also."[22] I must emphasize time and again, against the mopy liberal prognosis, that all of the nasty phenomena described above are occurring because of the fundamental weakness of the social system. Certainly we should take stock and understand that this struggle to create a radical questioning, an interrogation of the principle of reason, is part of a larger matrix of struggle that will be more intense still. But at the same time we should realize that we are in a position to make a great deal of trouble for the business of not-thinking as usual and for the structures of power behind this war on thought. We must strive to link up with marginalized people in this society who have every interest in taking this trouble-making to the point of basic social transformation.

As critical thinkers, what are we about if not this? What is the discourse and language of the other and the margin about if not this?

To resist the war on thought we must seize initiative, take the offensive. We must not simply cower in our supposed sanctuary and hope for better times. This initiative is especially a matter of engaging this struggle in a way that exposes the terms of the anti-PC/anti-multiculturalism camp and that allows us to get inside the terms of their post-Vietnam syndrome/New World Order "humanism" and to generate the terms of a language in which the other can be heard. Many aspects of this strategy will emerge fully only in the struggle itself. However, much more clarity is needed on at least three points.

First, this is not a struggle that should—or even can—be waged in careerist terms. There is too much at stake here. That is not to say that we should simply sit back and let the other side destroy what we have achieved institutionally. We fought hard so that certain questions could be raised in the academy, and so did a great many other people, who are themselves not in the academy. On no account should this ground be conceded. On the contrary: we should fight tenaciously to ensure that the anti-PC/anti-multiculturalism forces are not allowed to shut down any space for radical questioning, in the university or elsewhere. This does not mean that we will automatically win in every battle; on the other hand, to not wage the fight does mean that we will automatically lose. If we try to wage this struggle, however, simply in terms of "my career," then we have already lost.

Second, without naming names, some of those who have been appointed to represent "our side" seem more interested in self-aggrandizement than in winning. Some clearly like being in the spotlight, and that seems the main point of their involvement in these issues. Of course, some of the people on our side are appointed and promoted, as it were, by their side; after all, we don't control the airwaves or print venues.

Third, even though we will sometimes have to engage the anti-PC/anti-multiculturalism current on their ground, we cannot accept their terms and logic, which is predominantly a logic of the corporate media and television, a logic of the pernicious flattening of meaning that is the hallmark of authoritarian movements. We have to reject not only the 25-words-or-less, soundbite solution but, further, the idea that we have to play by their rules or to come off as "polite" so as to not "give offense." Nothing would please the anti-PC/anti-multiculturalism forces more. They have declared war, a cessation of civility, and they would love it if we were to respond in a civil manner.

Consider: it would have been a bad thing if people in south central

Los Angeles had responded in a civil manner to the legal legitimation of the idea that Black people are nothing, are non-human. It would have been a very bad thing if defenders of abortion rights had responded in a civil manner to Operation Rescue and other Christian fascist groups in Buffalo.

We must not fall into the trap of simply wanting a return to the previous civility, to the sanctuary of the university. As the crisis that has generated the diatribes of Bloom and company deepens, the (anti-) possibility of a return will become a dream only held dear by liberals (the real conservatives today). Why should we yearn for a return, when new possibilities are opening up, when the tasks that are part of our self-definition as critical intellectuals are being thrust upon us?

The important points of this general strategy can be struggled over and debated quite openly; after all, we have ideas and they don't. That's what their supposed love of canonical works, which most of them haven't read anyway, is really all about. Why else would they squirm and feel so insecure at the idea that, for example, women, of all people, might have ideas? Frankly, the cultural conservatives have every mark of being the ideological representatives of a desperate, decrepit, and dying class. It is not as though they are producing Shakespeares and Rousseaus and Tolstoys any more, so naturally Saul Bellow and Allan Bloom get worried when people start looking to Alice Walker and Chinua Achebe. The fact that they get worried shows clearly that they are neo-conservatives, not traditional conservatives, for no one who really cared about learning, even in the traditionally conservative sense, would accept the idea that we have to choose between Shakespeare and Walker. Anyone who really cared about learning would question the idea that education should be such a constrained activity that such choices have to be made in the first place. In any case, in the constrained model of "western civ," in which a student is supposed to be exposed to bits and pieces of the western intellectual tradition, there is little difference between teaching Walker, Shakespeare, or what-have-you. This model of education itself has little to do with real learning. Why is there such a shortage of time that only some people receive an education to start with, and why is it that even these people are only supposed to deposit a little bit of the world's rich intellectual heritage in their mental piggy banks? That we can describe the situation using the terminology of Paulo Freire, showing that there is no time for the community of questioning of which Derrida writes, straightforwardly demonstrates that the attack on Derrida and the concomitant attacks on multiculturalism and Political Correctness are primarily about power, not learning. The attacks are part of an emerging culture of reaction in which basic legal rights are stripped away, Black youth are sent to "boot camps," religious fundamentalism comes back from the dead, war is back in style, the Supreme Court rules that it is all right to execute the mentally retarded but against the law for homeless people to beg on the subway.

Richard Rorty would have us return to civility by showing that the kinds of questions that Derrida raises are really harmless. Jürgen Habermas would have us rethink our Enlightenment heritage, but also with an eye toward restoring the civility that is breaking down. These two paths may seem like options to some in the academy. When you talk with homeless people on the streets or with Black youths who see no future, and who brilliantly demonstrated the fact that they do not want the future of non-existence that this system has created for them by rising up in Los Angeles and elsewhere; when you see the outright barbarism of mentally retarded people being put to death in the electric chair; when you see that women are being told that they are not adults, they are children, who cannot be allowed to control their own reproductive processes; when you see the turkey shoot of the Gulf War (the massacre of an army in retreat), the sheer sport of murdering tens of thousands (one TV reporter put it: "The view here is fantastic; the skies over Baghdad are lit up like a Christmas tree"); when you see a million other ways that this society is coming apart at the seams, you see that the solution of recreating the academic sanctuary is unrealistic, apolitical, and irresponsible. Most of all it is irresponsible to the possibilities that are being called forth by the impossibility of the new, which would be destroyed in the cradle by the anti-possibility machinations of the war against *différance*. It is irresponsible to what responsibility might mean, what it might do.

Pat Buchanan and other outright fascists say that they want a return to European culture. In truth, this is the last thing they care about; however, as an answer to this invocation of the master culture, I will indeed make a trip to Europe, with Derrida as the guide.

Part 3

From other shores:
Derrida and the idea of Europe,
apropos of *L'autre cap*

And what about the *other* history, if its characteristic trait is not
to be a history—not in the sense of *Histoire*, or in the sense of
Geschichte (which implies the idea of unification)? What about the
other history, wherein nothing of the present ever happens, where
no event or advent measures or articulates? Foreign to the succession of moments, which is linear even when it is hindered and
as zigzagging as it is dialectical, the other history is the deploy-
ment of a plurality which is not that of the world of numbers. It
is a history in excess, a "secret," separate history, which presup-
poses the end of visible history, though it denies itself the very
idea of beginning and of end. It is always in relation with an
unknown that requires the utopia of total knowledge because it
exceeds this utopia—an unknown which is not linked to the irrational beyond reason or even to an irrationality proper to reason,
but which is perhaps the return to an *other* meaning in the labo-
rious work of "designification." The *other* history would be a feigned
history, which is not to say that it is a mere nothing, but that it is
always calling forth the void of a nonplace, the gap that it is, and
that separates it from itself.

—Maurice Blanchot

Apropos of *The Other Heading: Reflections on Today's Europe* . . . .
   This part presents a linear series of images and speculations (what
else is new?) that must become a constellation. The setting-off point
for these remarks is a close reading of a recent text of Derrida's *L'autre
cap*, translated by Pascale-Anne Brault and Michael Naas as *The Other
Heading*. Having discussed the translation of the title at length with

127

the translators, I know that they especially worried over the translation of *cap*, for, in addition to "heading," the word might have been
translated as "head," "capital," "capitol," or "cape," or at least all of
these terms are invoked by Derrida's reflections. I believe that the translators chose very well, focusing on what remains the most important
question: Where does humanity go from here? In what follows, I hope
to show how the other terms invoked by *cap* should be understood in
relation to this central question. Although I will deal here in the language of images and speculations, I have also created analytic separa-
tions between different questions that emerge in Derrida's text,
attempting to work through the different levels on which the text functions. Again, what else is new? But, in order to generate the constellation necessary for understanding *L'autre cap* as in some sense a complete
text—which is to say, as having made a statement—there must be some
principle of totalization. This, of course, is required as much, if not
more, by the logic of the present commentary as it is by Derrida's text
itself, and the question of totalization (totality, totalitarianism, etc.) is,
and must be, very much alive in this discussion. Attempting to avoid
all dissimulation, therefore, let me say here that the totalizing gesture
of this reading pursues the question, What does this constellation portend for the idea of Europe, which is to say, the idea of humanity, of
humanism?

Students of Derrida (and here I will always consider myself a student) will understand that, while there is every effort in Derrida's work
to postpone totality, this postponement occurs under the rubric and in
recognition of totality itself (the totality which is always, however,
absent). I will discuss further the ways that Derrida wrestles with Kant,
but this is surely one of the most important. For Kant, thinking is
"condemned" to metaphysics ("Human reasoning regards all knowledge as belonging to a possible system"); for Derrida, thinking is just
as necessarily condemned to struggle against metaphysics, even if always from "a certain inside." Without this struggle, without the question there is no thinking: thinking stops. This argument of Derrida's,
developed in texts as disparate as *of Grammatology* and *of Spirit*, is an
extension of Kant's argument. Responding further to the claims of pragmatism (especially of the Rortyan sort, and not so much to the pragmatism of Mead, where there is a deeper sense of the other), on the
one hand, and to Derrida's overarching concern for the unprecedented
(an *arche* that cannot be an *arche*, cannot be understood purely in terms
of a preestablished "logic of discovery"), something Adorno said is
helpful:

Hence the difference between dialectics and pragmatism, like every distinction in philosophy, is reduced to a nuance, namely, to the conception of that "next step." The pragmatist, however, defines it as adjustment, and this perpetrates the domination of what is always the same. Were dialectics to sanction this, it would renounce itself in renouncing the idea of potentiality. But how is potentiality to be conceived if it is not to be abstract and arbitrary, like the utopias dialectical philosophers proscribed? Conversely, how can the next step assume direction and aim without the subject knowing more than what is already given? If one chose to reformulate Kant's question, one could ask today, *how is anything new possible at all?*[1]

Recall also Adorno's famous dictum, against Hegel, that "the whole is the false"; in this context we might see that Adorno is interested in a dialectic with a difference. Adorno's sense of negativity, which makes itself evident especially in his style (his tone, recalling too that Derrida says of style at the conclusion of "The Ends of Man"—I will quote this passage soon enough), aims at not a mere difference but rather the difference of resistance. Here Derrida and Adorno are quite similar: they ask, What is both different and just? Can difference itself be justice, can deconstruction itself be the possibility of justice? These are questions that Kant, Adorno, and Derrida have in common. To pursue, in thought and practice, the infinite task set by the thinking of justice, this will provide the kind of totalizing ideal that is both necessary and resistant to closure.

Perhaps, speaking in the language of images and speculations, risking totalizations that some readers may wish to defer permanently, this part of the book will be what some people might call a discussion document. That would not be such a bad thing, as I am dealing, as Derrida likes to say, with an experiment. There are times when a rush to action is necessary, and actions represent judgments (at least for "we Kantians"). I will discuss the politics of speed in more detail in this part but at this point will thematize a distinction between a "frantic" or "feverish" politics and an urgent politics (and even an urgent philosophy, as discussed in the first part). Even so, the judgments embodied by actions, even actions driven by a sense of urgency, need not necessarily represent conclusions. To think otherwise is often to make a virtue of expediency. Here Adorno and Derrida, with their resistance to totality, have something to say to Marxism. And yet, because I believe that Marxism is the totalizing movement that has contributed the most to fighting "on the ground," as it were, capitalism's totalizing logic of the Same, it is especially toward the supplementation of Marxism that I want to offer these speculations on the experiment

of politics, the experiment of the thinking of the polis. This is the experimental approach necessary for keeping Marxism (and other post-
Hegelian radical theories or programs) from being inhabited and
recuperated by the logic of the Same.

The Other Heading is a work, shall we say, of journalism. It is not a
systematic theoretical work, even in the loose sense in which such a
designation might be applied to of Grammatology or even Glas. Many
themes in The Other Heading are left undeveloped and are presented
as probes (to use McLuhan's term). In this part I develop these themes
somewhat as though they were part of a system, even if of a speculative and experimental sort. But of which system? An anticipated one
which does not yet exist and which, always to some extent, postpones
its existence, which is to say, its completion. In anticipation of this
postponed system, I offer here a reweaving of the themes of The Other
Heading. Because Derrida's work is short, and in order to facilitate this
reweaving, I do not provide page numbers for quotations taken from
the text. This approach goes against the grain of what many readers
of Derrida think should be done with his work—and these readers
often express a somewhat ethical sense of this "ought." Somewhat in
the spirit of Derrida's Introduction to Husserl's "Origin of Geometry," I
have written a commentary that is as long as or longer than The Other
Heading. Concerning the question of systematicity and the question of,
to put it bluntly, whether I can get away with such a commentary, I
ask the reader to do two things. First, read Derrida's text.[2] Second,
think about whether these speculations are faithful to the spirit of
Derrida's project in The Other Heading and more generally. The impossible but necessary project, for both politics and philosophy, is to engage in the paradoxical, simultaneous thinking of system and the
subversion of system, closure and the resistance to closure. This is a
faithful formulation of Derrida's approach, despite (and, frankly, against)
the many readers of Derrida who believe that deconstruction is exclusively the resistance to closure.[3]

Vehicles of rhythm, with and without music

To reflect on Europe today is a dangerous profession. Derrida cites
Paul Valery concerning an "illness in the very structure of capital," a
"fever." The feverish movement of capital in the sense meant by Valery,
the stuff, the body of capitalism, but also in the sense of the head and
the center, makes discourse about the shape of the world, the world
for which Europe has been the head and the center, difficult. Derrida,
like Kant before him, has taken up this task—one might say, fever-

ishly: what we reflect and reflect upon today is fleeting. We know from Derrida, but also from Kant, that we cannot help but look for the center; and yet, clearly, we live in a period in which the center is being displaced and is even displacing itself. The very attempt to maintain the center through the most violent of means (marked by Derrida in the preface to these two essays, "Today," "in the midst of what is called the 'Gulf' War") is de facto recognition that the idea of the center is being reconstituted.

"I was thinking at first, while on board a plane. . . ." One thinks of Kant, never travelling far from Königsberg, in the heart of Europe; his "outer life was almost entirely uneventful" (I'm simply quoting from an encyclopedia, appropriately, for at the heart of modern Europe are Kant and the encyclopedia). He "admired Rousseau and the French Revolution from afar," he "conversed eagerly with travelers who brought him news of a wider world." This quasi-shut-in, Kant, perhaps we can call him the first global scholar, the first to think, in his "Universal History" essay, the idea of Europe—the first idea of the world, the first idea that the world has had, and thus far the only idea that the world has had. The closing passages of "Idea for a Universal History with Cosmopolitan Intent" have a beauty rare in philosophy, the beauty of a beautiful soul. Now Derrida is on a plane, he is a truly global scholar. (When I wrote "Now Derrida," at first I did not mean "today, right now, right at this moment." But this may indeed be the case, Derrida on a plane, now). For the most part he is not a "frenzied scholar" (and one imagines that the expression must be an oxymoron), but "today" he has taken up as a scholar a frenzied subject—the subject of Europe, which is for Derrida and for us the only subject, the only idea.

Some of the thoughts presented here are also "quasi-improvised reflections," a rhapsody of analyses. How could they not be, in the aftermath of the European idea? Not only do we not know what configuration will emerge in this aftermath, it is difficult to get a clear picture of the present configuration. I am even tempted to place a calendar date here, for the "present," even in the ordinary sense, is practically gone before we know it. Certainly the presence of Europe's configuration is what is open to question here. There is a certain kind of reading of Derrida that is so Eurocentric that it wishes only that the presence of Europe be secured, come what may. In this 500th year of the Columbus invasion, it is remarkable that such Eurocentrists still do not grasp what Europe's secure presence entails. On this question, more in due course. The further point is that in trying to get some perspective on what Derrida has written, I have found it necessary to attempt to slow things down a bit. I find, now, that some of what follows was indeed thought at first while on a plane. Even more of these thoughts came to me while on the various trains that I travel around a particular shore, an enclosed shore, the "shore" of Chicago.

Is this an other shore?

Can one think more clearly about the idea of Europe from this enclosed shore, while listening to the music of the train? For there is a music of the train that is a music, if not "of thought," at least a music that one can think to and with. Superficial, one may say (the one who is the subject, the only subject, the persona of Europe), but still compelling is the music of Gershwin, Jazzbo Brown's Blues that opens *Porgy and Bess* (George Gershwin wrote this music on a train), the music and the train that take us to another shore, of Catfish Row, Charleston, South Carolina. Far from the idea of Europe? (And, will one be able to think there, away from the frenzy of Europe?) What is less superficial here? Do we resist Gershwin's bastardization of the operatic form by returning, quickly, to the arms of Wagner or Mozart?

The different-but-same Europes of Mozart and Wagner: there is the essence of the question of humanism. And Gershwin: there is the essence of the aftermath. But no—there is no "essence" to the music of Gershwin.

What thought do we resist? Is this a thought mediated through Africa, through the Black slave brought to North America by Europeans?[4] Is the thought of Europe, and therefore the thought of humanity, thereby mediated through an Africa where one cannot think, where it is simply too hot to think, as Hegel would have it? Europe cannot think Africa, in this view, as Africa is outside the pale of the idea of humanity, and Africa cannot think itself, Africa cannot think period. And yet, a bastard thought emerges on an other shore, a thought mediated through Africa.

This superficial music of Gershwin, it is a bastard child of Europe, born on another shore. Who or what is the other parent, who or what has Europe "opened onto"? How stands this other of the heading in relation to the idea of Europe? What is the meaning of Africa as the other head of this household? It would be the easiest thing in the world to say that these are American questions, having little to do with the idea and destiny (heading) of Europe. But what could such a claim be other than the abdication of the heading, for there is no parental "right" to spill one's seed carelessly. Aimlessly, with no heading in sight. Europe: you see the African as a child when it suits you, but somehow not your child. How simple, how useful, but then how calculating it is to imagine that Africa, having no idea, representing no concrete individual (to take up again the Hegelian language that Derrida also interrogates), cannot respond; therefore there is no need to speak of a responsibility toward Africa or (by extension of the same argument) to the bastard children who are the result of the careless, aimless events of European history.

On another shore, yea, even unto the shores of Chicago, this aimlessness, this carelessness sounds an echo: We shall be "Europeans" in this matter also.

But, of course, this non-thinking of Africa, this thoughtlessness and irresponsibility backfires. But let me leave this Gershwin problematic for the moment. The structure of European irresponsibility will be set out in the specific language of *The Other Heading* as this commentary develops. However, let me take at this point, as a theoretical guide, the following formula: If Europe is uniquely the home of the idea of humanity and therefore of human responsibility, then it is also uniquely the birthplace of irresponsibility. For Europe to deny responsibility for this irresponsibility, Europe must also abandon its claims on humanism.

I cannot imagine a music of the plane, but perhaps I am not up to speed. And this, finally, is what is necessary to reckon (with) the course of Europe today, a politics of tremendous speed and a politics that can move at tremendous speed. Where the polis is frenzied, however, perhaps there is no polis; perhaps we are, at best, in the realm of the "quasi-political."

Here I begin, then, to reckon with the improvizations (is it European to improvize?) of Derrida, his reckoning with Europe today, its frenzied polis. But who is this Derrida who has been on many planes, who has traveled far beyond the heart of Europe but tells us that we cannot travel beyond this center? Who is Derrida to speak on the polis, at "this critical moment" (this moment of crisis where—emphatically where, for time is fully spatialized here, emphatically here—the frenzied pace may or may not allow space for criticism, for thinking), when "the finitude of Europe" is "beginning to emerge"? I find that, even in the space of commentary (the caboose, as it were), there is no slowing down. Forgive me then if, at this speed, the two essays (the first originally a conference presentation, the second an interview, both originally published as newspaper articles) that make up *The Other Heading* start to run together, one might say into a thematic doppler effect, but that's to assume we know whether we (who?) are coming or going.

The final nail: Derrida is not "political"

Derrida has managed to generate the ire of both the right, meaning the neo-conservatives, and what often goes by the name the left, meaning all sorts of things. On either side, from that of the right Hobbesians or the left Hobbesians, it is argued that Derrida is not political, that he is a distraction from politics. Thus Derrida cannot really be speaking of Europe (or for that matter, of not-Europe). Discovering this truth, based on the most painstaking close readings of Derrida (the sort that would do Bloom and D'Souza proud), one can come out into the sunshine, into the real world of politics, where Richard Rorty, Jürgen Habermas, Allan Bloom, William Bennett, and other realistic thinkers get down to business. Happy day—Derrida is, at best, a pleasant diversion from politics, his medium is postcards, not programs.

A catalogue of all those places where Derrida is already not speaking of politics or of Europe would take me back to his earlier work on Husserl. But there Derrida constantly speaks of Europe. What is wrong here? As it turns out, there is a problem with Derrida's scholarship. Derrida took Husserl's thought to be fundamentally about the idea of Europe; it is, of course, but in no political way. Derrida, it seems, was already caught up in the frenzy of the critical moment. That is, in taking Husserl's work to be, in an essential way, about Europe, Derrida was already in that no-man's land between discourses that do not speak to one another: transcendental philosophy and political science. These deconstructionists, who attempt to think outside of categories, no wonder they constantly make category mistakes! (Michael Naas has carefully traced the question of the "example" and the exemplary in his intro-duction, "For Example," to the English translation of *The Other Heading*.)

There seems to be a consensus, as well, among writers on both the social democratic (i.e., Eurocentric) left and the anti-communist right that whenever Derrida seems to be discussing colonialism or imperi-alism he cannot actually be saying anything, because colonialism and imperialism do not exist or at least they are only properties of the now defunct Soviet empire. More orthodox Marxists, to the extent that they are still able to understand the meaning of imperialism, do not see that Derrida is saying something about this subject. Of course, it is typical of Marxists who value orthodoxy that they do not see that anyone who does not share their particular orthodoxy could be saying any-thing of value regardless; I will turn to an example of this orthodoxy in a moment. Talk of imperialism and colonialism has been ruled out of the New World Order.

What is this blessed rage for order? It is a matter of making politics an arithmetic, a calculus, to be determined and disseminated by Guardians, a true political science. Anyone who questions this science or who fails to contribute to it is out of order and outside of the order. In attempting to raise the question of an impossible experiment, an impossible thinking of the polis against calculation, then, Derrida is indeed "not political."

If Derrida wants to speak to the New World Order, he will have to clean up his language. How might this decontamination be accomplished? Derrida must recognize that today the proper language of politics must shuttle between two well-defined poles: the pole of a self-contained European identity (reinforced, even as I write this, September 14, 1992, with the language of "Auslanders aus!") and the pole of the New World Order. Even putting the best face on the Eurocentric pole, we might say that Derrida, if he wants to get down to the business of politics, must learn to shuttle between Jürgen Habermas at the one (left?) end, George Bush at the other. But this is the political spectrum and conception of politics into which Derrida does not fit. Therefore, there is no room for Derrida's work in politics or social theory.

Derrida does not offer his equation, the European equation, to be compared with other accounts of Europe. How can Derrida settle accounts with Europe—the numbers just aren't there. For science there must be numbers, and Derrida offers us no numbers, therefore no formula, no chemistry, no science of Europe. He cannot say what will happen next in Europe—he cannot even say what Europe is—and therefore is unfit to appear on television. His words, his thoughts will not, simply cannot, be screened. What can he possibly be talking about when he refers to "an ethics confused with juridical calculation," "a politics organized within techno-science"? These will be, are, the ethics and politics of the New World Order, and thou shalt have no other gods. Derrida speaks of "the incalculable": *"if there is any"* it "never *presents* itself; it is not, it is never the theme of some scientific or philosophical objectification." Case closed!

Derrida is and is not European. He, most of all, cannot speak of Europe, any more than a cross-dresser can speak of gender. To mention that it has generally been men who guide the ship of state, to introduce this unscientific observation into the world of hard facts, of political science . . . who is he, he who is and is not European, to contaminate the discourse so? He cannot answer the question, Where do you stand on Europe? He speaks, for instance, of a Marxism that we have learned to resist, an ossified, solidified Marxism—on the one hand. But that was Marxism, that was the great utopian experiment, everyone can see the nowhere utopia of the Soviet Union and eastern Europe;

indeed, it would be hard to think of more utopian figures than Brezhnev, Ceausescu, Honecker. Yes, they were the great utopians of our day, but they failed—human nature and all that, people just weren't up to living in their utopias, they just weren't ready for the lofty goals presented by the Brezhnev generation. On the other hand—as though he has got a hand to play here—Derrida warns us of the dominance of the market. But we now know that these are the realistic choices: either a paternalistic state attempting the utopia of fully regulated commodity production, in which labor continues to be a commodity also, that is, fully regulated capitalism, in which the anarchy of the market is somehow brought completely under the direction of state ministries, or an all-encompassing market, hymns to which are now sung by all the legitimate political spokespersons. Or rather, our only legitimate choice is both the state and the market, for no globally articulated market can work without a great deal of political and military coordination. But let me not go too far: even *talking* about Derrida, if only to show that he is not relevant to our political science, lulls us toward an extremist mode, that sleep of reason. Most political scientists can explain to us the relation between politics and economics in a complex economy. That is all we need to know. Never let it be suggested that the key relation is that between economics and military force. Anyone so uncouth as to suggest that there could still be an outside to the science of politics, our logic of the Same applied to the polis, cannot truly be thinking politically.

Sarcasm aside: Response to an orthodox Marxist reading of Derrida

Alex Callinicos, a Marxist in the neo-Trotskyist tradition of Tony Cliff,[5] has written a critique of postmodern theory that makes an essential appeal to orthodox Marxism.[6] There is much in *Against Postmodernism: A Marxist Critique* that I find good, especially its focus on Lyotard and Baudrillard as the postmodern epigones most in favor of the aestheticization of politics and of thought generally. Callinicos clearly recognizes Derrida, on the one hand, and Foucault and Deleuze, on the other, as thinkers of a different caliber. However, he does charge these three with opening the pathway in thought that leads to Lyotard's and Baudrillard's "jargon of postmodernity."

Callinicos, like the two French followers of Leo Strauss whom he quotes often and with approval, Alain Renaut and Luc Ferry, argues that postmodernism is the aftermath of "68 Thought": "Postmodernism must be understood largely as a response to the failure of the great upturn of 1968–76 to fulfill the revolutionary hopes it raised" (p. 171). In itself, one would think, this is not necessarily a bad thing, but, Callinicos argues, "talk about postmodernism turns out to be less about the world than the expression of a particular generation's sense of an ending."

True enough. But then, Derrida does not ever talk about post-modernism. Callinicos feels justified, however, in placing Derrida in the camp of postmodernism, because of what he sees as a strain of Nietzschean romantic anti-capitalism; that is, "opposition to capital-ism in the name of pre-capitalist values" (p. 67).[7] This description also places Derrida firmly within the group of what Jürgen Habermas calls the "young conservatives," and in general Callinicos endorses the cri-tique of Derrida presented by Habermas in *The Philosophical Discourse of Modernity*.

Before discussing this claim about Derrida, which I find dubious— or perhaps overconfident and unhelpful would be the right terms— even if there is a kernel of truth to it, I must turn to the way that, for Callinicos, Derrida's supposed romanticism is intertwined with his "textualism," a term be takes over from Rorty.[8] Derrida's textualism, for Callinicos, has two chief aspects. First, it regards all species of writing and thought as literary genres. Textualism thus places the literary at the center of all cognitive pursuits. Second, and concomitantly, this focus on the literary leads to an "aestheticizing of language":

> The practice of deconstruction denies theoretical texts their appar-ent cognitive content, reducing them to an array of rhetorical de-vices and thereby effacing any difference between them and explicitly literary texts. (p. 70)

According to Callinicos, the critique of various texts from various genres becomes primarily a critique of style. Callinicos approvingly quotes Habermas on this point:

> Derrida proceeds by a critique of style, in that he finds something like indirect communications, by which the text denies its manifest content, in the rhetorical surplus of meaning inherent in the literary strata of texts that present themselves as nonliterary. (p. 70; from Habermas, *Philosophical Discourse*, p. 189)

What Callinicos and other commentators have found puzzling about Derrida's work is that, instead of moving from positions such as these (as understood by these commentators—I will soon turn to the ques-tion of the accuracy of the characterizations) toward either the cri-tique of metaphysical realism à la Wittgenstein, Quine, Sellars, Goodman, etc., or toward a kind of historicized hermeneutics à la Gadamer, Derrida

moves toward what looks like a new kind of transcendental philosophy, where the "obliterated origin of absence and presence" is discussed using the terms trace, archewriting, and, most famously, *différance*.

Interestingly, Callinicos describes this move, in terms taken from
Peter Dews' *Logics of Disintegration*, as "a quest for the ground of transcendental consciousness" (p. 75). Actually, Callinicos seems at pains
to find various descriptions of Derrida's arguments that will make things
look bad. While at one point describing Derrida's work as "a radically
anti-realistic philosophy of language which denies us the possibility
of knowing a reality independent of discourse" (p. 81),[9] he elsewhere
agrees that "textualism does not deny the existence of extra-discursive
objects" (p. 76). These two positions are not in contradiction, however, if understood in a Kantian framework, as Callinicos argues.
However, as with most orthodox Marxists, for Callinicos "Kantian" is
a term of abuse.

> If textualism does not deny the existence of extra-discursive objects,
> it does deny our ability to know these objects. For such knowledge
> would seem to require some reliable mode of access to that object.
> But for Derrida the notion of such access is an instance of the meta-
> physics of presence, involving the idea of some direct, unmediated
> contact with a reality outside the play of signifiers. One might com-
> pare this position with that of Kant, who believed that we could not
> know things in themselves, but only sense-impressions organized
> by the categories of the understanding inherent in the structure of
> transcendental subjectivity underlying experience. The difference is
> that Derrida sets *differance* in the place of the unknowable *Ding-an-
> sich* and, resolving the subject into the play of presence and absence,
> sets the categories themselves in motion. (p. 77)

In short, Derrida rethinks the categories of subjectivity in terms of the
question of language. My question, however, is: Is what Callinicos
describes simply Nietzschean "radicalizing of Kant" or is it a materi-
alizing of the categories?

Having begun with a broad characterization of Derrida as a romantic anti-capitalist in the Nietzschean mold, then turning to a general
characterization of Derrida's philosophy as a species of Kantianism,
Callinicos ends by returning to political questions. Unfortunately,
Callinicos half-heartedly cites, but does not pursue, arguments by Frank
Lentricchia and Christopher Norris that bring out the possibilities of
joining deconstruction with oppositional politics. Callinicos calls Lentricchia's *After the New Criticism* a "devastating critical survey of Derrida's
American followers [that] has shown how the notion of deconstruction
can legitimize a genuine idealism narcissistically preoccupied with an

endlessly self-generating textuality" (p. 77), but he does not mention Lentricchia's later *Criticism and Social Change*, which mentions Derrida's work in a positive light, comparing it to that of Kenneth Burke (the main focus of the book) and Antonio Gramsci. In Norris's more recent work, Gramsci's influence is much more in the foreground. Callinicos writes:

> Norris offers a reading of deconstruction as, not "a species of Nietzschean irrationalism," but as, in the hands of Derrida and de Man at least, a form of *Ideologiekritik* whose "point of departure is to argue with the utmost *logical* rigour to conclusions which may yet be counter-intuitive or at odds with common-sense (consensual) wisdom." (p. 77; from Norris, *The Contest of the Faculties*, p. 18)

Which sounds, to me, much like what Gramsci, on the one hand, and Adorno and Horkheimer, on the other, were doing. But Callinicos does not pursue this point; I mention this brief encounter with Lentricchia and Norris to demonstrate the simple ungenerousness of the orthodox cast of mind.

Wondering if Norris himself is applying the procedure he describes to Derrida's texts in order to invent a political meaning that may not be there, Callinicos allows (in a sentence with an amusing typographical error) that "Nevertheless, Derrida herself is concerned to establish the politically oppositional character of his philosophy." However, Callinicos argues, Derrida is unable to "rationally ground" his political commitments "because he denies himself the means either to analyse those existing social arrangements which he rejects or to justify this rejection by outlining some more desirable state of affairs" (p. 79). Callinicos also claims that Derrida's commitments "do not seem in any case to rise much above a fairly commonplace left liberalism."

As an example of the supposed ineffectiveness of deconstructive social critique, Callinicos discusses Derrida's "Racism's Last Word," an essay on South African apartheid, and a response to Derrida written by two American literary theorists. (Derrida wrote his essay as part of the catalogue for an exhibition of anti-apartheid art.) "The main philosophical point at issue was whether or not Derrida's denial of the existence of the *hors-texte* was responsible for his failure to attend to the evolution of racial domination in South Africa" (p. 78). It is interesting that, having charged Derrida with this failure, Callinicos goes on to quote Derrida's statement that apartheid is a "concentration of world history," more specifically of "a European 'discourse' of the concept of race bound up with the operation of the Western multinationals and nation-states." Furthermore, Derrida argues, the opposition to apartheid depends on "the future of another law and another force lying beyond the totality of this present." Callinicos centers his critique, however, on two main points: first, Derrida's claim that the nature of this other law and force (Callinicos puts these terms in quotation marks) cannot be anticipated: second, Derrida's comment about the anti-apartheid paintings, that "their silence is just. A discourse would compel us to reckon with the present state of force and law. It would draw up contracts, dialecticize itself, let itself be reappropriated."

As with the discussion of Rorty, I find myself chomping at the bit to dig into the problems that I find with Callinicos's positions, especially the wilfull misreading of passages such us those just quoted. (In "Biodegradables," Derreda invents the term *ne "pveut" pas lire* to describe those who can't/won't read; the term suits many of Derrida's critics well, including the one under discussion.) However, I want to take care in spelling out the full extent of the critique.

Here are Callinicos's conclusions regarding what he thinks himself to have read and considered:

> So the resistance to apartheid must remain inarticulate, must not seek to formulate a political programme and strategy: any attempt to do so would simply involve reincorporation into "the present state of law and force" and perhaps even into the "European discourse of racism." If this argument is valid, then the resistance was lost long ago.... the contention of these [oppositional] discourses [Callinicos names a number of them operative in South Africa]—the stuff of any real liberation struggle—for Derrida presumably amounts merely to variations on the theme of the "present state of law and force." No wonder that Ferry and Renaut talk about Derrida's "negative ontology": we can only allude to, but not (at the risk of "reappropriation") seek to know anything lying beyond "the totality of the present." ... Apartheid is "the archival record of the unnameable" because it represents the culmination and therefore the truth of the European civilization which, not only produced the "discourse" of race but which, reproduced now on a world scale, is the source of the categories in terms of which we are all compelled to think. It is therefore the *alternative* to apartheid which is unnameable, because it lies beyond these categories. (pp. 78–79)

Right! With this last passage Callinicos is finally on to something! Sarcasm aside: let me go somewhere closer to the language of deconstruction, for a moment, taking a pause just as I did in the discussion of Rorty. It is the singular achievement of the New World Order, this postmodern capitalism, this economic/political/military logic of the Same, that irony is set aside, ruled out of (the) order. Spectacular capitalism (one recalls Susan Sontag's "Fascinating Fascism") has organized a massive failure of the imagination. Kant, thinker of the imagination, where are you now? It is declared that the federation you wanted is now coming into being: a federation of European states; a world federation that took on the Gulf War, the date of Derrida's address—to the ship of state? to the "captain" of the ship?[10] Clearly professor Derrida cannot address, as you did, the enlightened rulers of Europe. But Derrida has no address, he can neither send nor receive, he has no heading, no letterhead, no direction. Kant, where are you now? Political thinking for you is thinking without categories, it is in the realm of the imagination. There are no categories for us now, even if there is not a "new Europe"—Europe is unprecedented but it is not new; Derrida says that he is a "tired European"; the fact is that he is in a tired Europe. This Europe is a product of the failure of socialism—on this all parties can agree, but for my part it is the failure of socialism to replace tired, capitalist Europe, which will get more tired still if it lunges into yet another go-round of market frenzy, more fascination with today, today, today, there is no other day. "Has the day ever been the measure of all things"—to what end? Kant, where are you now? The Gulf War, a political event? therefore beyond categories? What is the structure of an event in which humans massacre other humans? Of course, there was no massacre: it was a turkey shoot, it was shooting fish in a barrel. Those who are outside the idea of Europe cannot die for or because of that idea: those outside do not exist. Some, Habermas (his "reservations" about the war, his "critical support," aside) apparently is one of them, are already saying, "This is the perpetual peace that Kant dreamed of, a federation of nations restoring order." This is thinking beyond categories, beyond humanism. Kant, where are you now? Something called political science has been at the ideological forefront of this organized failure. Something called deconstruction, from somewhere else, the very space that the spectacle attempts to keep open for so long that it becomes permanent, a blinding sun, this "deconstruction," something called that, addresses itself to Europe? How does it set sail for the destination, Europe, if it only knows "someplace else" as its point of departure? This sounds like a very dangerous way to sail, from "someplace else." And yet, one also thinks of the danger of the "explorers," those who know where they come from, though not where they land; Columbus, for instance, who needed to know nothing about his destination, only that he encountered gentle, curious folk there, all the better to be conquered—they will make fine slaves for the emerging world order.

Better that the someplace else cannot be fully specified. Better that

Europe does not know the address of the other; perhaps now the idea
of Europe will stay home? But where is Europe's home? Europe has
made the world its home, and therefore the world is no longer home
to the other of the heading. Indeed, one (one such as Derrida) has to
go first to Europe, or rather be first in Europe, be first a creation of
Europe, in order to go someplace other and then to set sail, once again,
for Europe. This folding of space, in which one appears to have moved
not at all (on a plane or otherwise), always not to leave Europe (for
how can it be a place to leave—what is "it"?) is exceedingly difficult
to conceptualize as politics—there is no space in political discursivity
for such thinking as Derrida does. Derrida is not political, his work is
a fold in political space.

Yet there is a shape to this fold, that can be set out albeit in a necessarily limited way, a shape that can be found by looking at political-
discourse-as-usual, on the one side, and texts by Derrida that do, in a
straightforward way, refer to this political discourse, on the other side.
Such texts do not always display the shape of a fold in political space—
in some sense they are a kind of compromise—but they are also a
key, a pointer, a quasi-saying toward the unsaid. Derrida writes in *of
Spirit*, in *The Other Heading*, and in other recent works that we would
be very foolish simply to abandon the language of humanism and indeed
of liberalism. I will take up this subject with a different spin in a moment,
when I turn to the politics of speed. I am already close to the politics
of the unprecedented. But not (t)here yet, to this question. (My destination, my question; setting off, also, from a question, but a question
of the question or a question in question.) The point, however, is that—
because of or in spite of such remarks about the unavoidableness of
the humanist vocabulary—Derrida nowhere works within the parameters of this vocabulary. Indeed, Derrida's entire *oeuvre* may be considered a gigantic avoidance of this vocabulary. An essay such as "The
Ends of Man" may be read as a statement about autonomy (and that
is what the essay is about), but not as a text that fits very comfortably
with the canonical discourse on the subject. In the wake of Reagan,
Thatcher, the initiation of the New World Order, in other words, now,
today, the term anti-humanism, which is sometimes applied to Derrida's
work (as well as Foucault's Deleuze's, etc.), seems unfortunate.

The term has in contemporary philosophy and social theory (which
is to say the theory of today?) two sources, which seem quite distant
from one another: Heidegger and structuralism. These are sources that
motivate Derrida's texts. What does one get when one rubs two anti-
humanists together? Whatever the answer is, it would seem a species
of being that one would do well to stay away from. Except that we

cannot stay away. Our thoughts wander to Saussure and to Levi-Strauss, but also to Althusser. His presence in Derrida's text often goes unmarked and unremarked. Today, of all days, I read a slight against him in the Chicago Tribune.[11] The "New Philosophers" are being revived: they were already the anti-PC warriors of their day. (If you are here, with us, today, you will need no explanation of these comments.) These "ex-Maoists." There is another name already present in this discussion; I will say that name in a moment. "History is a process without a subject." Who will inscribe this, today, upon their banners? Althusser presented his program, his theoretical practice, under the heading of an anti-humanist Marxism. Now all may stand back from Europe, whatever this Europe is and whatever this Europe may be, and see that the process without a subject is playing itself out on both sides of the line between eastern and western Europe. There is no more line; more and more there is a single process, without a subject. What could Althusser have meant? Surely not this. If Althusser had only said, "Capitalism is a process without a subject," he would have gone no further than Marx, who in his later writings (and Althusser was of course *the* Marxist of the later writings, especially *Capital*, and of the "epistemological break") continually remarked on the unconscious nature of the invisible hand. This hand that now guides all Europe—and has guided all Europe for some time, but now we sing hymns to the hand: the market is all, thou shalt have no other master, no other god (and Moneybags is so lucky!).

Althusser meant, of course, that there is no collective subject; his is a response most of all to the ontologizing of the proletariat accomplished by Lukacs in *History and Class Consciousness*. Funny that Althusser is continually called a Stalinist in some quarters, for it was this ontologizing move that characterized Stalin's particular form of dogmatized Marxism. (Of course, both Lukacs and Althusser are called Stalinists. Can you have it both ways—or, does this really say that repeating "Stalinism" like some sort of mantra does not help very much if the goal is to understand the world in order to change it?) Derrida himself everywhere displaces this ontologization, including the onto-theology of Stalin. However, is history a process without a subject for Derrida, this Derrida who is continually accused of having done away with the subject? If this is so, who is this Derrida who everywhere writes of the other and of responsibility? Is it also a writing against the coldness of Being? One thinks of Heidegger, but one also thinks of Sartre, the "last humanist." For many in "Derrida's camp," that *l'autre camp*, it is true, there is nothing to be said of Sartre except that he is a bad reader of Heidegger, just as there is nothing to be said of Habermas except that he is a bad reader of Derrida and Heidegger. Does one read in the *Critique of Dialectical Reason* the last (meta-)language of humanism, the last word on the subject? And what does one read in Derrida's "Cogito and the History of Madness," a text on one of the first words of the subject? The first is displaced: there is no first (contrary to Foucault), even if there is the first word, the subject's first word (and the first word is not "mama," it is "I"). Does Sartre, if not in his *Critique* (his unfinished *Critique*, his unfinished everything), then in his *Flaubert* speak humanism's last word? This question must be asked, because, despite Derrida's insistence that the last word of humanism has not been spoken, Derrida nowhere speaks the language of humanism. Is this the expression of a nostalgia, today? For the language of humanism, the language of the subject, the language of Europe? It would be quite simple to answer, "No, there cannot be any nostalgia in Derrida," but I am not absolutely sure that this is what someone who calls himself an old, tired European would say.

Significantly, the charge of anti-humanism is often advanced by either those on the right, those Reaganites or Thatcherites who can hardly be called humanists themselves, or by a still somewhat orthodox left which does not know (indeed, rarely asks) in what its humanism consists. That is, in the latter case, a left that still speaks the language of humanism (even in questioning that language—here the trick is to switch to the sub-dialect of secularism) without intending to, without wanting to (and even denying that it is doing so) speak the language of Europe.

Sartre and Althusser: Who could be further apart, the great "last humanist" and the great "anti-humanist"? And yet, in one thing they were quite similar: both attempted to think beyond Eurocentrism. They are a crucial part of Derrida's genealogy, for it is certainly not from Nietzsche and Heidegger that one receives the expressly political motivation to think the not-West, as much as they are crucial to thinking the West. And yet, Derrida never truly speaks the language of not-Europe nor does he believe it possible for him, for "us," to speak that language, if indeed a language is what we are necessarily concerned with here. Let us face the question squarely: Derrida is one of the great practitioners of the "European language." Except that Derrida, of course, and according to his own thinking, is not a practitioner of anything. Derrida does not speak Europe, Europe speaks Derrida . . . and what is Europe speaking when it speaks Derrida . . . is Europe a process without a subject . . . and is the name of that not-subject Derrida? Or, at least, something called deconstruction?

How would Derrida escape the charge of anti-humanism, when he seems to cast the vocabulary of humanism into the void? With his whole mouth, it seems that Derrida does not speak (the language of) humanism. There is no "on the one side" and "on the other side" here; is Derrida univocal on this point? Where is the double-gesture, its possibility?

To all appearances, there only seems to be the gesture of two voids— one an avoidance, a denial of speaking, the other a writing from someplace outside.

But there is no outside and there is no inside, there is only an inside, or one might as well say there is only an outside—for the terms only go with the distinction. But Derrida is not there, not at the outside, not at the inside; he is, rather, at the fold.

What an ironic gesture, what play with language, it would now be to speak of an eastern Europe that is "returning to the fold." Yes, this is your "new" Europe, a very old, a very tired Europe.

Thus we find, page one, page-one news, Derrida the pamphleteer, Derrida the journalist, who is taken to task now, in the United States, perhaps elsewhere, for his "attack on journalism," because he takes issue with the way that U.S. newspapers and magazines have treated the case of Paul de Man's wartime journalism. Ah, more journalism, which is, what?—more "todayism"? "Journalism is history's first draft" (could Derrida really be involved in such an enterprise?)—who will raise the "question of the day." What better medium—the journal, the pamphlet—to raise this question. This Derrida who nevertheless herself is concerned to establish the politically oppositional character of his philosophy. But the medium is not adequate to the hope and fear of what Europe may be; there will be no answer to this question, today. Whoever gives an answer is a liar, claiming to see, to know the face of Europe, the language to be spoken. ". . . the signs which come to us from everywhere in Europe, where, precisely in the name of identity, cultural or otherwise, the worst violences, those which we recognize all too well without yet having thought them through, the crimes of xenophobia, racism, anti-semitism, religious or nationalist fanaticism, are henceforth unleashed, mixed up, mixed up with each other, but also, and there is nothing fortuitous in this, mixed in with the breath, the respiration, the very 'spirit' of the promise." What language is adequate to these signs? The language of humanism, in whose name the worst violences have sometimes been perpetrated? This language which seems old, even though in historical perspective it is not very old and even though it has not yet taken root in the larger, non-European world (to speak the Hegelian variant of that very language)? This language of *droit*? Where will we be without it? Without speaking this language, Derrida asks this question. One might extrapolate. The signs of the worst violence, intermingled, "and there is nothing fortuitous in this," with the breath of Europe's promise: possibility, possibilities inseparable from counter-possibilities. Where will we be in setting sail for the possibilities, for the "spirit" of the promise, without this language, this humanism? Where are the possibilities without this language, and where is the polis? "From what exhaustion must the young old-Europeans that we are set out again?" Even from "another shore," if indeed there is such a thing, one feels this exhaustion. Europe has exhausted all of us, even those who are not-European (especially those); but who is not European? This amounts to saying, Who is not political? Then politics remains at the limit of Europe and in the folds of Europe; something called deconstruction seeks that limit and looks into those folds.

Sarcasm aside, let me consider the particulars of Callinicos's argument. It is ironic that Callinicos shows so little appreciation for what might be called, after Adorno, ironic resistance. It is ironic that Callinicos himself would remark that

> the kind of ironic distance from the world which was so important a feature of the great works of Modernism has become routinized, even trivialized, as it becomes a way of negotiating a still unreconciled reality which one no longer believes can be changed. (p. 170)

It is ironic that Callinicos would characterize Derrida with the words "we can only allude to, but not (at risk of 'reappropriation') seek to know anything lying beyond 'the totality of the present'" (p. 78). This formula might easily serve as a characterization of Adorno's philosophy, which Callinicos generally cites with approval.

However, the question of irony aside (did I not say earlier in this letter that perhaps irony should be foregrounded as a key concept in critical theory?), let me now assess Callinicos's arguments.

First, let me respond to the question of the supposed aestheticism of Derrida's work. Callinicos has defined this as a preoccupation with style, to the exclusion of an emphasis on content. Callinicos quotes Susan Sontag on this point toward the end of the book: "Aestheticism involves 'an attitude which is neutral with respect to content'" (p. 170). Furthermore, not only is Derrida preoccupied with the critique of style, his contribution to philosophy consists in nothing but style. Callinicos approvingly quotes the sarcastic comment of Ferry and Renaut that "while, for example, 'Foucault = Heidegger + Nietzsche,' 'Derrida = Heidegger + Derrida's style'" (p. 76).

Actually, there are three broad claims here, all presented under the banner of the critique of aestheticism. First, Callinicos is claiming that Derrida is a mere formalist, that he takes no concrete political positions. This is simply not true, and I will deal with this claim at more length.

The second claim is that Derrida merely recapitulates Heidegger. This is also not true. While there is some truth to the claim that, as Habermas puts it, "Derrida's deconstructions faithfully follow the movement of Heidegger's thought" (cited in Callinicos, p. 76), neither Habermas nor Callinicos has, with any degree of care, understood the meaning of this "faith." Contrary to Habermas, "the Heideggerian theme of the self-occultation of Being" is not simply "repeated in the conception of *différence*." (This is Callinicos's description of Habermas's argument.) Certainly Derrida has a basic affinity with Heidegger in that both are reading against the grain of Husserl's transcendental phenomenology. Derrida attends carefully to the specificities of Heidegger's *destruktion* of the western tradition of ontotheology. Part of the problem with Callinicos's argument (and Habermas's) is that he writes as though there is no point, in any case and come what may, to following out Heidegger's thinking. When I use the expression "come what may," I mean, in part, come what may to the Marxist tradition that Callinicos continually invokes as the alternative, the Marxist tradition that has nothing to learn from Heidegger or from anyone who pursues the contours of Heidegger's thought. Part of what I hope to establish in this study is that one can remain a Marxist (and not necessarily just a purely academic Marxist) and yet reject this kind of orthodoxy. I would go so far as to say that one *must* reject this orthodoxy in order to remain committed to a Marxism that is more committed to radically changing the world than it is to ontotheological purity.[12]

Still, it must be said that Callinicos is simply wrong in claiming that Derrida merely recapitulates Heidegger. One would think that the very fact that Callinicos devotes quite a few pages to Derrida would serve as refutation of this claim. Perhaps for Callinicos and Habermas this is nothing more than a minor detail, but the fact is that Derrida's reading of Heidegger is aimed at showing that Heidegger is no more able to escape metaphysics than is Husserl. As Rodolphe Gasché puts it,

> Like Heidegger, Derrida criticizes Husserl's phenomenological reduction, but he also questions Heidegger's interpretation of that method as a method of inquiring into the meaning of Being. If, as Derrida writes in *Writing and Difference*, referring to the *Cartesian Meditations*, that "in criticizing classical metaphysics, phenomenology accomplishes the most profound project of metaphysics" (*WD*, p. 166), then the same can be said of Heidegger's destruction of the Occidental tradition of ontology and of his focus on Being. (p. 119)

Although it is the case that Derrida originally used the term deconstruction as a translation of Heidegger's terms for destruction and dis-
mantling, the word came to have, mainly through the efforts of Derrida's
North American students, a broader meaning, as the name for Derrida's
work as a whole.[13] In this broader context, *différance* is not merely
Derrida's stylized substitute for Heidegger's *Sein*. While Heidegger is
concerned to reach outside of the temporality of western ontotheology,
in order to think the radical essence of Being, Derrida argues that this
gesture places thought even more firmly within the confines of the
tradition it would dismantle. Derrida's aim is not *destruktion* in this
sense but rather what he calls (in "Ousia and Gramme" and *of
Grammatology*) "de-sedimentation." To be blunt: clearing a space for
the other is a matter of stirring things up. Why any Marxist would
reject this I do not know.

I will discuss the politics of de-sedimentation further. However, beyond the charge that Derrida accomplishes no more than a "French"
("warm-blooded"?) rewriting of Heidegger—beyond a certain point
one wants to answer this charge with one word: Read!—let me deal
with the third claim that Callinicos presents in his critique of Derrida's
supposed aestheticism, namely, Derrida's preoccupation with style. The
claim is that Derrida's only concern is with the style of other writers
and with creating his own style. This claim raises the question of genre.

Derrida is undeniably engaged with the question of style. In concluding "The Ends of Man," he remarks upon the "dominant style" of
thought in France today—"today" meaning the autumn of 1968, the
aftermath of the events of May. This style, which I would identify
with Sartre, though Derrida does not explicitly make this attribution,
Derrida contrasts to another, "that of the Heideggerian questions."
Interestingly, he refers to both styles as forms of deconstruction. Derrida
calls for "a new writing," one that "must weave and interlace these
two motifs of deconstruction." Capping this line of analysis (other
dimensions of which I pursue in *Matrix and line*, Chap. 2), Derrida
claims that "what we need, perhaps, as Nietzsche said, is a change of
'style'; and if there is style, Nietzsche reminds us, it must be plural"
(p. 135).

Perhaps I tend to read these lines too "straightforwardly," or at least
to want such a reading that might need to be complicated further, but
it seems to me that Derrida is calling here for a style of thought and a
kind of writing that allows the interweaving of critical thoughts, methodologies, questions, and practices, an interweaving that aims at
answering the question given in the penultimate sentence of the essay, "Is there an economy of the eve?" The reference becomes clearer,

though never absolutely clear (nor could there or should there be such "clarity"), in the context of the final lines of the essay:

> Must one read Nietzsche, with Heidegger, as the last of the great metaphysicians? Or, on the contrary, are we to take the question of the truth of Being as the last sleeping shudder of the superior man? Are we to understand the eve as the guard mounted around the house or as the awakening to the day that is coming, at whose eve we are? is there an economy of the eve?
>
> Perhaps we are between these two eves, which are also two ends of man. But who, we?

May 12, 1968 (p. 136)

Are we to understand the eve as that which stands guard against the appearance of the other or as that appearance itself? Is the eve the final, completing motion of the humanist project or does it portend the opening to another project? What is it to be between eves? I would say that it is to be in the space of the transformation of humanism.

But who, we? For the end of man was set, by Kant, Hegel, and other formulators of a universal human project, first of all for European man. All humankind might be heading toward the end of man, but in this race, so to speak, European man is destined to arrive first, to be the first true man.

But Derrida complicates this race and the idea of its completion. Why the resistance to this complexification? Is it simply because complexity speaks the language of "style"? But what other language could be spoken here? For the question is one of genres, of the supposed purity of genres, of some imperative to not mix genres. One can already hear the objections to this line of reasoning, which takes us to Derrida's essay, "The Law of Genre": the orthodox Marxist response would be that we are not simply afloat in the universe of discourse here, there are material grounds of genres. It is commonly taken by orthodox Marxists or others who believe that deconstruction is just an excuse to play around (sometimes the line of reasoning is employed precisely by these more "playful" deconstructionists) that Derrida is somehow unaware of the claims of materiality. On the contrary, it is in the attempt to grasp the materiality of "the law of the law of genre" that Derrida materializes genre's necessary impurity and contamination.

Perhaps this point can be best brought out by testing what would seem to be its contrary. What would it take for the law of genre to rule as "imperiously" (Derrida's word, "The Law of Genre," p. 225) as "the guard mounted around the house"? What measures would have to be taken against contamination? The resonation of "imperious" with

imperialism is not accidental. What is the "style" of this singular human project, this humanism? Is the style singular or plural—in other
words, if there is any energy left to the universal human project conceived by Kant, if there is any inspiration in reading again the texts of
that project (especially in Kant's post-critical work), we must ask if
there is any more an inspiration to be found in the sense of universal
as uniform, as the establishment of a singular genre of "man." Is this
the "end of man," the only end of man?

This is the genre question that more orthodox forms of Marxism
(Callinicos's analysis is hardly the worst) has yet to confront. I am not
entirely sure that the answers will come from Derrida, but then, it is
the mark of orthodoxy that there must always be immediate answers,
sometimes before there are even questions. (Lenin once said, incidentally, that we—we communists—would do well to come up with a
good question.)

This formulation from Derrida's essay, "White Mythology," is a challenge and a question to Marxism (and to Kant and Hegel):

> Metaphysics—the white mythology which reassembles and reflects
> the culture of the West: the white man takes his own mythology,
> Indo-European mythology, his own *logos*, that is, the *mythos* of his
> idiom, for the universal form of that he must still wish to call Rea-
> son. Which does not go uncontested. (p. 213)

Now, a clever rejoinder to this formulation might be to say that Marx
was never so concerned with "Reason," that for him the more fundamental category is "practice." Well and good, this is an advance in
my view. But, how do diverse practices (and their governing laws)
become one practice, one practice of humanity? Should such diverse
practices become a single practice? Isn't it the bourgeois epoch and
the international market that create the reduction of all quality to
quantity such that a single practice can emerge?

Derrida's work, especially concerning genre, raises this question and
provides useful formulations for pursuing the question—without an
answer. Is Derrida concerned with universality as it has been conceived in the West? He says that he is, in texts as diverse as *of Spirit*
and *The Other Heading*. What sort of universalism? One possibility,
which is not in the spirit of "impossibility" as Derrida uses the term,
but rather the agent of counter-possibility, is universalism as the im-
position of a single "style." Derrida rejects this "possibility" that is
the cancellation of possibility. Where Derrida cannot give an "answer"
to the question of a different universalism is where he also provides a
model of "the fold." The "edge, borderline, boundary, and overflow-

ing . . . do not arise without a fold" ("The Law of Genre," p. 235).

It is not a matter of "leveling the genre distinction," as Habermas charges. Callinicos agrees with the charge—so does Rorty, for that matter, but he likes the idea. Earlier I discussed Derrida's interrogation of the reason of reason; Derrida is also interested in questioning the genre of genre:

> The genre has always in all genres been able to play the role of order's principle: resemblance, analogy, identity and difference, taxonomic classification, organization and genealogical tree, order of reason, order of reasons, sense of sense, truth of truth, natural light and sense of history. (p. 252)

Derrida's concern is not so much that there are different genres—of writing, of living—but that to question the fixed boundaries and to raise the possibility of folds seems so problematic, an opening to madness, to irrationality. This must be kept at bay, on some other shore, at all costs. But: 1) What is the cost?—and what is the cost of not asking, as Callinicos and Habermas do not ask—what the political import of interrogating the genre of genre might be? 2) Is this madness, this other of reason, simply an invention of the clever Professor Derrida, who in one blow will bring down all of the hallowed distinctions upon which political modernity and Enlightenment rationality rest?

Derrida addresses the most urgent political questions in an often less than urgent way. One may question this strategy and its occasional tendency to go off into what seems to be sheer aestheticism. I find the strategy to be not so different from that deployed by Adorno, who also had some strong aestheticist tendencies. Perhaps it is simply wrong, and I mean this in an ethical as well as a strategic sense, to give in to this pleasure of the text. Perhaps it is simply fiddling while Rome burns. But I do not think so. Against the ungenerous reading of Callinicos, I would recommend finding four merits to Derrida's strategy (this does not mean that I find these merits present in equal measure in all of Derrida's diverse texts). First, what appears in some cases as aestheticism might also be taken as a demonstration of Adorno's ideal of the autonomous work of art. That is, Derrida's texts resist the immediate commodification and assimilation that sucks in most straightforwardly intended artifacts of the culture of resistance and rebellion. In a culture in which commodity logic has taken hold of even the material of everyday language, to work at the limits of meaning can be an important means for radical questioning. Of course, any Marxism that does things by the numbers and is so occupied by positivism itself is unlikely to see the merit of this approach.

Second, Derrida is, if anything, too analytical at times, giving in too much to the violence of abstraction. Or so it seems. The truth is that any commentator on Derrida's work, pro or con, and including myself, will tend to abstract from Derrida's work those passages where a thesis is being put forward. In fact, however, Derrida's theses are always fully interwoven with narratives that tend to demonstrate the materiality of language and the impossibility of laying down the law of genre. Derrida provides these material demonstrations with the intention, I think, of also showing the undesirability of laying down this law. Without really reading Derrida's texts, but instead always and only abstracting from them a set of neo-Kantian or neo-Nietzschean/ Heideggerian theses, this materiality is covered over. It is highly significant, crucially significant, that this covering can only occur through the reestablishment of the law of genre, especially through enacting a sharp distinction between the literary and philosophical "uses" of language. Fearing madness, perhaps in this reenactment we cut ourselves off from thinking the profundity of practice and materiality.

Third, what of these "theses," which do not seem immediately available for appropriation by the classical Marxist framework? If Derrida is too "idealist" for Callinicos and many other more orthodox Marxists, why are they not able to suspend the rush to judgment for long enough to imagine that Derrida might stand to contemporary Marxism (the best of it, that is, not purely dogmatic calculation) as Hegel did to Marx? Is there not a dialectic here to be grappled with? When did Marxism ever replenish itself with other "materialisms," classically understood? Marx did not look to Hobbes, he looked to Hegel and the German idealist tradition. It is a big mistake to think that the book is closed on the history of that dialectic.

Fourth, taking one "thesis" in particular, and thinking in terms of the three merits of Derrida already enumerated, we might attempt to think of the relation of the fold and the opening created by questioning the genre of genre, especially in terms of the genre of all genres, the European idea of "man." We might do this—I think that we have to do it.

But I have no desire to write as uncharitably of Callinicos as he does of Derrida. Although I have serious reservations about a theory that steps back from the seeming abyss of postmodernism only in order to make arguments for "radicalized Enlightenment",[14] I am generally sympathetic to Callinicos's final words:

Unless we work towards the kind of revolutionary change which would allow the realization of [human potentials unleashed by modern society] in a transformed world, there is little left for us to do, except, like Lyotard and Baudrillard, to fiddle while Rome burns. (p. 174)[15]

Of course, there will be those "practical" souls who will say that all philosophical and theoretical work nowadays consists in such fiddling. (I should point out, by the way, that the choice of metaphor is itself somewhat indicative of the Eurocentrism of Trotskyism and radical democracy; if we are communists and internationalists, isn't it our work to see that "Rome" burns? And that something quite unlike "Rome" is built in its place?) Clearly Callinicos is not saying this, though that will not stop certain kinds of postmodernists from claiming that he is. Such claims of reductionism have become a chief ploy in the strategy of those postmodernists who have no perceptible (even in the most charitable reading) orientation toward transformative social practice. This detachment, part of postmodern fascinations, is itself the true and most dangerous reduction. Against the logic of pure fascination, the import of deconstruction must be that it helps in the work of imagining and building the polis beyond the logic of the same.

I have numerous disagreements with Callinicos's interpretation of both Marxism and deconstruction. Perhaps these disagreements come down to one thing. Callinicos argues that postmodernism reflects the failed aspirations of 1968. Derrida's formative work, of course, predates May 1968, but I have no great difficulty with seeing him as part of the 68 generation. I wonder, however, if what might set Derrida's work and my own articulation of Marxism and deconstruction apart from Callinicos's interpretation is the idea that 1968 was not a failure.

The world's one and only idea

We read not only that Derrida is not political, but, on the contrary, that he is the arch-politician of our time, the source of an all-out attack on the West. Again we are in the company of the painstaking close-readers (there's that sarcasm again). Perhaps the best thing to do is to set aside the polemics and the polemical tone, for I do not want to have to say again the names of these anti-PC warriors who have no arguments, whose works are not published, publicized, and debated on television and in other channels of the corporate media because of the unforced force of reason. Well, they are waging a war of sorts, they have even called for a Gulf War against "enemies at home," and some of them have identified Professor Derrida as the source of all the trouble. But, let me leave that polemic for another day, yesterday, simply marking here the danger, indeed, the threat, that is posed by the question of the heading of the other. Even the posing of the question is a danger to some. That Europe's "eyes" (Derrida again cites Valery on the "face" of Europe, and, pursuing the image, says that this *cap*, this cape or head, "also has eyes, it is turned on one side, and it scans the horizon, keeping watch in a determined direction") look out onto a West which is indeed the not-West-which-becomes-West-for-having-been-seen-by-the-West (seen, that is, by the idea of Europe) conjures a troubling scene for the keepers of the monoculture. Elsewhere, Derrida refers to "Islamic memories" and the uncertain borders of Europe. Clearly these are troubling images from a political perspective that fears "contamination" above all.

In a sense, and under a reading that has to be called Hegelian (and which is fully amenable to Hegelian and Marxist ways of thinking, at least where these forms of thought remain critical), much of Derrida's writing, including *The Other Heading*, says the following. The world has only had one idea, and that is the idea of Europe. Or, with a different emphasis, we might say that the first and only idea to become a world idea has been the idea of Europe. Now that idea seems to be in a state of exhaustion. The question is whether the world can come up with another idea. Where will this idea come from? Derrida's answer, and his contribution, is to say that this idea can only come from the one idea that we already have, but that this "new" idea must come from the margins of this "old" idea. (Put this way, if the formulation is correct, it may be interesting to ask whether the anti-PC trend is afraid of Derrida because they do not understand him or because they do.)

But this is not "the question facing us." There is the further question, but perhaps it is the first question, the question before the question, of the singularity of this "idea," whether it is the only idea that we have—we who are defined by having only had this idea—or if it is some "other idea." We have to interrogate not only the singularity of the idea, but, crucially, we must even more interrogate the politics of the question which only asks after the possibility of a singular "other" idea. But this is to interrogate this "we" who quests always after singularity.

When Derrida asks to what real individual the name Europe might be assigned today, he is speaking Hegelian. Unlike Hegel, Derrida is not confident that we can name this individual, nor can we see its face, nor can we be sure of its persona. Something new is happening, but there is also a feeling of being very old. "We are younger than ever, we Europeans, since a certain Europe does not yet exist." Hegel might have said that, he might have remarked that the day was just beginning for Europe. But Hegel would not say what Derrida must say: "We are like these young people who get up, at dawn, already old and tired." I suppose that there might be two kinds of young people that Derrida could have in mind; either children of poverty, who must get up early and work long hours every day, or children who are tired from having too much—too much wealth, television, drugs, etc. Derrida says of the "young-old Europe," "we are already exhausted." I believe that he must have the latter group of young people in mind; to put it bluntly, the jaded. Europe is a jaded society. So that Europe (and the well-off children of the industrialized world) can be jaded from having had too much, there are children tired from long hours and malnutrition who live and work on other shores. There is, to speak Marxist, a dialectical relationship between "these young people," these young-old-tired Europeans and these young-old-tired laboring people from another shore. Something called Critical Theory, in dancing around the question of imperialism and even what was already basic in *Capital*, has not always done such a good job of showing the relation of these two poles—so that Professor Rorty can say that, contrary to Adorno, it isn't domination that we are talking about but some other relation.

But keeping this relationship in mind, a relationship that must be described in terms of political economy as well as in other terms if it is to be understood with any degree of specificity, we understand, to speak Derridean, that to frame the relationship in terms that are either Eurocentric or anti-Eurocentric will not do justice to either the idea of Europe or the new idea which the world has not yet had. When Derrida refers to "the exhausted programs of *Eurocentrism* and *anti-Eurocentrism*," his line of reasoning must be understood on two levels. First, and perhaps more clearly, the program of anti-Eurocentrism simply reinscribes the terminology of Eurocentrism. With such reinscription as the primary strategy, Eurocentrism is unbeatable. However, the more difficult point is to grasp that, on the one hand, there is no "new" idea which is simply "not" the idea of Europe, and, on the other hand, the "new" idea must be an idea that already exists in the margins of the only idea that we have already had. And, again, if this idea is singular (recall here the remark about plurality of styles in the final part of "The Ends of Man") then, whatever claim it may have to anti- or non-Eurocentrism, it is, all the same, European to the core. Derrida believes that it is a very dangerous thing, with the possibility of the most violent consequences, to simply lunge toward what appears to be the "wholly other" of Europe and its idea. The point, as I will take it even if many of Derrida's interpreters will not, is that this attempted radicality simply reinscribes the most violent aspects of exhausted Eurocentrism. Unfortunately, it must be said, that this fact never takes the onus from Eurocentrism, never licenses a new (old, exhausted, but propped up for one more performance) Eurocentrism.

If I may advance a thesis here purely for the purpose of provocation: perhaps the Khmer Rouge strategy is an example of such an anti-Eurocentrism, one that remains singular and tied to the exhaustions of Europe. This strategy was refracted through Marxism, which can hardly break free of its roots in the European idea, but perhaps that also contributed to a kind of double-bind that must necessarily accompany the attempt to constitute ourselves—whoever "ourselves" happen to be, but the point is that in some fundamental sense ourselves will be European—as "universal men," while at the same time attempting an absolute break with the European idea. The case of the Khmer Rouge is complex. I have just now given one reason why it cannot be separated entirely from the idea of Europe; there is another reason, however, that returns me to the question of a dialectical relationship of the shores, namely, the destruction of agriculture in the Kampuchean countryside by the United States. This line of thinking, which brings together deconstruction and political economy, needs to be further developed. Here I would also have to develop questions of agriculture more generally and the question of the relationship between city and countryside in particular.[16] Derrida remarks that "the feeling of being 'men of universality' is not reserved for the French. Not even, no doubt, for Europeans." What if, for example, people in the Andes felt themselves to be universal men? What if a person in the Andes woke up one morning and said, "I am universal man"? We have not even begun to think the possibilities, but I believe that what Derrida provides in *The Other Heading*, but also in his earlier work, is the basis for at least an opening to such a thinking.

The scene is more complex. Europe is exhausted, it is jaded, but in some respects its idea is still young and not tired. The idea of Europe still has some energy. Derrida speaks of "the emancipation of responsibility," in the context of asking, "What if Europe were this: the opening onto a history for which the changing of the heading, the relation to the other heading or to the other of the heading is experienced as always possible?" In formulating his question in this way, Derrida is not reaching for some "wholly other," he is attempting to find a space for the other through refolding our "old" idea, the idea of Europe, which is, by another name, the idea of responsibility. The question is, Can this responsibility be emancipated? This now becomes the European question. I am heartened by the fact that political reactionaries find this a dangerous question, even though no question could be more European.

The irony, then, is that Derrida represents the threat of multiculturalism primarily by calling Europe to a new responsibility to itself, to its idea. How is it that the "new traditionalists," the cultural conservatives, perceive this threat? First of all it must be in terms of Derrida's questioning of capital, for here two essential questions come together: the question of the head, and even of the avant-garde, and the question of the hand, that is, the invisible hand. The new traditionalists, after all, are for the most part neo-conservatives, which is to say, they are not concerned so much with culture as with the dominance of a particular culture. They are concerned to maintain the dominance of *one* culture. This, with absolutely no question, is one aspect of the European idea, one aspect of the "universality" of humanism. (Leave aside, for now, the not inconsiderable fact that neo-conservatives typically attack "secular humanism.") The neo-conservatives have severed the question of culture, about which they are not particularly interested after all, from the question of dominance, about which they are very interested.

In this light, let me turn to Derrida's remarks concerning the "traditional discourse of modernity." Again I am in the vicinity of a politics of speed, for when Derrida refers to the "old modern Europe" he evokes the fact that modernity became old before its time, before the time of a Europe that has yet to be born. Modernism speeds up the aging process. But let me resist, for now, the headlong rush toward a frenzied politics, and focus instead on the irony of the term the modern tradition. Sooner or later there would have to be a tradition of the new, which is to say a tradition of anti-tradition. But clearly this is a moment of exhaustion. What is striking is that there are at least two forms of the exhaustion of modernity, one capitalist, the other Marxist, both with a certain fetish for progress, originality, and the new. In the European context (but not in the larger world) the Marxist anti-tradition found itself exhausted by the capitalist anti-tradition, to the point where the orthodoxy of eastern Europe became indistinguishable from the capitalist orthodoxy of western Europe. This transformation of the one anti-tradition into a mirror of the other, with the chief difference being that there were, until recently, two heads of capital in Europe, passed through a fundamental moment of rupture when Khrushchev made rising living standards, and not the self-emancipation of the masses, the sine qua non of socialism. Wherever this point of rupture is not recognized, analysis seems to devolve into a much too general discussion about "totalitarianism." Derrida's analysis in *The Other Heading*, and sometimes in other places, is in danger of such a de-evolution, even as Derrida gives us the conceptual tools for analyzing the question and the possibility of violent totalizations. (Here is another possible meeting place of Derrida and Adorno, but more work is needed to achieve an articulation that has a real edge, an Adornian edge.)

For example, Derrida remarks that, in 1939, Europe felt "the *imminence* of a tremor that was not only going to reduce to rubble Europe in the name of an idea of Europe . . . ." Derrida goes on to say that

> the "Western Democratic" nations, in their turn, and in the name of another idea of Europe, prevented a certain European unification by destroying Nazism, allied as they were for a limited but decisive time to the Soviet Union.

A few things are far from clear here. Was there really another European idea that constituted itself against the Nazi vision of a new Europe? It was perhaps Stalin and Georgi Dimitrov who argued most forcefully for the idea that there was a fundamental difference between the fascist countries and the "bourgeois democracies," even as the latter capitulated one after another to Hitler and maneuvered in various ways to ensure that the main thrust of the Wehrmacht was aimed at the Soviet Union. This is one of the great ironies of history, Stalin's and Dimitrov's "deviation" from Marxism on this point. Where, however, was the other (or another) idea of Europe, and what role did it play in the prevention of the Nazi unification? Was this idea present at Stalingrad, where the Wehrmacht decisively broke its back?

There, too, was real exhaustion, of a socialism that was never not embattled, that was already deformed by dogmatism (which, however, must be understood in all its historical complexity, without too quick recourse to the rhetoric of totalitarianism), that had come unstuck from the idea of the self-activity of the masses. Or, as Sartre put it, "Marxism stopped." To get the socialist project going again in the Soviet Union would have required another revolution, a revolution in the revolution, toward *this* idea of Europe: self-activity. Such a revolution was not forthcoming, not in the Soviet Union—but also, and decisively, not in the "Western democracies" either. The only "other" idea of Europe that seemed to emerge from the prevention of the Nazi unification of the cape (or camp) was the idea that capital would rule. The irony is that the energies of the then-socialist Soviet Union were spent so that capital could rule "democratically," while, on another level, a level that Stalin and Dimitrov would have grasped had Marxism not stopped for them, it is not absolutely clear that what began in 1933 ended in 1945.

And yet, Derrida is absolutely right to focus on the question of the idea of Europe which is, as he says, "in a constitutive way," the very idea of responsibility itself. This idea of Europe has yet to be born, even if it is foreshadowed in Kant, this little man of middle Europe with whom Derrida continues to wrestle. When Derrida remarks that Europe, but therefore also the world, has need of a "new culture," "one that would invent another way of reading and analyzing *Capital*, both Marx's book and capital in general," one thinks of a wrestling and a wrangling that is implicit in much of what Derrida writes, between two relationalities, one that is dialectical, the other which is other and partakes of something other, something incalculable. In other words, a wrestling and tangling of Marx and Kant. Only Europe can stage this match, but this is not to say that the match will not be staged on other shores. Or, I should say, the idea of Europe, this "new" idea of Europe, will necessarily take its heading from other shores.

When Gershwin and Stravinsky and others exploited the resources of jazz (I choose these words carefully), they were hailed by some for doing something new. What they did, however, was to incorporate the heading of the other, under the banner of the exotic, into the European idea (of music, but not only of music). Derrida's Europe as "the opening onto a history for which the changing of the heading, the relation to the other heading or to the other of the heading is experienced as always possible" must move to another rhythm, something qualitatively distinct from the emerging cultural esperanto of "world beat." There must be specificity beyond and fetish of the new and original. The anti-tradition of modernity, in its exhaustion, is giving way to a jaded, cynical, always already exhausted postmodernity. The neo-conservatives who despise Derrida in the name of tradition (a tradition they seem to know little about, either with regard to its still latent energies or its barbarous underside) are no less jaded, and a good deal more fearful of the future, even as they themselves amplify the frenzied march of the politics of speed.

Transparency

Re-enter Habermas, who could have easily written: "I do not believe that anyone has spoken seriously of public opinion without the model of parliamentary democracy and as long as an apparatus of laws did not permit or promise the formation, expression, and especially the 'publication' of this opinion *outside* of these political or corporative representations." Habermas would not, however, have written these words: "But everything that is not of the order of judgment, decision, and especially representation, escapes *both* present-day democratic institutions *and* public opinion as such." To continue in this way, as

Derrida does, would seem to place Habermas in a double-bind, except
that Habermas does not accept the terms of the second quotation.
Habermas might accept Derrida's continuation of the first quotation,
where he remarks that the politics of speed, in the form of "a zone
that is being extended and differentiated today in an accelerated way,"
poses "serious questions about the present functioning, if not the very
principles, of liberal democracy." Derrida would reject, however,
Habermas's solution to this problem, which I will now turn to under
the rubric of the question of transparency. I think it important that we
set up an engagement of the two most important minds of Europe on
the way toward (I still resist the fevered rush) our encounter with the
politics of speed. A comparison of the ideas of Habermas and Derrida
is one form of the comparison of the only two ideas that we have, an
exhausted idea of Europe which can genuinely claim to know no other
idea (and so we'd best make do) and a yet to be born idea whose
music can only be heard in the margins. Both ideas, which is now to
say, both Habermas and Derrida, wrestle with Kant.

Here is Habermas's idea, as presented by Derrida:

> Under the pretext of pleading for transparency (along with "con-
> sensus," "transparency" is one of the master words of the "cultural"
> discourse I just mentioned), for the univocity of democratic discus-
> sion, for communication in public space, for "communicative action,"
> such a discourse tends to impose a model of language that is sup-
> posedly favorable to this communication. Claiming to speak in the
> name of intelligibility, good sense, common sense or the democratic
> ethic, this discourse tends, by means of these very things, and as if
> naturally, to discredit anything that complicates this model. It tends
> to suspect or repress anything that bends, overdetermines, or even
> questions, in theory or in practice, this idea of language. With this
> concern, among others, in mind, it would be necessary to study cer-
> tain rhetorical norms which dominate analytic philosophy or what
> is called in Frankfurt "transcendental pragmatics."

In many respects, Derrida and Habermas do not seem so far apart in
the political positions that they take, which are usually to be found
somewhere in the spectrum from liberal democratic to radical democratic. And yet, in speaking of "everything that is not of the order of
the judgment, decision, and especially representation," Derrida must,
to be consistent, challenge a certain model of language that is now
common to both positivism and Habermas. This model seems so harmless, so innocuous, so common-sensical (perhaps, however, it is a peculiarly positivistic, and perhaps even peculiarly "English" mistake to
equate common sense with the *sensus communis*) that it is rarely brought

to the surface as a model, much less compared to another conception. This is the model of language as communication and as medium. Derrida fundamentally rejects this model, though he does not reject the idea that there is communication, however problematized by his own work, and it is only in this rejection that Habermas has recently taken up the defense of this model as a model (in *Philosophical Discourse of Modernity* and other recent texts). Prior to the "Heideggerian" challenge, Habermas did not recognize that there was any other way of conceiving of language, and therefore there was for him no "model" of language, only "language."

Here the conflict (which I analyze at length in *Matrix and line*, Chap. 3) can only be presented in condensed form. For Habermas, the essence of communication is the "validity claim," a sentence to which one can say either yes or no. All other forms of language use are parasitic upon the validity claim. Habermas is after the traditional virtues of the anti-metaphysical program, as set out, for example, by Rudolf Carnap in "The Elimination of Metaphysics through Logical Analysis of Language." These virtues are especially those of logical transparency (that is, our sentences are not permitted to play tricks with syntax) and a procedure for determining the truth of assertoric sentences. For Carnap, the procedure is empirical verification, while Habermas opts for the broader (Popperian) criterion of requiring that assertions be, in principle, subject to falsification. For Habermas, the idea is that, with decision procedures based on transparency and the principle of falsifiability, consensus can be reached by means of the unforced force of reason, and therefore the autonomy of all members of the speech community can be respected and taken into account. For both Carnap and Habermas, the enemy is Heideggerian obscurantism, and there is little appreciation for the idea that Heidegger was after a truth that is obscure, indeed, that is obscured by the reductionism proffered by Carnap and Habermas.

Both Carnap and Habermas see great danger in the sort of thinking and language use offered by Heidegger. They are not wrong, I think, to see this danger. Habermas's solution, however, is to argue for what he sees as a politics without danger. Furthermore, Habermas sees the prerequisites for his ideal speech situation already present in the parliamentary democracies of western Europe; indeed, everything is already present in these democracies. Nothing remains to be invented.

In this context, perhaps it could only be the act of a massive dissimulation to offer, again, but now in the name of Heidegger, Hölderlin's famous dictum that "Where there is danger, there too the power of rescue grows." Still more would it be dissimulation to turn the dictum against Habermas, in the name of Heidegger, by saying, "Where there is no danger, there is no saving power either."

But it is not entirely clear that there is no danger to be found along the path of the ideal speech situation. I can think of three dangers in particular.

First, the "normal" functioning of the democratic systems that Habermas seeks to reform in the direction of the ideal speech situation is fraught with dangers for those pressed into the margins of society. One wonders, too, if the program of anti-Eurocentrism (in a more flatfooted sense) is exhausted in comparison with Habermas's exclusive focus on Europe, where there is no attention given to the heading of the other or the other of the heading. Thus the Gulf War, today's example, is considered in entirely Eurocentric terms.[17] Habermas wants most of all to avoid apocalyptic eruptions, in theory or in practice. There is no place in Habermas's thinking for the strategy of attempting "to change terrain, in a discontinuous and irruptive fashion, by brutally placing oneself outside, and by affirming an absolute break and difference." This strategy, which Derrida counterposes to a Heideggerian strategy of attempting "an exit and a deconstruction without changing terrain, by repeating what is implicit in the founding concepts and the original problematic," must necessarily fail. This strategy of discontinuity, discussed by Derrida in "The Ends of Man," is identified as "the one which dominates France today" and which I believe we are entitled to call Sartrean. This strategy, Derrida argues, cannot help but reinscribe "more naively and more strictly than ever" what "one declares one has deserted." And yet, Derrida does not reject this strategy but offers that the essence of deconstruction is the interweaving of the Heideggerian and Sartrean strategies. We cannot effect an absolute break, but we still must attempt to do this very thing. (We must attempt an impossible praxis.) Otherwise there is no possibility of encountering the other of the heading. This is a moment that does not exist for Habermas, nor, it must be said, for most Derrideans. (Perhaps I am wrong and willful in thinking that Sartre is present at the end of the essay, but I do not think so.) To think that there is no danger in avoiding apocalyptic discourse (the key references here are the anti-apocalyptic apocalyptic discourses of Derrida's "No Apocalypse, Not Now" and "Of an Apocalyptic Tone Recently Adopted in Philosophy") is the naivety, which becomes chauvinism, of thinking that there is no danger in a desert storm. One must wonder if Habermas is only thinking that there may be no danger to Europe. He may be right, there may be no practical, calculable, pressing reason to re-encounter Islamic memories, and therefore there may be no pressing, practical reason to work beyond the logic of decision and validity claims. Yes, he may be right that there is a kind of responsibility to Europe that sees no larger responsibility. And it is not hard to imagine a certain Heidegger agreeing on this point. This takes me back to the ethics of Eurocentrism discussed in Part 1. Is this ethics one destination of the adventures of immanence? Is the exhaustion of Europe the outcome of this adventure?

Second danger: What would it really take to instantiate something approaching the ideal speech situation, or at least to make qualitative progress toward that ideal? Given the force that capital is able to marshal on its side, can we really, decisively, break through to a situation in which reasonable discussion is conducted toward consensus formed through the unforced force of reason? Even assuming that we accept the ideal as Habermas formulates it, I think it naive in the extreme to think that, for example, and as Derrida puts it, "democracy without reciprocity" would give way to any substantive alternative without a real struggle. My term for Derrida's "democracy without reciprocity" is "anti-participatory democracy"; in either case we are talking about a "democracy" that is not about a society that is run by the people, a society that has as its foremost goal the elimination of structures and habits that treat people as means and not ends. I wonder if Habermas, as Kantian as he is at times, has not fundamentally given up on this goal of a participatory socialist society. He seems to accept that the complexification of society by advanced capitalism is simply a fact of social life, and therefore there is nothing to do but to inhabit the structures of techno-capital. The only struggle is between the more "democratic" and the more "dictatorial" technocrats. I suppose that there is no danger to the masses here, because people do not really fit into this equation.

For Derrida, the third danger is that we accept a certain conception of the ideal speech situation as the goal or at least as the regulative principle. This is the primary danger; for the long run, beyond the day which imposes itself as the measure of all things, Derrida is right about this. There is tremendous irony in the somewhat parallel Eurocentrisms of Habermas and Heidegger. There is a further irony in the somewhat parallel decisionisms of Habermas and Carl Schmitt. Derrida, in what may seem a cruel twist, remarks that Schmitt's "influence is still alive, whether he is cited or not, (on the) left and (on the) right, in every analysis of public space, for example in Habermas." Of course, Habermas rejects Schmitt's "right-Nietzschean" approach to the moment of decision that is created by the breakdown of parliamentary democracy (even while the right-Nietzscheans do everything in their power to ensure this breakdown). Habermas does not propose a left-Nietzchean alternative (I suppose he might apply this label, along with left-Heideggerian, to Derrida, but without seeing, fundamentally, what in Nietzsche and Heidegger Derrida is building upon). But to accept that language, which is to say, public discourse, which is to say, discourse, which is to say, communication, comes down to validity claims, is to accept the logic of decision in its most reductive form. Habermas accepts this reduction and takes it to be a virtue of his theory of communicative action, for it is in the reduction to validity claims that one finds the *telos* of language, the transcendental pragmatic structure of the necessity, on the whole, for speakers to attempt to advance the truth.

For Derrida, this is a part of what it means to "use language," although he speaks more of a promise than a truth claim. This is a larger difference than may be clear at first, since for Derrida, one can promise meaning but not absolutely guarantee its delivery, because language is not simply an object that language users can get a purchase on and deploy. Habermas has recently conceded that there is a "function" of language that may be called world disclosive, or poetic, but that this function is parasitic on the primary function of language, which, in Habermas's view, is pragmatic (see *Postmetaphysical Thinking*, p. 42). Of course, to define the poetic as a function is already to prejudice things in favor of Habermas's view. What follows from this view, among other things, is the idea that only those who accept the pragmatic function as primary have any possibility of offering a theory of language. Therefore, Habermas looks primarily to linguists (especially Chomsky) and analytic philosophers (especially speech act theorists) for a theory of language that can be incorporated into a larger, comprehensive theory of society. In this view, language is an activity that can be understood as a distinct human (or rational) function. Contrast this to the Heideggerian view that all human activities appear amid language. In this view, there is no separate sphere of intellectual inquiry called philosophy of language that can then be inserted into a general social theory. But neither is it correct, obviously, to say that only those who view language as fundamentally pragmatic have important things to say about language.

Habermas must be given his due, despite these criticisms, in leading social theory toward the linguistic turn. And yet, what he claims about language is problematic not only in itself but also, and this is the point that Derrida is driving at in his remarks on Habermas and the program of transparency, in its conception of the polis. What will be accepted as a validity claim, as something to which the language community can say yes or no? What is excluded by this procedure of yes or no? These questions bind the three dangers into one, perhaps even into Derrida's question, "What philosophy of translation will dominate in Europe?"

What, then, is Derrida up to when he says:

> If it had a proper place (but that is the whole question), public opinion would be the forum for a permanent and transparent discussion. It would be opposed to nondemocratic powers, but also to its own political representation. Such representation would never be adequate to it, for it breathes, deliberates, and decides according to other rhythms.

If I may be pardoned a massive summation, one might say that Derrida is making a move similar to the one at the close of "The Ends of Man." It is always a question of a double strategy. Derrida does not reject everything about the Habermasian program. If anything, Derrida requires the most radical reading of that program, always toward a radical democracy. But even radical democracy is not enough, for it can have the effect of simply reinstating, albeit in a radical form, the presuppositions of the already constituted polis, whereas Derrida evokes (for he cannot calculate) the polis that is responsive and responsible to and for the other of the heading, even the other of the radically democratic heading.

But here, even in view of the critique of calculation, and even more against the ethic of calculation, much remains to be said. Left in the form of an evocation, Derrida's formulation has some of the same problems found in the Bataillean "critique of project." The point which especially needs to be developed is that, in his formulation, Derrida is not simply counterposing representative democracy to "direct democracy," however radicalized either may be. No direct democracy, or rather, no democracy, however direct, can do without forms of representation, and it is the latter which must, transparently, remain open to critique. This, I hope it is clear, is a different ideal of transparency than that proposed by Habermas.

The age of speed

Derrida opens his "No Apocalypse, Not Now" with the words, "In the beginning, there will have been speed." In the first sentence of *The Other Heading*, Derrida is already worried about the spectacle (translated as "event") of the intellectual conference. There is a connection, a very close one, between the politics of speed and the spectacularization of even the obscure intellectual event, namely, compression into the moment and the rhythm of the moment, the collapsed time of what has yet to be born but which is already old and exhausted, the de-temporalized space of jaded society, the televisual "democratization" which "never represents without filtering or screening": there one has it, there one never has it, the onrush of flattened dots on the television screen, between channels.

The danger, too, of a left-Heideggerian politics falling into the spectacle of the momentary gesture, is readily apparent.

Has the rhythm of the day—by which is meant the tyrannical day, which cannot see beyond itself and cannot hear other rhythms, the day of the jet airplane and the global telecommunications network—always had as its destiny the rhythm, which cannot be a rhythm, of the singular moment? This day of the metropolis, which begins with the clock and the cannon? This Cartesian meditation without flesh, which cannot sing, which has no music?

"If this meeting had any chance of escaping repetition": not only the meeting at which Derrida first delivered *The Other Heading* but every meeting, every polis—if there is any chance to escape repetition, the always first time of the *cogito*, the inability to recognize or connect with any other moment, "it would only be insofar as some *imminence*, at once a chance and a danger, exerted pressure on us."

What imminence?

Derrida seems to rule out the possibilities that one might typically offer: either something we already know or something that we do not know. He is simultaneously suspicious of "the absolutely new" and of "repetitive memory," of *both* anamnestic capitalization *and* the amnesic exposure to what would no longer be identifiable at all." These possibilities (or counter-possibilities) leave us in the moment. Again there is need for a double strategy: there must be an "act of memory which consists in betraying a certain order of capital in order to be faithful to the other heading and to the other of the heading." (I take heart in this radicalization of memory which so troubles the neo-conservatives and their violently false sense of tradition.) This is an impossible strategy, beyond calculation, beyond "political science." The latter is perhaps the best organized academic attempt to legitimate a politics of the moment which is in turn founded upon the material basis of calculation (a basis in which people cannot be ends). If calculation is the best methodology in politics, whatever system calculates best is the best political system. In this respect, the professors of Marxism-Leninism of eastern Europe lost out to the political scientists of the West. The calculating contest was lost by eastern Europe, but in either *capital* the victory was one for calculation. A Marxism of calculation—

always a part of Marxism but not the only part and not the defining characteristic; the point is that in reversing the classical priority of ethics over politics Marx prepared the way for the eventual victory of calculation—has been defeated by calculation pure and simple. A new universalism is declared, and the crucial element in this declaration is speed.

Before you know it, the liberal tradition in politics is erased by economic calculation. Derrida wonders about the de-linkage of capital from capitals, transnational capital, on the one side, the metropolis, on the other. Arguing that "the question of the capital remains completely intact," Derrida asks whether the "old states" will help resist the aporia of "neither monopoly nor dispersion." This is a question where there is no substitute for specialized investigation in political economy, even if the other theoretical concerns raised by Derrida should never be too far away. It is not clear that capital has come unhinged from its traditional basis in nation states and their military machines. True enough, the old states may play some role in the resistance to the New World Order (a kind of world dictatorship of U.S. capital that is inherently unstable) where there is some possibility of the constitution of another capital, but in the name of what? Is "local control," meaning control by the old states, preferable to "remote control" (moving now to the media of speed politics)? Or, at any rate, are these the alternatives? Is the question simply at what pace we will run the speed race toward the politics of calculation? If so, then the old states have already lost, and the project of a polis with a different heading could only lose by joining in this race.

The alternative is the "experiment of the possibility of the impossible." But this must also be a race, a race against speed. What forms will it take? The question of the media is crucial. First, a comment about not playing the game of the market, which, in its complexification of the economy, necessitates every aspect of the speed race of feverish capital. We hear, incessantly, of the "resurgence of the right." A friend of mine who is a political activist commented recently, "Yes, there is a resurgence of the right, it's on the left." There are many aspects of this resurgence of the right, but, at the expense of angering some who still consider themselves on the left, I want to point to "market socialism" as one of the key aspects. It is often pointed out that the first experiment in planned socialist economy, in the Soviet Union, involved an economy in which there was a need to plan the production and distribution of about 300 items. The champions of the market, right or left, point out how much more complex the economy is today, when we are talking about thousands of items. They never seem to question

whether this complexity itself could be the problem. Their only question, even if from a left perspective, is whether we can get up to speed
with this complexity. We have to wonder, however, what is destroyed,
in humanity and in the environment as a whole, by this speed race
and the acceptance of it as the sole arbiter of value.

If asking such questions makes me a Luddite, then so be it.

It is against this "realism," this conception of the "possible," that
Derrida supplies some conceptual tools.

Nowhere is the dominance of speed more apparent than in the workings of the media, which is simultaneously an extension of the speed
race of feverish capital and the organizing force of the inhabitants of
the race. Derrida criticizes as "naive and crude" the view that public
opinion is simply "produced" or "formed" or "influenced" by newspapers (the rhythm of the day) and the electronic media (the rhythm
of the moment), even when he goes on to speak that language himself. There is, here as well, a double-bind of the "public" of public
opinion: on the one side, the resistance that is constituted by the marginal (im)possibility of responsibility, which is to say by personhood
in the Kantian sense; on the other side, the reconstitution of that ability to respond in the asymmetry of a media predicated on the absence
of the right to respond.

Perhaps Derrida sees this reconstituted responsibility in the possibility of the telephone:

> We know that a totalitarian system can no longer effectively fight
> against an internal telephone network once its density has exceeded
> a certain threshold, thereby becoming uncontrollable. Indeed, no "mod-
> ern" society (and modernity is an imperative for totalitarianism) can
> refuse for very long to develop the technico-economico-scientific serv-
> ices of the telephone—which is to say, the "democratic" places of
> connection appropriate to operating its own destruction.

I wonder if Derrida is a bit optimistic here; it depends, I suppose, on
what counts as totalitarianism and what counts as its destruction. Suppose
one sees the reconstitution of a public sphere in eastern Europe through
the use of the telephone. Then we might report, optimistically, that
there is a reconstitution of responsibility even in the technical apparatus established at first to destroy all autonomy. Well and good, and I
have nothing against optimism. What, then, are we to make of the
western democracies, where there are plenty of telephones (and fax
machines, photocopiers, etc.) but the public sphere has been effectively
"malled," that is, reduced to the consumer paradise of the shopping
mall, where, in the United States, oppositional political speech is pro-

hibited. Derrida himself, with regard to the "free press," asks how this freedom is actually a name for censorship. How does the telephone, especially, provide an opening for the overcoming of techno-capital? Derrida hints that the telephone erases the barrier between public and private. I'm skeptical or, at least, I wonder if this erasure is a good thing. There are also the issues of atomization and surveillance. Is there really any community in AT&T's advertising slogan of "worldwide telecommunity"? Perhaps there is only that community which exists as the underside of techno-capital, a responsibility that is invoked even in the asymmetry of corporate power and the denial of the right to respond, a responsibility that, ironically, makes advertising slogans which invoke community appealing. That is something, it is real, it is where responsibility finds itself today. I am just unsure about the role of the telephone here, and I suspect that Avital Ronell (*The Telephone Book*) may be on to something when she says that when we answer the telephone we say yes to fascism.

About the main point I am more sure. Derrida is enthusiastic about the telephone because with it there is some possibility of response and reciprocity. These are the main issues at stake, which cannot be resolved primarily through technical means. The example of the telephone is representative of an overflow of desire toward and for the other. Meanwhile, however, in the today of the West, Derrida emphatically notes that "the right of response hardly exists." Derrida asks,

> Why does one so often pretend (a fiction *of* democracy) to ignore the violence of this dissymmetry, along with what can or cannot be reduced in it? Why the hypocrisy, the denial or the blindness before the all-too-evident? Why is this "all-too-evident" at once as clear as the light of day and the most nocturnal face of democracies as they are, *presently*?

It is difficult not to call the tone of these questions prophetic. Reading these questions in this way, I return to a passage a few pages before the one just quoted, where Derrida asks, "Is the power of the media unlimited?" His answer, I hope, can be read in light of a militant responsibility: "Untimely developments that escape its [the media's] grid of readability might one day take over without any resistance at all."

From another shore, I also wonder about the institution of the journalism school, despite the fact that, in the form familiar in the United States, it does not exist in western Europe. But the nature of the speed race, especially its new form, the New World Order, is that we can safely predict *USA Today, Europe Tomorrow*. To know what journalism schools will be like in Europe tomorrow, one need only look at them in the United States today, where critical thinking is exactly what students are taught not to engage in, and where journalism schools are the home base, generally, for advertising departments—advertising being an academic discipline. That is, unless untimely developments intervene.

When Derrida argues, therefore, that "democracy's most precious good," "freedom of the press," "remains to be invented," "and democracy along with it," we must wonder if this "remaining to be invented" is not at the same time a place of hope, for the right of response and for a fundamental responsibility, as well as a rhetoric which both gives rise to and comforts the jaded society. After all, the Gulf War resurrects the idea of a war to make the world safe for democracy, especially for a cynical democracy that incorporates the media apparatus fully within its cynicism. We must get up to speed with the politics of speed, but only in order to create a different conception of the polis. To invent the freedom of the press, the "free press" will have to be destroyed. This is not a call for terrorism, but we must be clear that to inhabit the media, even "critically," is overwhelmingly to play into the logic of the politics of speed. This is not a call for terrorism but for the right of response. The right of response is a right but it is also, insofar as it partakes of a more fundamental responsibility, beyond calculation and the mechanisms of calculation, not something to be abandoned to the fates set for it by those mechanisms. We cannot take our responsibilities lightly nor let them fall prey to fascination with the spectacle. The right of response is a special kind of right, beyond but not precluding radical democracy, conferring responsibility beyond calculation.

An impossible praxis

Throughout *The Other Heading*, Derrida stresses a double imperative which is, strictly speaking, impossible. First, the old idea of Europe cannot be simply abandoned, on this shore or any other, while, at the same time, the exhaustion of Europe necessitates a reinvention of this idea and a rigorous listening and opening for the other of the heading, the idea that the world must now invent. On the one hand, borders and differences should not be cultivated for their own sakes. On the other hand, "it is necessary to make sure that a centralizing hegemony (the capital) not be reconstituted." It is worth repeating, at some length, the description that Derrida gives to the general, but impossible, law of this "double contradictory imperative":

Responsibility seems to consist today in renouncing neither of these two contradictory imperatives. One must therefore try to *invent* gestures, discourses, politico-institutional practices which inscribe the alliance of these two imperatives, of these two promises or contracts: the capital and the a-capital, the other of the capital. That is not easy. It is even impossible to conceive of a responsibility that consists in being responsible *for* two laws, or that consists in responding *to* two contradictory injunctions. No doubt. But there is no responsibility that is not the experience and the experiment of the impossible.

Derrida goes on to compare this double responsibility to "a responsibility [that] is exercised in the order of the possible," which makes of action the applied consequence. I am struck by the way that Derrida radically reconstitutes Kantian ethics in the wake of the European idea. Then comes the most difficult question:

Nevertheless, one will always be able *de jure* to ask what an ethics or a politics that measures responsibility only by the rule of the impossible can be: as if doing only what were possible amounted to abandoning the ethical and political realms, or as if, inversely, in order to take an authentic responsibility it were necessary to limit oneself to impossible, impractical, and inapplicable decisions.

Derrida writes, then, against the *de jure*, the legal, order of the day, which demands only the possible. For Derrida to raise the possibility of an ethics and a politics oriented otherwise, to the impossible, places him again squarely in the tradition of what two of France's leading cynics have termed 68 Thought.

Kant might also have written, "Be reasonable, demand the impossible!"

This may seem a naive, hopeful, and nostalgic place to end the discussion. I hope not too naive; a bit nostalgic, yes, for the last time the world was shaken up by the impossible, the struggle of other voices to be heard despite the anti-rhythms of the day (I miss the music, too, the attempt at its cooptation in the name of the Big Chill notwithstanding); and there can be nothing but hope for what, after today, will be born.

Afterword

Destinations after Europe (and points for further research and discussion)

To what extent does coappearance resemble the character of a coincidence, a contingency? Perhaps it will seem too much of a coincidence for the reader to believe true: on the day when I wrote the words (in Part 3), "What if a person in the Andes woke up one morning and said, 'I am universal man'," I see on the ABC Evening News that Abimael Guzman has been captured by the Peruvian government. I felt as if I had been struck by lightning. From that day, Sunday, September 13, 1992—Dr. Guzman was actually captured the day before—until early November I was unable to work on this book. I could not stick to my schedule for intellectual production because I had things to do. My work as a radical intellectual—essentially reading, writing, teaching, "conferencing"—was seriously disrupted. It was like being on a roller coaster: little sleep, much work, lots of meetings. I am used to these things, but at that point the genres of intellectual work and political activism were mixed to what seemed an untenable degree. The temptation to reinvoke the law of genre ran strong.

What is it to be a radical intellectual? The term radical, has been much abused in recent years—it has become innocuous. Attempting to think in terms of a practice that comes before ontology, to give a Levinasian gloss on a Marxist claim, it is tempting to hold that radical is as radical does. Fortunately, things are not that simple, and much of the argument of this text has been directed at countering this and other pieces of instrumental reasoning. "Radical is as radical does" leaves little space for thinking the polis. If one purpose of this book has been to conceive of that thinking itself as a practice and as always necessarily interwoven with practice(s), this orientation has not been meant as any sort of rapprochement with political pragmatism.

In the last days of October 1992, I joined a delegation of five others to go to Lima, in order to shine the light of bad publicity on the Peruvian government. At the first public appearance of the delegation, a press conference, we were surrounded by machine-gun-carrying soldiers of the Peruvian National Police, detained and interrogated by "anti-terrorism experts" for about a day and a half, and ultimately deported. At the time we were arrested, again in an ironic coincidence, it was my turn to speak at the press conference. At the point when the soldiers came in, I was discussing the philosophy of Immanuel Kant, so important for thinking about humanism and its aftermath, especially his arguments concerning ethical universalism and universal human rights. (Abimael Guzman, in earning his Ph.D. in philosophy, had written a dissertation on Kant and Einstein.)

Was Peru always the destination of *Humanism and its aftermath*? Or is this simply the logic of the day? There is not only a difficulty to carrying out intellectual work in the terms of this logic, there is the weight of intellectual practice itself, which can perhaps imagine the aftermath of humanism as emanating from the work of some French (or French language) philosophers, but not from Peru or any other countryside. French postmodernism, *oui*, Quechua postmodernism, no.

The logic of the day; in the middle of writing this text I became that oxymoron, a frantic scholar. The text bears the marks of this transformation, so there's no point to trying to hide this fact. Is it the sort of work that can be sustained, that of a frantic scholar? If not, where is the space for a kind of oppositional writing that tries to strike at the heart of oppressive social systems? Is this space in the margins of the university, at the point where the principle of reason is interrogated? In the United States, at any rate, there is little space for intellectual work outside of the academy. And yet, the difficulties of living with and within the academy sometimes overwhelm me.

These difficulties have a great deal to do with the class nature of the academy, its role as a reproducer of the management structure of advanced capitalism. What are we doing in the colleges and universities these days? What can we do? Much of what is being attacked as multiculturalism and Politically Correct is, to my mind, good. But we have to find ways to take these trends much further, to connect these trends more deeply with their social basis, with the people who are marginalized by the traditional model of humanistic learning.

There is too much politics and not enough philosophy in this text; this I say without irony, simply recognizing the winds that blow the scholarly questions and possibilities presented here into a frenzy.

I tried to speak to this condition in the subtitle of the book, given its final form by my colleague, David Krell (for which I thank him). The original subtitle had been "Deconstruction and the thinking of the polis." In writing the book I felt that I had only scratched the surface of this topic, thus the original subtitle was not justified. Having now written two books on the subject of deconstruction and politics, I am painfully aware of the continuing preliminary nature of the enterprise. There are some good reasons for the preliminary character of the sorts of speculations that one finds in the vicinity of deconstruction and politics, but there are some bad reasons too. The good reasons have to do with "politics," while the bad reasons have to do with "philosophical" questions that have been postponed for too long. In responding to the call of decisive political questions, I may have contributed too much to the postponement of the philosophical discussion, which, seen in a larger frame, will be necessary for sorting out what deconstruction might contribute to a thinking of the polis.

This thinking begins with the earliest texts of western philosophy; this thinking has not yet begun. My belief is that certain long-range global social trends are coming to a head, and that the possibilities of deconstruction are as tied up with this developing conjuncture as anything else is. Given certain tendencies in the development of the discussion around deconstruction and Derrida's work in general, I felt compelled to speak to the broad question of the "fate" of deconstruction. All of this talk is a bit melodramatic, but I do believe that deconstruction finds itself at a crossroads: either it will become much more engaged with political questions, in somewhat the way that Marxism has been, or it will continue to devolve into nothing more than a sterile, even if sometimes funky, rhetoric.

And yet, politics faces this same dilemma. The reason for discussing the shared fate is twofold. First, I wanted to avoid the sort of thing that I see in a good bit of orthodox Marxism, which seems to already know that there is nothing to be learned from deconstruction and is simply going to offer an assessment of deconstruction from a secure vantage point. Second, and relatedly, the social trends that are coming to a head—and will not be headed off simply by chanting mantras about "the death of communism"—will require the reinvention of the thinking of the polis. Here, in its stress on what is beyond calculation, even on what is "impossible," I think that the fates of politics and deconstruction are inseparable.

The intellectual project still requires a great deal of development. A number of recent works seem to be fundamental contributions on the major themes of this text (I hope to discuss them in depth in my own work to come). Among these would be Drucilla Cornell's *The Philosophy of the Limit* (New York: Routledge, 1992), Simon Critchley's *The Ethics of Deconstruction* (Oxford: Basil Blackwell, 1992), John Llewelyn's *The Middle Voice of Ecological Consciousness* (New York: St Martin's Press, 1991), and Robert Young's *White Mythologies: Writing History and the West* (New York: Routledge, 1990). I cannot speak for these other writers, but I would imagine that we would agree we have all only begun the work of the intellectual project of deconstruction and politics. Before concluding with a few superficial comments about dimensions of that project that I think need pursuing, allow me to say again that the long-range project must begin to come together with a more engaged sense of politics and transforming society.

Attacks on 68 Thought (Ferry and Renaut) and the like are expressions of a certain politics of memory. Deconstruction can play a very important role in thematizing this politics for Marxism. This is especially important in this period of heightened capitalist amnesia (think of the Clinton administration theme song, "Don't stop thinkin' about tomorrow—yesterday's gone, yesterday's gone!"). Another area where deconstruction could make a decisive difference, especially in its more Levinasian aspect, would be with what I would call the question of totality and infinity in Marxism. I do not believe that radical politics can do without a sense of totality, even if this also means that there is the possibility of vicious totalization, a term I prefer to totalitarianism. I do not think that the thesis of totalitarianism, especially in its Arendtian or typically crude vernacular forms, has been firmly established; indeed, they are so intertwined with cold-war politics that it may not be possible to get very far with the language of totalitarianism. Like Sartre and Mao, I do not believe that the Stalin question can simply be cast away. But, on the other hand, what is needed is a Marxism of infinity that is the dialectical/differential other side of the Marxism of totality. Marxists should not let the seeming apolitical or reactionary or outdated aspects of certain canonical thinkers of infinity, especially Plato, Kant, and Levinas, keep them from responsibly taking up this question.

The other side of this coin, continuing in a Levinasian mode, is that the question of "otherwise than being" needs to be understood politically as the question of "otherwise than imperialism." Until the impasse of the dance around the question and fact of imperialism is broken, deconstructive politics will never get beyond the Eurocentrism that is so much a part of this rhetoric today.

Notes

Part 1: Amicus brief: De-sedimenting deconstruction, its possibilities for social theory

1. I say "most likely" because part of what is in question is de Man's claim (see, e.g., Lindsay Waters' "Introduction" to de Man, *Critical Writings*, especially the letter from de Man to Henry Levin) to have participated in the Resistance in Belgium. The assumption is that, writing as he did for a collaborationist newspaper and writing several articles that were antisemitic or pro-fascist, de Man could not have at the same time done things to help the Resistance. The assumption is unwarranted in any case, but it also seems that de Man did perform some acts for the Resistance, as noted in Jacques Derrida, "Like the Sound of the Sea Deep Within a Shell: Paul de Man's War."

2. Some readers will undoubtedly protest that they are not conservatives, they are liberals, and that the university remains a fundamentally liberal setting. In response, take a look at a couple of paragraphs from an article by Alexander Cockburn and Andrew Kopkind, "Democrats, Perot, and the Left":

   > Last month [political theorist Theodore] Lowi and a pollster, Gordon Black, published an opinion survey that provides the first categorical assay of the revolt that has moved beyond specific issues, such as taxes, the congressional pay raise, the deficit and talk-radio favorites like the fifty-five-mile-an-hour speed limit, mandatory seat belts and the spotted owl, to serious electoral reform.
   >
   > "The most moderate, middle of the road voters are the voters most in favor of fundamental reform in the American political system," Lowi wrote in his introduction to the survey. Those identifying themselves as conservatives were next, and liberals were far and away the least amenable to radical change. In other words, liberals have become the most conservative element in American politics where systemic change is concerned. (p. 86)

   The article is only dealing with voters; my view is that anyone who puts much stock in voting as having much of anything to do with politics (with the shape and character of the polis) is already pretty conservative. Still, it is significant that self-identified liberals are the most conservative even in these terms. The poll and Cockburn's and Kopkind's interpretation of it accord with my own observations.

3. Quantification logic, as developed by Frege, made it even more difficult to ask the question of being. Furthermore, the relation between this question of Leibniz's and Heidegger's and the ontological argument is brought out even more in light of quantification. Recall Quine's famous argument

177

that "to be is to be the quantity of a bound variable." In this respect, the question of being and the ontological argument both seem to assume that there could be a quantification that looks something like "For all x, x is all." Put this way we see more clearly why Kant argued that the onto-logical argument is a purely formal argument, one that can prove noth-ing. But then, the question might hinge on exactly what, if anything, the question of being hopes to "prove." I am perfectly willing to accept the positivist argument that the question of being cannot be a well-formed question, and yet this argument does not end all of my anxiety about the question of being or my feeling that the question is still a kind of limit question for scientific inquiry, much in the same vein as Wittgenstein's claim, "It is not how the world is, but rather *that* the world is, that is a mystery."

4. In today's radio-station programming, "classic rock" means the Jefferson Airplane playing "Don't You Want Somebody to Love?" not "Volunteers" or "Crown of Creation"; Sly and the Family Stone playing "Dance to the Music" and "Hot Fun in the Summertime"—which all the same have their political dimension, as did "Dancing in the Streets"—rather than "Stand"; Jimi Hendrix playing "Foxey Lady" rather than "Freedom."

5. Patrick Hayden comments: "I'm not sure that the position (at least in regard to Bataille) should be characterized as *anti*-project, because for Bataille the very *demand* for 'project(s)'—which he never ignored or de-nied—is precisely what necessitates an intense, close, and critical exami-nation of just what 'we' think 'project' to be (immanent critique, if you will). Granted, I believe that many use this criticism today in order to justify their own political apathy or quietism, but those who do so would be scathingly denounced by Bataille as simply repeating the same stand-ard gestures of the past: *either* apathy and political withdrawal, *or* com-plete, non-critical control of all political discourse or practice" (personal communication with the author, in my possession).

6. The discussion in this section is fundamentally indebted to Patrick Hayden and Kathy Dow. Part of my strategy is to bend the stick in the direction away from especially Blanchot and Nancy, in order to straighten things out a bit. Hayden took me to task for this, rightly pointing out all of the important truths in Bataille, Blanchot, and Nancy that should not be ob-scured by my critique. In this regard I think it important to cite more of Hayden's criticisms:

> I don't think that [Blanchot's reading of May 1968] can necessarily be equated with [the idea of a big "Love-In" or with "the present wave of apolitical sixties nostalgia], although I would agree to some *overlap*. It seems to me that Blanchot's evocation of phrases like "without project" or "not going anywhere" are intended to underscore the importance of the Events of May '68 to an understanding of political action with re-gard to the *unknown*. The people involved were not unconcerned with the social and political conditions they faced, for they *were motivated* to act by these conditions (which is the major difference from today's "apolitical nostalgia"). What is significant is that these actions weren't *directed* by a single authoritative discourse that told *everyone* how to act or think, or that had a single, specific goal to achieve, i.e., *complete*. In this way, as Blanchot says, an unknown kind of communism de-clared *itself*, rather than having its existence being declared by *someone*

or some committee or leadership council—"we have instituted communism, according to our plan. Now do not deviate in order to preserve..." etc. The task, it would seem, would be to try to understand how this kind of freely moving power and coming together can benefit political action without denying it, discrediting it as juvenile, or altering it through too rigid a project. It this impossible? Yes and no.

I believe that we can think of events like this as "instants" ("instances") of the impossible, in that they are not articulation points of a progressive social dialectic, but those very moments when the very *possibility* of a social dialectic is defined. Yet we should neither valorize this event, for then we would turn it into a model or "example" and reinsert it into a dialectic, nor should we denounce it, for then we deny its validity as a social experience and experiment (of the impossible, à la Derrida). This brings us back to the contradictory "yes" *and* "no" status of the impossible, which hopefully we can let come into our thinking without sublating, resolving, or putting its negativity to "work" in the traditional manner.

There is a great deal to grapple with here. As I argued in the main body of the text, the Stalin question is very much present in this discussion. In particular, there has been a tendency by many, in light of the negative aspects of the Stalin period, to negate the idea of leadership and organization altogether. The fact that the Communist Party of France did everything to destroy the uprisings of 1968 adds fuel to the fire of the rejection of "Stalinist" leadership. For me, the yes and no question, or the question of the impossible, has to do with thinking that there has to be a way to combine both the broad and somewhat anarchic initiative and inventiveness of people with the sort of leadership that could direct this initiative in such a way that, on the day after the rebellion, things don't simply return to business as usual. Mao reached a whole new level of understanding on this question, and of course the attack on Mao was a major part of the PCF strategy in 1968 (one important aspect of which was the expulsion of five thousand members of the youth branch of the PCF for supposed Maoism).

On the question of "mutual exchange," Hayden writes:

Although [Blanchot and Nancy] indicate this "mutual exchange" as already existing, the point is to develop an understanding of politics (political action) which enhances rather than forecloses this prior "exposure." Rather than seeing this "exchange" as purely a realm to be constituted by humans (which would be, I think, Nancy's notion of immanentism—creating our "essence" through work, such that our "essence" is our work) the goal would be to do all we can to cultivate our "common alterity" while recognizing that no *one* political theory or program can encompass the transcendence of this alterity (an alterity and singularity not restricted, additionally, to "humans," but also, say, to the environment, etc.). I believe that a big difference with liberalism emerges here, because alterity does not "belong" to any "one" and thus cannot be "utilized" in the manner of liberal politics. Granted this brings *many* problems with it, but I'd rather confront these problems than resign myself to being a liberal.

Hayden reminds me that Bataille does not equal Blanchot. There is a more Heideggerian element to the latter (as well as to Nancy), which Hayden argues has more to do with what appears to be "retreat from the political

brand of existentialism" in Blanchot and Nancy. Furthermore, Hayden
stresses that my claim that "there is an overarching rationalism here; . . .
there is no consideration of traditional communities or so-called 'elective
communities,'" is simply not applicable to Bataille.

Finally, the question of the morbid element in all of this:

> Let me pose a question: Is the fascination with death, and I would say
> generally with those *other* elements of existence that we "set apart"
> from us yet are nonetheless *compelled toward* such as sexual or religious
> ecstacies . . . or what have you, is this fascination "Bataille-inspired,"
> as if this fascination exists solely as if produced by Bataille and wouldn't
> exist if it weren't for Bataille, or is this fascination something integral
> to "humanity" that writers like Bataille only explore *because* of our de-
> sire for this fascination?—Remember that Bataille doesn't make up this
> fascination, but explores the ways that humans have dealt with it; for
> him, "death" is not some abstract "bad thing" to simply nihilistically
> glorify, but rather a fact of *life* that has a profound effect on the prac-
> tices of human communities, manifest through rituals, myths, relation-
> ships, etc. The wake, for example, could be viewed I suppose as a nihilistic
> glorification of death, but I tend to agree that it is a moving and beau-
> tiful way to affirm life without thereby denying *loss*, absence, lack of
> control or power over time, etc. I would hope that the word "death"
> does not simply inspire or conjure up images of war or murder (al-
> though it does do this in part, and that's *profoundly moving*), but more
> importantly of human relationships, the ones we love, reasons for af-
> firming life, and so on. Sure, there *are* nihilists who view death only in
> terms of *destructive* loss, divorced from any *feeling* of finitude, but I
> would defend Bataille whole-heartedly against those who attribute this
> view to him, or who claim him for their "inspiration," as grossly mis-
> reading Bataille. Perhaps we will never agree on this, but I think that
> one can dance and celebrate life at a wake while *honoring* death, too,
> just as much as one can at, say, a wedding or birthday party (which is,
> paradoxically, an implicit affirmation of one's finitude—which I say is
> *good*!). Maybe one could say that nihilists have no sense of life *or* death;
> they are simply empty shells.

Again, a great deal to grapple with here. I would like to, eventually,
place Bataille's complete *Accursed Share* next to Sartre's quasi-complete
Critique of Dialectical Reason, and see what percolates. (This material is
from a personal written communication with the author, and is used by
permission.)

7. Lenin's theory of imperialism sat undeveloped for decades, in large part
   covered over by the theory and practice of the Stalin period, including
   the "democracy versus fascism" model of the Comintern, as developed
   by George Dimitrov (see *Against Fascism and War*, New York: International Publishers, 1986). I believe it can be shown that Trotsky never accepted Lenin's theory. In recent years Bob Avakian has put forward the
   thesis of "lopsidedness," which has been developed by Raymond Lotta
   as part of articulating Lenin's theory. (See Avakian, *For a Harvest of Dragons*,
   pp. 137–52, and Lotta, *America in Decline*, Part 1, "Political Economy in
   the Era of Imperialism and Proletarian Revolution.")

8. Mao Tsetung made a further practical and theoretical contribution in showing what the proletariat must do to wage a successful national liberation
   struggle that does not result in merely working out a better deal with

the oppressor nations. On this point, see Avakian, *Mao Tsetung's Immortal Contributions*, pp. 1–37.

9. An especially creepy version of the "downstream" strategy is proposed by Lawrence Summers, recently the chief economist of the World Bank; as of this writing he has been nominated for a post in the Clinton administration (which he is expected to get). In a memo of Dec. 12, 1991, a copy of which was obtained by *The Economist*, Summers proposes that much more toxic waste should be sent to Africa. Doug Henwood, writing in *The Nation*, summarized Summers's argument:

> In his memo, which criticized a draft of the bank's *World Development Report*, Summers was applying cost-benefit analysis, which measures the value of a human life by the stream of wages remaining to it. Say it will cost Global Megatoxics $1 million to install a state-of-the-art scrubber in its chimney. If Global determines that not spending this sum will shorten the lives of five people by ten years apiece, all that would be lost would be present value of these fifty years of wages. At a wage of $1,000 a year, the cost of the five lives can be figured at $41,000, thanks to the magic of compound interest; at $30,000 a year, they're worth $1.2 million. As Summers said in his memo, "health-impairing pollution should be done in the country with the lowest cost, which will be the country with the lowest wages."
>
> Since the costs of pollution—always priced in dollars or their equivalent—rise with development, Summers argued, it makes sense costwise to dump in Africa. If a pollutant is going to cause "protrate" [sic] cancer, a disease of old age, why not locate it in countries where people aren't likely to live long enough to get it? He concluded this section by saying that disagreement with this logic suggests the belief that things like "intrinsic rights to certain goods, moral reasons, social concerns, lack of adequate markets, etc. could be turned around and used more or less effectively against every Bank proposal for liberalization."

Henwood concludes: "It makes no sense for Summers to resign; he expressed the bank's logic perfectly. It's a bank, and acts like one." This example poses sharply the question of what logic will dominate the world—or rather, the question is, will the world be dominated by the logic of calculation, or will there be the fundamental disruption of this logic by an ethic that stands against calculation?

10. I will pursue these questions, and many others relating to the possibilities of Marxism, especially a Marxism beyond calculation, in a book that I am working on at present, "The meaning of Mao."

11. These arguments are mutations of ones found in the work of Donald Davidson; they are developed more systematically in my "Interpretation and responsibility: excavating Davidson's ethical theory" (which will appear in the Davidson volume of the "Library of Living Philosophers"). The anomaly in Davidson's "anomalous monism" thesis is also found in Derrida's work. Under various names (the impossible, the undecidable, that which resists calculation, the unprecedented, etc.). Among those I am referring to as reductive materialists are Jerry Fodor, Fred Dretske, and Patricia Churchland. In both Davidson and Derrida, valuation is at the heart of the question, and the motivation for the argument for the anomaly of human thinking and responsibility is essential Kantian.

12. A conversation with Michael Lind helped me grasp this point.

Part 2: Transformations of humanism (current events)

1. Habermas develops this argument throughout *The Philosophical Discourse of Modernity*, as well as in *Moral Consciousness and Communicative Action*, p. 99, and "The Unity of Reason in the Diversity of Its Voices."
2. See Habermas's characterization of Heidegger and his circle of disciples in *Philosophical-Political Profiles*, pp. 55–62.
3. I believe that the argument that Adorno's *Minima Moralia* is fundamentally a Nietzschean work is much overdone. Kathleen League's reading of Adorno has been influential here.
4. The Davidson essay most relevant here is "On the Very Idea of a Conceptual Scheme."
5. Without going into detail, it should be mentioned that both Derrida and Habermas were involved in the student movement of the sixties, and in a real sense both can be said to have been formed by this experience. Habermas has played an exemplary role in the "Historian's Debate" in Germany; there was also a scandal several years ago involving the attempt to blacklist Habermas's students. Derrida has been one of the prime movers in a number of projects aiming to further the teaching and dissemination of philosophy in France, including GREPH and the International College of Philosophy. In recent years, he has taken initiative in calling on the French government to acknowledge the role of the Vichy government in the Holocaust, and he has called for educational opportunities for (mainly Arab) immigrants and guest-workers.
6. The characterization is from Kermit Parsons, *The Cornell Campus: A History of Its Planning and Development*.
7. The Heidegger text that Derrida is commenting upon is *Der Satz vom Grund* (*The Principle of Reason*).
8. George Trey makes a distinction between "descriptive" and "normative" postmodernity, associating the former with Jameson and the latter with Lyotard and Baudrillard.
9. This characterization of Freire is provided by Henry Giroux, *Schooling and the Struggle for Public Life* (Minneapolis: University of Minnesota Press, 1988), pp. 148–49. Giroux is a critical theorist and liberatory educator in the school of Freire.
10. Rorty's appeal to Michael Sandel's *Liberalism and the Limits of Justice* (in Rorty, *Objectivism, Relativism, and Truth*, p. 200) is interesting; I don't think that it holds up, at least, I don't think Rorty's use of Sandel's argument is what the latter had in mind—that's fine, but pursuing Sandel's argument leads one to a far different place than where Rorty takes us.
11. For example, see Honi Haber, "Richard Rorty's Failed Politics," and my response, "Liberalism: modern and postmodern," in *Social Epistemology*, 7.1 (Jan.–Mar. 1993), pp. 61–74, 75–81.
12. See, e.g., John Heinerman and Anson Shupe, *The Mormon Corporate Empire* (Boston: Beacon Press, 1985).
13. As well as making this argument in *Matrix and line*, I also develop questions of community in a series of essays that will eventually be published as a book, *Politics in the impasse*. (Albany, NY: Suny Press, 1996).
14. The inspiration for these two epigraphs, respectively, comes from Rebecca Comay, "Interrupting the Conversation," and Rick Roderick, "Reading Derrida Politically."

15. For a discussion of the meaning of "detournement," a term and practice that has some affinities with deconstruction, see: Ken Knabb, *Situationist International Anthology* (Berkeley: Bureau of Public Secrets, 1981), pp. 8–14; Sadie Plant, *The Most Radical Gesture: The Situationist International in a Postmodern Age* (London: Routledge, 1992), pp. 86–89; Greil Marcus, *Lipstick Traces: A Secret History of the Twentieth Century* (Cambridge: Harvard University Press, 1989), pp. 168, 170, 179, 372.

16. Roderick goes on to argue that Rorty is after "Sartrean freedom." I didn't quote this because I think that Roderick is wrong; in Sartre's view, one must take responsibility for one's historical situation. This sense of responsibility is entirely lacking in Rorty's arguments.

17. The "ear" statement comes from personal communication with Ron Scapp. The passage quoted is from Scapp's dissertation in philosophy, cited in bell hooks, *Black Looks*, p. 13.

18. Teachers for a Democratic Culture, an organization set up to fight the attacks of multiculturalism and Political Correctness, has done a number of studies showing that the money for the operations of D'Souza, Kimball, etc., comes from sources such as the John D. Olin Foundation, organizations set up to generate partisan university research in favor of free market, neo-conservative goals.

19. At the 1991 meeting of the Sartre Society of North America, Annie Cohen-Solail remarked in a lecture that people are often surprised when they see Professor Derrida for the first time, expecting to see someone who in his physical appearance matches his reputation as a barbarian and demonic crusader against all that is good. Dr. Cohen-Solail went on to compare the attacks on Derrida that are typical today with the attacks on Sartre in the fifties and sixties—an apt comparison, to my mind. My experience is that people are also surprised by Derrida's lecturing style: that he does not jump up and down, rave, pull rabbits out of a hat; indeed, that he makes the audience work for the experience that they have come for.

20. I do not want to wade back into the cesspool of this text to find the page reference, but I assure the reader that I can find the line I am referring to. Unlike Lehman, et al., I feel some responsibility to actually read the works of authors I comment upon and condemn. And condemn them I do.

21. The reason I point out that Plato, Wittgenstein, and Woolf were all homosexual is that, in one of the first attacks on PC, "Taking Offense: Is This the New Enlightenment on Campus or the New McCarthyism?" (*Newsweek*, Dec. 24, 1990), there is the bizarre (idiotic, really) claim that some PC educators want to remove Plato from the canon and replace him with readings from gay writers. I can only echo Michael Berube's warning that, if the anti-PC people are the best defenders of the canon out there, then the canon and western civilization are in deep trouble!

22. There are various translations of this line from Hölderlin; in Part 3 I return to the translation that is more popular in continental philosophy circles these days, mostly because of the influence of Heidegger.

Part 3: From other shores: Derrida and the idea of Europe,
apropos of L'autre cap

1. This passage is from *Prisms*, quoted in Comay, "Interrupting the Conversation," p. 119.
2. Because *The Other Heading* is in part a work of journalism, of "political commentary," readers without wide experience reading Derrida may find it more approachable than some of the other shorter works, e.g., *Of Spirit*. I say this because we all know that people who want to "check out" Derrida, largely so that they can say they've read Derrida—often so that they can then say that it didn't make any sense, generally look for the slimmest texts, whereas they would do better to read one of the thicker works. I still believe that the best places to start are *Speech and Phenomena* and *of Grammatology*.
3. My article, "Nomad and empire: Nietzsche, guerilla theatre, guerilla war," *Arena*, 77 (1986), pp. 88–95, was an earlier attempt to deal with the problem of closure and open-mindedness, though with reference to Deleuze and Foucault rather than Derrida. On this question Derrida is significantly different; his "an-arche-ism" is not mere anarchism.
4. I use "black" to refer to people who have their origin in Africa, and "Black" to refer to the Black nation that exists within the borders of the United States.
5. The neo-Trotskyist traditions of Tony Cliff and Raya Dunayevskaya maintain that capitalism was restored in the Soviet Union in the late twenties with the consolidation of Stalin's leadership. This is in contrast to the more orthodox Trotskyist view that, with the ascendency of Stalin, the Soviet Union became and remained a "degenerated workers' state." See Tony Cliff, *State Capitalism in Russia* (London: Bookmarks, 1988; orig. 1948), and Raya Dunayevskaya, *The Marxist-Humanist Theory of State-Capitalism* (Chicago: News and Letters, 1992). I deal with their arguments in detail in "The meaning of Mao," Chap. 2, "Segment of the spiral." My understanding of the Stalin question is much influenced by Bob Avakian, *Conquer the World? The International Proletarian Must and Will* (*Revolution Magazine*, 50, Dec. 1981); see esp. p. 29.
6. By the term "orthodox Marxism" I do not mean any particular form of Marxism. Some Trotskyists, some CP Leninists, some classical Marxists, and perhaps even some Maoists (as much as I, who call myself a Maoist, might wish otherwise), despite their differences, appeal not to the same orthodoxy but, at any rate, to the idea that there should be an orthodoxy. The orthodox form of thought proceeds as follows: "I am an X, therefore I believe Y," rather than, "I have come to believe Y, so that would make me an X." This does not mean, in my view in any case, that it is always wrong for a person to try to figure out what the Marxist (or Derridean or whatever) thing to think is, and to think that this Marxist view is therefore a good view to hold; orthodoxy sets in, however, when Marxism becomes simply a form of calculation, so that one always already knows what to think, without thinking. In the spring of 1991 I was involved in a debate with some of Callinicos's fellow enthusiasts of Tony Cliff-style Trotskyism (supporters of the International Socialist Organization), concerning the book by Callinicos that is under discussion here, *Against Postmodernism*. Part of the debate came to focus on Derrida. Indeed, in

unreservedly defending Callinicos's text, my debating opponent had only terms of abuse for Derrida and his work. When I asked the person I was debating (and others in the audience who were also with the ISO) exactly which texts of Derrida's he wanted to discuss and take issue with (which I think is the question that should always be asked in this sort of "discussion," the sort that I have mostly had with analytic philosophers), he had to admit that not only had he not actually read any of Derrida's books, he didn't even know the titles of these books. I would not even mention this little encounter, which in itself is of virtually no significance, if it were not so typical of the orthodox cast of mind, which is ultimately against thought. Lest the reader suspect that I relate this incident for purely sectarian reasons, let me say that: 1) Callinicos himself is generally far more careful than this; 2) I find much to admire in Callinicos's works generally, and I believe that any critical thinker would benefit from reading his works; 3) while I have some basic differences with the general theoretical framework of Tony Cliff, differences which go to what I think is the essential Eurocentrism in all Trotskyism, I take his arguments, especially his theory of capitalist restoration, seriously, and I believe that there is much to be learned from an engagement with these arguments; 4) some of my fellow Maoists have been just as guilty, at times, of a dismissive orthodoxy. The danger is inherent in the need to think systematically; to avoid this danger would be, I have argued in a Kantian and Derridean frame, to give up on the attempt to think, period. When it comes to condemning books that we haven't read and philosophies toward which we have not put any effort to understanding, however, the answer is quite simple: This is dangerous and irresponsible knownothingism. Cut it out!

7. I am quoting Callinicos quoting Robert Sayre and Michael Lowy; I've removed the italics that were in the original.

8. See esp. Richard Rorty, "Nineteenth-Century Idealism and Twentieth-Century Textualism," in *Consequences of Pragmatism*, pp. 139–59.

9. Without running down too many examples, I should point out that "realism" and "anti-realism" have been used to mean quite a number of different things in recent years, such that many of the philosophers who were using that vocabulary, e.g., Hilary Putnam, Michael Dummett, Donald Davidson, W.V. Quine, were talking at cross-purposes. What one meant by "realism," the other might have meant by "anti-realism." Lately, Rorty has had the benign influence of encouraging many philosophers to find a better vocabulary.

10. When I wrote these words unification appeared inevitable; now, less than a year later, unification appears far from certain. Where things will be when this text is published is anyone's guess.

11. Sharon Waxman, "No Exit. Communism's Collapse Leaves Once-Revered Heirs of Sartre at a Loss to Fill the Intellectual Void," (*Chicago Tribune*, Nov. 5, 1991; Sec. 5, pp. 1–2). Gee, isn't it fun to say "the collapse of communism" over and over again? In a real sense, it is the hot air generated by the chanting of this mantra that powers capitalism—for now. But, if I get going on this it will be difficult to stop!

12. Callinicos's way of defining the Marxist tradition is significant here, his invocation, a litany really, of "the tradition of Marx, Engels, Lenin, Trotsky,

Luxemburg, and Gramsci." In what systematic sense is this a tradition? Again, not to be sectarian about this, but both Luxemburg and Trotsky explicitly rejected major aspects of Leninism, and Lenin rejected major aspects of their approaches as well. There are still many questions here that need to be struggled through and understood, despite the distance that many readers of Derrida (or readers of post-1968 European philosophy generally) have from them. One often hears from Trotskyists the argument that, in 1917, Trotsky came into agreement with Lenin on the "organizational question," as though that was all that divided them. Even on this point, I don't think that Trotsky(ism) ever grasps that Lenin's position, as first developed in *What Is to Be Done?*, is first of all a question of epistemology; the question is, Through what means can the basic masses, with the proletariat at their lead, come to self-consciousness so that they can enact self-activity? However, the larger, more important point at this juncture is that it is difficult to see the virtues of the kind of orthodoxy (of Marxism or of anything else) that seems to already know that it has nothing to learn from "outside sources" (Heidegger, etc.).

13. Rodolphe Gasche, in *The Tain of the Mirror*, writes:

> In the debates following the presentation of "L'Oreille de l'autre" in 1979 in Montreal, Derrida recalled that when he employed the word *deconstruction* in his early writing, he did so only rarely, and with the understanding that it was only one word among others, a secondary word, translating Heidegger's terms for destruction and dismantling. It is a word, he has said elsewhere, that he has never liked, and whose fortune has disagreeably surprised him. Only after others valorized the word in the context of structuralism—which Derrida claims, did not primarily determine his usage of the word—did Derrida try to define *deconstruction* in his own manner. (p. 118)

What's in a name? A great deal, according to Derrida. (I develop this question in *Matrix and line*, Chap. 5) Drucilla Cornell has recently proposed that Derrida's work should be called not deconstruction but rather, "the philosophy of the limit" (see Cornell's book with this title). This expression captures Derrida's project quite well.

14. Radical Enlightenment, radical democracy, and radical trade unionism, i.e., the left, perhaps even far left, end of what already exists is the standard thesis of Trotskyism and, more and more, or much of what calls itself the Left. The basic idea is that socialism equals radical democracy, as evidenced, e.g., in the well-received work of Ernesto Laclau and Chantal Mouffe (other important examples are Roberto Unger and, of course, Jurgen Habermas). The greater militancy of Callinicos notwithstanding, there are problems with the entire spectrum that runs from Habermas to more militant radical democrats. The question is alterity, uncovering the repressed margin of representation. From a Marxist perspective, I find Bob Avakian's critique of the radical democracy thesis helpful; see *Democracy: Can't We Do Better Than That?* However, still more needs to be done to capture theoretically the spirit of Mao's fully internationalist application of Marx and Lenin. (I will address these questions in "The meaning of Mao.")

15. In fact, the potential that Callinicos refers to is not simply that created by political modernity. Callinicos refers to "both sides of Marx's perspec-

tive on capitalism—not simply the destruction it wreaks, but the potential expansion of human capacities it involves" (p. 174). This formulation also takes us into debate over the radical democracy thesis—and shows again that Callinicos is part of a continuum with Habermas, representing simply the left, militant end of that continuum; that a certain side of Marx is also on this continuum cannot be disputed (so, if it is simply a question of going back to classical Marxism—a popular trend these days— then I agree that the Trotskyists are on to something; but I do not think this is the question). However, my point is that there has to be a way to critically open the archive that is both presented to and concealed from us by political modernity, and even by the ideal of the "unforced force of reason." Here Derrida's work is powerful and exemplary, even if he, in my humble opinion, sometimes valorizes the idea of democracy too much (and even if he always speaks of a "democracy that is yet to come and little resembles what goes by this name today").

16. Here I would also have to develop questions of agriculture more generally and the relationship between city and countryside in particular. Here too I would have to ask about the relationship between the polis and the metropolis. Even where Derrida raises this question, in his thematizing of the "quasi-political," he does not thematize the fundamental connection with the problem of agriculture. Of course, he is not alone here. (On these subjects I am writing a short book, "The urban ideology: Wendell Berry and the countryside of social theory." The point will be to ask about the possibilities after Wendell Berry and the ecological-communitarian critique of industrial society.) However, something that Derrida said elsewhere (in a public presentation) is perhaps useful for further exploration of these questions:

> This afternoon we heard something about the city—philosophy, architecture, and the city—not only about these but also about politics—the polis. Once we reach an epoch in history where the polis is not the ultimate unit of social space . . . well, now, in this post-city age, the social space in which we live may no longer be organized in the form of a polis. This has a number of consequences. The very *concept* of Graeco-Western politics, which was structured by the Greek polis, is not adequate any longer to all the interconnected concepts, to everything we are discussing here. Perhaps "politics" is not a good name for it all. Which does not mean that we are becoming apolitical. Perhaps whatever we are discussing here in terms of politics is already beyond the city, beyond polis, beyond politics. ("Response to Daniel Liebeskind," *Research in Phenomenology*, [1992], p. 89.)

17. In the midst of the Gulf War, Habermas gave an address in Copenhagen in which he expressed "qualified support" for the war, citing especially his concern for the security of Israel. This argument has been heard from many liberals, during the war and since that time. My position on the question of Israel and the Jews is more complex than what is generally put forward by Marxists. But it is hard for me to see that the question of the fate of the Jews is advanced one iota by the slaughter in Iraq, and may have been set back considerably in the long run. The real issue is that Habermas and other left-liberals do not see any solution to basic social issues that lies outside of existing parameters. See Anson Rabinbach, "German Intellectuals and the Gulf War," *Dissent*, Fall 1991, pp. 459–63.

References

Adorno, Theodor. *Negative Dialectics*. E. B. Ashton, trans. New York: Continuum Publishing, 1983.

———. *Prisms*. Samuel Weber and Shierry Weber, trans. Cambridge: MIT Press, 1981.

Althusser, Louis. *Lenin and Philosophy*. Ben Brewster, trans. New York: Monthly Review Press, 1971.

Aronson, Ronald. *Sartre's Second Critique*. Chicago: University of Chicago Press, 1987.

Avakian, Bob. *Democracy: Can't We Do Better Than That?* Chicago: Banner Press, 1986.

———. *For a Harvest of Dragons*. Chicago: RCP Publications, 1983.

———. *Mao Tsetung's Immortal Contributions*. Chicago: RCP Publications, 1979.

Bataille, Georges. *The Accursed Share*. 3 vols. Robert Hurley, trans. New York: Zone Books, 1988 (Vol. 1), 1991 (Vols. 2–3).

———. *Visions of Excess*. Allan Stoekl, trans. Minneapolis: University of Minnesota Press, 1985.

Barthes, Roland. *S/Z*. Richard Miller, trans. New York: Hill and Wang, 1974.

Baynes, Kenneth. *The Normative Grounds of Social Criticism: Kant, Rawls, and Habermas*. Albany: State University of New York Press, 1992.

Berube, Michael. "Public Image Limited: Political Correctness and the Media's Big Lie." *The Village Voice*, 36, n. 35 (June 18, 1991), pp. 31–37.

Blanchot, Maurice. *The Unavowable Community*. Pierre Joris, Trans. Barrytown, NY: Station Hill Press, 1988.

Bloom, Allan. *The Closing of the American Mind*. New York: Simon and Schuster, 1987.

Bordo, Susan. *The Flight to Objectivity: Essays on Cartesianism and Culture*. Albany: SUNY Press, 1987.

Bove, Paul. *In the Wake of Theory*. Hanover, N.H.: Wesleyan University Press, 1992.

Burrows, Jo. "Conversational Politics: Rorty's Pragmatist Apology for Liberalism." In Alan Malachowski, ed., *Reading Rorty*, Oxford: Basil Blackwell, 1990; pp. 322–38.

Callinicos, Alex. *Against Postmodernism: A Marxist Critique*. New York: St. Martin's Press, 1990.

Carnap, Rudolf. "The Elimination of Metaphysics through Logical Analysis of Language." Arthur Pap, trans. In A. J. Ayer, ed., *Logical Positivism*. New York: The Free Press, 1959; pp. 60–81.

Cochrane, James L., Samuel Gubins, and B. F. Kiker, *Macroeconomics: Analysis and Policy*. Glenview, IL: Scott, Foresman and Company, 1974.

Cockburn, Alexander, and Andrew Kopkind. "Democrats, Perot, and the Left."

The Nation, 255, n. 3 (July 20/27, 1992).

Comay, Rebecca. "Interrupting the Conversation: Notes on Rorty." *Telos*, 69 (Fall 1986); pp. 119–30.

Corlett, William. *Community Without Unity: A Politics of Derridian Extravagance*. Durham, N.C.: Duke University Press, 1989.

Cornell, Drucilla. *The Philosophy of the Limit*. New York: Routledge, 1992.

Davidson, Donald. "Expressing Evaluations." The Lindley Lecture. University of Kansas, 1982.

———. "On the Very Idea of a Conceptual Scheme." In Davidson, *Inquiries into Truth and Interpretation*. Oxford: Oxford University Press, 1985; pp. 183–98.

de Bolla, Peter. *Harold Bloom: Towards Historical Rhetorics*. London: Routledge, 1988.

de Man, Paul. *Allegories of Reading*. New Haven, CT: Yale University Press, 1979.

———. *Blindness and Insight*. 2nd ed., rev. Minneapolis: University of Minnesota Press, 1983.

———. *The Resistance to Theory*. Minneapolis: University of Minnesota Press, 1986.

———. *The Rhetoric of Romanticism*. New York: Columbia University Press, 1984.

Derrida, Jacques. "Biodegradeables: Seven Diary Fragments." Peggy Kamuf, trans. *Critical Inquiry* 15 (Summer 1989), pp. 812–73.

———. "Cogito and the History of Madness." In *Writing and Difference*, pp. 31–63.

———. "From Restricted to General Economy: A Hegelianism without Reserve." In *Writing and Difference*, pp. 251–77.

———. *Glas*. John P. Leavey, Jr. and Richard Rand, trans. Lincoln: University of Nebraska Press, 1986.

———. *Edmund Husserl's "Origin of Geometry": An Introduction*. John P. Leavey, trans. Stony Brook, N.Y.: Nicholas Hays, Ltd., 1978.

———. *L'autre cap*. Paris: Editions Minuit, 1991.

———. "Like the Sound of the Sea Deep within a Shell: Paul de Man's War." *Critical Inquiry*. 14 (Spring 1988), pp. 590–652.

———. *Margins of Philosophy*. Alan Bass, trans. Chicago: University of Chicago Press, 1982.

———. "No Apocalypse, Not Now (full speed ahead, seven missiles, seven missives.)" Catherine Porter and Philip Lewis, trans. *Diacritics*, 14, n. 2 (Summer 1984), pp. 18–31.

———. "Of an Apocalyptic Tone Recently Adopted in Philosophy." John P. Leavey, trans. *The Oxford Literary Review*, 6, n. 2 (1984), pp. 3–37.

———. *of Grammatology*. Gayatri Chakravorty Spivak, trans. Baltimore: Johns Hopkins University Press, 1976.

———. "Ousia and Gramme: Note on a Note from *Being and Time*." In *Margins of Philosophy*, pp. 29–67.

———. *Positions*. Alan Bass, trans. Chicago: University of Chicago Press, 1981.

———. "Racism's Last Word." Peggy Kamuf, trans. *Critical Inquiry* 12 (Autumn 1985), pp. 290–99.

———. *Speech and Phenomena, and Other Essays on Husserl's Theory of Signs*. David B. Allison, trans. Evanston, IL: Northwestern University Press, 1973.

————. "The Ends of Man." In *Margins of Philosophy*, pp. 109–36.

————. "The Force of Law: The 'Mystical Foundation of Authority.'" Mary Quaintance, trans. In *Deconstruction and the Possibility of Justice. Cordozo Law Review*, 11, n. 5–6 (July/August 1990); pp. 920–1045.

————. "The Law of Genre," Avital Ronell, trans. In *Acts of Literature*, Derik Attridge, ed. New York: Routledge, 1992.

————. *The Other Heading: Reflections on Today's Europe*. Pascale-Anne Brault and Michael B. Naas, trans. Bloomington: Indiana University Press, 1992.

————. *The Post Card: From Socrates to Freud and Beyond*. Alan Bass, trans. Chicago: University of Chicago Press, 1987.

————. "The Principle of Reason: The University in the Eyes of Its Pupils." Catherine Porter and Edward P. Morris, trans. *Diacritics*, 13, n. 3 (Fall 1983), pp. 3–20.

————. "Violence and Metaphysics: An Essay on the Thought of Emmanuel Levinas." In *Writing and Difference*, pp. 79–153.

————. "White Mythology: Metaphor in the Text of Philosophy." In *Margins of Philosophy*, pp. 207–71.

————. *Writing and Difference*. Alan Bass, trans. Chicago: University of Chicago Press, 1978.

Dews, Peter. *Logics of Disintegration: Post-Structuralist Thought and the Claims of Critical Theory*. London: Verso Books, 1987.

Dow, Kathy. "Ex-posing Identity (Derrida and Nancy on the (Im)Possibility)." Unpublished manuscript.

D'Souza, Dinesh. *Illiberal Education: The Politics of Race and Sex on Campus*. New York: The Free Press, 1991.

Eagleton, Terry. *Against the Grain*. London: Verso Books, 1986.

Eribon, Didier. *Michel Foucault*. Betsy Wing, trans. Cambridge: Harvard University Press, 1991.

Fanon, Frantz. *Black Skin, White Masks*. Charles Lam Markmann, trans. New York: Grove Weidenfield, 1967.

Ferry, Luc, and Alain Renaut. *French Philosophy of the Sixties: An Essay on Antihumanism*. Mary Schnackenberg Cattani, trans. Amherst: University of Massachusetts Press, 1990.

Foucault, Michel. "Nietzsche, Genealogy, History." In Foucault, *Language, Counter-Memory, Practice*. Donald F. Bouchard, ed. Donald F. Bouchard and Sherry Simon, trans. Ithaca, N.Y.: Cornell University Press, pp. 139–64.

Fraser, Nancy. "Solidarity or Singularity? Richard Rorty between Romanticism and Technocracy." In Alan Malachowski, ed., *Reading Rorty*. Cambridge: Basil Blackwell, 1990; pp. 303–21.

Fried, Marlene Gerber. *From Abortion to Reproductive Freedom: Transforming a Movement*. Boston: South End Press, 1990.

Gasche, Rodolphe. *The Tain of the Mirror: Derrida and the Philosophy of Reflection*. Cambridge: Harvard University Press, 1986.

Grossberg, Lawrence. *We gotta get out of this place: Popular Conservatism and Postmodern Culture*. New York: Routledge, 1992.

Habermas, Jurgen. *Moral Consciousness and Communicative Action*. Christian Lenhardt and Shierry Weber Nicholsen, trans. Cambridge: MIT Press, 1990.

————. *Philosophical-Political Profiles*. Frederick Lawrence, trans. Cambridge: MIT Press, 1985.

——. *Postmetaphysical Thinking: Philosophical Essays*. William Mark Hohengarten, trans. Cambridge, MA: MIT Press, 1992.

——. "The Idea of the University—Learning Processes." John R. Blazek, trans. *New German Critique*, 41 (Spring-Summer 1987); pp. 3–22.

——. *The Philosophical Discourse of Modernity: Twelve Lectures*. Frederick Lawrence, trans. Cambridge: MIT Press, 1987.

——. "The Unity of Reason in the Diversity of Its Voices." In Habermas, *Postmetaphysical Thinking*, pp. 115–48.

Hamacher, Werner, Neil Hertz, and Thomas Keenan, eds. *On Paul de Man's Wartime Journalism*. Lincoln: University of Nebraska Press, 1989.

Hayden, Patrick. "(Re)thinking community: responding to Bataille." Unpublished manuscript.

hooks, bell. *Black Looks: Race and Representation*. Boston: South End Press, 1992.

Horkheimer, Max. *The Eclipse of Reason*. New York: Continuum, 1974.

Jacoby, Russell. *The Last Intellectuals: American Culture in the Age of Academe*. New York: The Noonday Press, 1987.

Kant, Immanuel. *Fundamental Principles of the Metaphysics of Morals*. Thomas K. Abbott, trans. New York: Macmillan Publishing Company, 1985.

Kimball, Roger. *Tenured Radicals: How Politics Has Corrupted Our Higher Education*. New York: Harper and Row, 1990.

Knabb, Ken, ed. and trans. *Situationist International Anthology*. Berkeley, Calif.: Bureau of Public Secrets, 1981.

League, Kathleen. "Problems of Deconstructive Communitarianism." Unpublished manuscript.

LeGuin, Ursula K. *The Word for World is Forest*. New York: Berkley Medallion Books, 1972.

Lehman, David. *Signs of the Times: Deconstruction and the Fall of Paul de Man*. 2nd ed. New York: Poseidon Press, 1992.

Lenin, V. I. *Imperialism: The Highest Stage of Capitalism*. New York: International Publishers, 1939.

——. *Materialism and Empirio-Criticism*. Peking: Foreign Languages Press, 1972.

Lentricchia, Frank. *After the New Criticism*. Chicago: University of Chicago Press, 1980.

——. *Criticism and Social Change*. Chicago: University of Chicago Press, 1983.

Lotta, Raymond, with Frank Shannon. *America in Decline*. Chicago: Banner Press, 1984.

Mao, Tsetung. *A Critique of Soviet Economics*. Moss Roberts, trans. New York: Monthly Review Press, 1977.

Martin, Bill. "Blindness and Hindsight." *Canadian Journal of Political and Social Theory*, 13, n. 3 (Fall 1989), pp. 26–28.

——. *Matrix and line: Derrida and the possibilities of postmodern social theory*. Albany: State University of New York Press, 1992.

McBride, William L. *Sartre's Political Theory*. Bloomington: Indiana University Press, 1991.

McCarthy, Thomas. "The Politics of the Ineffable." In McCarthy, *Ideals and Illusions: On Reconstruction and Deconstruction in Contemporary Critical Theory*. Cambridge: MIT Press, 1991; pp. 97–119.

McCumber, John. "Reconnecting Rorty: The Situation of Discourse in Richard

Rorty's *Contingency, irony, and solidarity. Diacritics*, 20, n. 2 (Summer 1990), pp. 2–19.

Mendes-Flohr, Paul. *From Mysticism to Dialogue: Martin Buber's Transformation of German Social Thought*. Detroit: Wayne State University Press, 1989.

Nancy, Jean-Luc. "The Compearance: From the Existence of 'Communism' to the Community of 'Existence.'" Tracy B. Strong, trans. *Political Theory*, 20, n. 3 (August 1992); pp. 371–98.

———. *The Inoperative Community*. Peter Connor, Lisa Garbus, Michael Holland, and Simona Sawhney, trans. Minneapolis: University of Minnesota Press, 1991.

Norris, Christopher. *Paul de Man: Deconstruction and the Critique of Aesthetic Ideology*. London: Routledge, 1988.

———. *The Contest of the Faculties: Philosophy and Theory after Deconstruction*. London: Methuen, 1985.

———. *Uncritical Theory: Postmodernism, Intellectuals, and the Gulf War*. Amherst, MA: University of Massachusetts Press, 1992.

Parsons, Kermit. *The Cornell Campus: A History of Its Planning and Development*. Ithaca, N.Y.: Cornell University Press, 1968.

Rasmussen, David. *Reading Habermas*. Cambridge: Basil Blackwell, 1990.

Roderick, Rick. "Reading Derrida Politically (Contra Rorty)." *Praxis International*, 6, n. 4 (January 1987), pp. 442–49.

Ronell, Avital. *The Telephone Book: Technology, Schizophrenia, Electric Speech*. Lincoln: University of Nebraska Press, 1989.

Rorty, Richard. *Consequences of Pragmatism*. Minneapolis: University of Minnesota Press, 1982.

———. *Contingency, irony, and solidarity*. Cambridge: Cambridge University Press, 1989.

———. "Is Derrida a transcendental philosopher?" In Rorty, *Essays on Heidegger and Others*. Cambridge: Cambridge University Press, 1991.

———. *Objectivity, Relativism, and Truth*. Cambridge: Cambridge University Press, 1991.

———. "On Ethnocentrism: A Reply to Clifford Geertz." In *Objectivity, Relativism, and Truth*, pp. 203–10.

———. *Philosophy and the Mirror of Nature*. Princeton: Princeton University Press, 1979.

———. "Postmodernist bourgeois liberalism." In *Objectivity, Relativism, and Truth*, pp. 197–202.

———. "The priority of democracy to philosophy." In *Objectivity, Relativism, and Truth*, pp. 175–96.

———. "Thugs and Theorists." *Political Theory*, 15, n. 4 (November 1987), pp. 564–80.

Sartre, Jean-Paul. *Critique of Dialectical Reason*. Alan Sheridan-Smith, trans. Jonathan Ree, ed. London: Verso Books, 1976.

———. *Search for a Method*. Hazel E. Barnes, trans. New York: Vintage Books, 1968.

Scapp, Ron. "Rorty: Voice and the Politics of Empathy." Unpublished manuscript.

Sophocles. *Antigone*. Robert Fagles, trans. New York, Penguin Books, 1987.

Spender, Dale. *The Writing or the Sex? Or Why You Don't Have to Read Women's Writing to Know It's No Good*. New York: Pergamon Press, 1989.

Stalin, J. V. *Economic Problems of Socialism in the USSR*. Peking: Foreign Languages Press, 1972.

Sykes, Charles J. *Profscam: Professors and the Demise of Higher Education*. New York: St. Martin's Press, 1988.

Taylor, Mark C. *Altarity*. Chicago: University of Chicago Press, 1987.

Van der Linden, Harry. *Kantian Ethics and Socialism*. Indianapolis: Hackett Publishing Company, 1988.

Warren, Mark. *Nietzsche and Political Thought*. Cambridge: MIT Press, 1988.

Waters, Lindsay. "Introduction. Paul de Man: Life and Works." In Paul de Man, *Critical Writings, 1953–1978*. Lindsay Waters, ed., pp. ix–lxxiv.

Winn, Kenneth H. *Exiles in the Land of Liberty: Mormons in America, 1830–1846*. Chapel Hill: University of North Carolina Press, 1989.

Index

Achebe, Chinua, 125
Adorno, Theodor, 1, 3, 8, 26, 59, 70, 72, 128–29, 139, 151, 155, 158
Africa, 132–33
Agriculture, 156, 187n. 16
AIDS, 123
Alterity, 62, 72, 83
Althusser, Louis, 24, 36, 42, 51, 73, 143
Analytic philosophy, 28, 49, 60, 73–74, 85, 101, 110–11, 160, 164
Analytical Marxism, 30
Antigone (Sophocles), 25
Anti-humanism, 142–44
Apartheid regime (South Africa), 139–40
Arendt, Hannah, 176
Aristotle, xi, 48, 88, 117
Aron, Raymond, 20
Aronson, Ronald, 24
Autonomy, 16, 23, 53, 76, 118, 142, 146, 161, 168
Avakian, Bob, 184n. 5
Ayer, A. J., 49

Barthes, Roland, 18, 114
Bataille, Georges, 21–26, 47, 57, 165, 178n. 5, 178–80n. 6
Baudrillard, Jean, 58, 136, 153
Baynes, Kenneth, 59
Benjamin, Walter, 17
Bennett, William, 122
Berkeley, George, 60
Berube, Michael, xiv
"Biodegradables" (Derrida), 140
Blanchot, Maurice, 21–26, 87, 127, 178–80n. 6
Bloch, Ernst, 17
Bloom, Allan, xiii, 113–18, 122, 134
Bloom, Harold, 6

Book of Mormon, 87, 110
Bordo, Susan, 47, 51–53, 57
Bove, Paul, xiii, 27–29, 114, 116–17, 122
Brault, Pascale-Anne, 127–28
Brezhnev, Leonid, 136
Buber, Martin, 23
Buchanan, Patrick, 126
Buddhism, 33
Burke, Kenneth, 139
Burrows, Jo, 98
Bush, George, xv, 36, 97, 119, 123, 135

Callinicos, Alex, 136–53, 184n. 6, 185n. 12, 186n. 15
Carnap, Rudolph, 21, 50, 161
Cartesianism, 24, 50–57, 166
Categorical imperative, 41–42
Cheney, Dick, 122
Cheney, Lynn, 122
Chomsky, Noam, 164
Church of Jesus Christ of Latter-day Saints (Mormons), 86–88
Class, xv, 10–11, 30, 39, 86–87
Clifford, James, 107
Clinton Administration, 176
Closure, 130
"Cogito and the History of Madness" (Derrida), 53–57, 144
Colonialism, 38, 134
Columbus, Christopher, 131, 141
Comay, Rebecca, 96–97
Communicative action, 160, 164
Communist Party of France, 21
Community, 24–25
Contamination, 149, 154
Continental philosophy, 28
Corlett, William, 53–54
Cornell, Ezra, 67
Cultural Revolution in China, 14

195